Phebe A. Hanaford

Field, gunboat, hospital and prison

Thrilling records of the heroism, endurance, and patriotism displayed in the Union army

Phebe A. Hanaford

Field, gunboat, hospital and prison
Thrilling records of the heroism, endurance, and patriotism displayed in the Union army

ISBN/EAN: 9783744748940

Printed in Europe, USA, Canada, Australia, Japan

Cover: Foto ©Andreas Hilbeck / pixelio.de

More available books at **www.hansebooks.com**

Field, Gunboat, Hospital, and Prison;

OR,

THRILLING RECORDS

OF THE

HEROISM, ENDURANCE, AND PATRIOTISM

DISPLAYED IN THE

UNION ARMY AND NAVY DURING THE GREAT REBELLION.

BY

MRS. P. A. HANAFORD,

AUTHOR OF "LIFE OF ABRAHAM LINCOLN," "THE YOUNG CAPTAIN,"
"OUR MARTYRED PRESIDENT," ETC.

"Be a hero in the strife." — LONGFELLOW.
"The Lord hath done great things for us, whereof we are glad." — Ps. cxxvi. 2.

BOSTON:
C. M. DINSMOOR AND COMPANY.
1866.

Entered, according to Act of Congress, in the year 1865,
BY MRS. P. A. HANAFORD,
In the Clerk's Office of the District Court of the District of Massachusetts.

STEREOTYPED AND PRINTED BY
GEO. C. RAND & AVERY, No. 3, Cornhill.

To

LOYAL HEARTS EVERYWHERE

IN OUR

Rescued Land;

TO ALL WHO APPRECIATE THE

NOBLE SELF-SACRIFICE, PATRIOTIC SENTIMENTS, HEROIC EFFORTS,

PATIENT ENDURANCE, AND SUBLIME ACHIEVEMENTS,

OF OUR

UNION SOLDIERS,

WHICH HAVE CROWNED THEM WITH

IMMORTAL HONOR;

AND ESPECIALLY TO THOSE WHOSE DEAR ONES

DIED FOR FREEDOM;

THIS

RECORD OF THRILLING SCENES

IN

FIELD, GUNBOAT, HOSPITAL, AND PRISON,

IS NOW

INSCRIBED.

PREFACE.

In the days of chivalry, when troubadours sang in ladies' bowers, the heroic deeds of brave and gallant knights were often the theme of the minstrel's ballad; and earlier yet, in the classic eras, the exploits of mighty warriors were told in song and story. Even the sacred writings show that this was customary in the childhood of the world; and the triumphal song of Deborah, the majestic utterances of the prophets, and the unsurpassed poetry of the monarch-bard, are evidences that bravery, heroism, fortitude, and the mighty arm of God displayed in the hour of military triumph, were deemed the legitimate and worthy themes of the poet and historian.

The same idea prevails in our own day, while we have almost infinitely greater facilities for making world-wide the name and fame of our gallant heroes. The printing-press, like a thousand-tongued troubadour, sings the praise not only of the men who fought at Thermopylæ and Waterloo, at Lexington and Bunker Hill, but sings also, and with clarion notes, of the champions of liberty, no less brave and patriotic, who battled for the right upon the sanguinary fields of Bull Run, Ball's Bluff, Antietam, Gettysburg, Pittsburg Landing, Shiloh, and many another field of blood and glory, as well as on the decks of our monitors and gunboats, which have thundered at doors which opened wide only at their summons.

Principles, and not mere preferences, were at stake; and our heroes fought as if they believed this.

It is to keep in memory some of the heroic deeds of daring, the Christian acts of self-denial, the unshrinking fortitude, the patient endurance, the pure patriotism, of "our brave boys" who followed the "dear old flag," that this volume is prepared.

It aims to give a graphic picture of Spartan virtues and chivalrous exploits as displayed in the army and navy of the Union during the dark and terrible years of the great Rebellion.

The material has been gathered from various sources, and the anecdotes are believed to be mainly authentic. Some of them are altogether new. As such, they are presented to a public that enjoys truthful pictures of thrilling events and incidents, with the hope that each one as he reads will be led to lift up his heart in devout recognition of that Hand which has guided the nation through seas of unexampled horror and suffering to the harbor of a peace, that, we trust, will be as permanent as it is acceptable.

Other writers have collected anecdotes, and prepared valuable works for reading and reference: this is designed for a niche yet unoccupied, as it is thought, and is sent forth with the humble yet sincere hope, that it may do its part in fostering a true sense of the real dignity of humanity, the value of free institutions, and the immeasurable worth of Christian principles, so that God shall be honored, and his laws revered, till his kingdom shall come, his will shall be done, and a ransomed world sing evermore, *Te Deum laudamus!*

P. A. H.

READING, MASS.

CONTENTS.

CHAPTER I.
RECORDS OF THE GREAT UPRISING . . . . . .

CHAPTER II.
COURAGE, BRAVERY, AND PATRIOTISM ON THE FIELD .

CHAPTER III.
GALLANT EXPLOITS OF OUR NAVY . . . . . .

CHAPTER IV.
BATTLE-SCENES IN CONNECTION WITH THE POTOMAC ARMY

CHAPTER V.
BATTLE-SCENES IN THE WEST AND SOUTH-WEST . . .

CHAPTER VI.
HOSPITAL-SCENES . . . .

CHAPTER VII.
PRISON-HORRORS . . . .

CHAPTER VIII.

SKETCHES OF CHRISTIAN LIFE IN THE ARMY AND NAVY

CHAPTER IX.

LAST HOURS OF SOME OF FREEDOM'S CHAMPIONS .

CHAPTER X.

THE MARTYR OF MARTYRS . . . .

Field, Gunboat, Hospital, and Prison.

CHAPTER I.

RECORDS OF THE GREAT UPRISING.

> "Toll, Roland, toll
> This side the sea!
> No longer they, but we,
> Have now such need of thee!
> Toll, Roland, toll!
> And let thy iron throat
> Ring out its warning note
> Till Freedom's perils be outbraved,
> And Freedom's flag, wherever waved,
> Shall overshadow none enslaved.
> Toll! till from either ocean's strand
> Brave men shall clasp each other's hand,
> And shout, 'God save our native land!'
> And love the land which God hath saved.
> Toll, Roland, toll!"
>
> THEODORE TILTON.

THE American nation stands foremost among the nations of the earth. Such, at least, is the opinion of the American people; and if the Icelander, in his rugged land and inhospitable clime, is allowed to retain the opinion which he everywhere fearlessly expresses, — that there is no land so desirable as his geyser-renowned island, and that the sun shines upon no spot so beautiful as Iceland, — surely the people of our broad, fair country may boast of its place among the lands, and of our rank among the nations, of the earth. In arts and sciences, in all that exalts humanity, the American nation could defy competition, or at least successful rivalship, with any other people, before the great Rebellion. Only one blot was on its escutcheon before the terrible war which has just closed; and that conflict, righteous but awful as it was, has not only shown the martyr-like heroism, the Spartan endurance, and the more than Roman patriotism, of the people of these United States of America, but it has removed the foul stain; and our star-spangled banner, torn and tattered in the death-struggle between Liberty and Slavery, yet waves in its more than pristine beauty, and with its newly won glory, above a country that is now truly

"The land of the free and the home of the brave."

Let us recall the past. Looking across the war-scarred years since 1860, what do we behold? A land prospered and prospering. The original thirteen States increased, till, silver stars added one after another to our beautiful flag, at last it showed no less than thirty-four. But there are mutterings of treason along the horizon. A dark cloud is rising, and many loyal hearts are fearful that the night will be bereft of stars. One* who has just passed to the eternal day, asked, in that hour of terrible suspense, —

"Are ye all there, are ye all there,
Stars of my country's sky?
Are ye *all* there, *are ye all there*,
In your shining homes on high?

---

* Mrs. L. H. Sigourney.

> 'Count us, count us!' was their answer,
>   As they dazzled on my view,
> In glorious perihelion,
>   Amid their field of blue.
>
> I cannot count ye rightly;
>   There's a cloud with sable rim:
> I cannot make your number out;
>   For my eyes with tears are dim.
> O bright and blessed angel
>   On white wing floating by!
> Help me to count, and not to miss,
>   One star in my country's sky."

But, alas! one after another the stars were shut out by the murky cloud of secession, till there remained but twenty-three. Eleven States — North and South Carolina, Alabama, Arkansas, Louisiana, Mississippi, Tennessee, Texas, Florida, Georgia, and Virginia — no longer gleamed as stars in our country's firmament. We may not pause to narrate the history of their unwise secession: if we did, it would be to go back to the time of John C. Calhoun, and wish, vainly, that flint-faced Jackson had occupied the place of the timid Buchanan when Jeff. Davis imitated Calhoun, and shook his treasonable fist in the very face of the United-States Government, but was unmolested. We pass on over the months that intervened after the election of Abraham Lincoln — a man of the people, and emphatically *a man for the times*, though comparatively few understood it then — till the time of his inauguration. That was a brilliant and imposing ceremony. More than two thousand soldiers were on parade that day. The fine appearance of cavalry, artillery, and infantry, in their splendid uniforms, awakened universal admiration. Yet they were but holiday soldiers, and little dreamed that they were to be constituted real knights of Fatherland, and receive a baptism of blood and glory.

Southern disunionists preached secession, till it was evident they meant to secede; but many at the North talked of "compromise," and hoped the matter would be settled without bloodshed. The country was unprepared for a sanguinary conflict. It had not been her motto, "In time of peace prepare for war;" for she had not dreamed that the sons of Revolutionary sires could re-enact the sad tragedy of Paradise, and the cruel Cain of the South lay violent hands on his brother at the North, whose "free soil, free speech, and free men," were more acceptable in the sight of God than desolated homes, parted families, and suffering bondmen. Jefferson Davis and John B. Floyd had so directed in the War Department for eight years, that the South had more than its share of Government aid in a preparation for an aggressive assault, while the North was left nearly defenceless. Floyd, the infamous thief, sent arms and ammunition to Southern arsenals, depleting the North; and our little navy was scattered, its best portion being ordered to faraway seas. The Confederate States, as the seceding portions of our country called themselves, elected Jefferson Davis to the Presidency in February, 1861. He was inaugurated on the 16th of that month, and Alexander H. Stephens also inaugurated as Vice-President. The nominal head of the nation, a mere party tool, looked on all this treasonable conduct with unpardonable pusillanimity, and perhaps with dismay, and a cowardly dread of the South. Probably he found in those hours, that

"Uneasy lies the head that wears a crown;"

and he longed for the time when the giant of the West would take the burden from his shoulders. So, instead of crushing the viper in the egg, he let treason grow to a hydra-headed monster, fit to frighten vast armies, such as at least only vast armies could utterly overcome.

Lincoln came to the chair of State a prepared man for the hour of a nation's destiny; but he had Quaker blood in his veins, and he preferred peace to war. Yet justice and liberty should triumph, he thought, at any cost.

The South desired to secure the forts along their shores; but this President Lincoln could not allow. His oath of office must be religiously kept. He had the spirit of a martyr, but not a particle of traitor blood in him. He could bear to be a stoned Stephen, but not a despised Arnold; and so he forbade the surrender of the forts into Southern hands: and, when supplies were needed, he was ready to furnish them, that the glorious old stars and stripes might still float over those defences of Southern harbors.

Meanwhile the traitors were busied in building forts, and preparing to take forcible possession of those over which waved the starry flag.

The loyal United-States soldiers who occupied the forts in Charleston Harbor were in need of food and ammunition. Government attempted to supply them; but the steamer

"Star of the West," which was sent to relieve the starving garrison, was fired upon, and unable to enter the harbor and draw near the forts. At last the parricidal hands of Southern traitors were raised against their country; and "at twenty minutes past three, A.M., of the 12th of April, 1861, Major Anderson was duly notified that fire would be opened on Fort Sumter in one hour. Punctual to the appointed moment, the roar of a mortar from Sullivan's Island, quickly followed by the rustling shriek of a shell, gave notice to the world that the era of compromise and diplomacy was ended; that the slaveholder's confederacy had appealed from sterile negotiations to the last argument of aristocracies as well as kings. Another gun from that island quickly repeated the warning, making a response from battery after battery, until Sumter appeared the focus of a circle of volcanic fire. Soon the thunder of fifty heavy breaching cannon in one grand volley, followed by the crashing and crumbling of brick, stone, and mortar around and above them, apprised the little garrison that their stay in those quarters must necessarily be short." *

The casemates of Fort Sumter were shell-proof, so that the loyal defenders were tolerably safe; and, in fact, not one was killed on either side. "So bloodless was the initiation of the bloodiest struggle that America ever witnessed. But, though almost without casualty, the contest was not, on the side of the Union, a mere mockery of war: it even served to develop traits of heroism." Says one of those who participated in the perils of the defence,—

* Greeley's History of the American Conflict.

"The workmen (Irish laborers, hired in New York for other than military service) were, at first, rather reluctant to assist the soldiers in handling the guns; but they gradually took hold, and rendered valuable assistance. Few shots were fired before every one of them was desperately engaged in the conflict. We had to abandon one gun on account of the heavy fire made upon it. Hearing the fire renewed, I went to the spot. I there found a party of workmen engaged in serving it. I saw one of them stooping over, with his hands on his knees, convulsed with joy, while the tears rolled down his powder-begrimed cheeks.

"'What are you doing here with that gun?' I asked. 'Hit it right in the centre,' was the reply; the man meaning that his shot had taken effect in the centre of the floating battery."

Says another eye-witness, "The firing of the rifled guns from the iron battery on Cummings's Point became extremely accurate in the afternoon of Friday, cutting out large quantities of the masonry about the embrasures at every shot, throwing concrete among the cannoneers, and slightly wounding and stunning others. One piece struck Sergeant Kernan, an old Mexican-War veteran; hitting him on the head, and knocking him down. On being revived, he was asked if he was hurt badly. He replied, 'No; I was only knocked down *temporarily;*' and he went to work again." [*]

With the fort on fire, and the men as busily engaged in fighting flames as fighting rebels, with provisions gone, and

---

[*] Horace Greeley's History, &c.

powder rolled into the sea to keep from explosion, the garrison was compelled to surrender; but they asked and obtained honorable terms. "When the baggage had all been removed, a part of the garrison was told off as gunners to salute their flag with fifty guns; the stars and stripes being lowered with cheers at the firing of the last gun. Unhappily, there was at that fire a premature explosion, whereby one of the gunners was killed, and three more or less seriously wounded. The men were then formed and marched out, preceded by their band, playing inspiring airs, and taken on board the 'Isabel,' whereby they were transferred to the Federal steamship 'Baltic' awaiting them off the bar, which brought them directly to New York; whence Major Anderson despatched to his Government this brief and manly report: —

'Steamship "Baltic," off Sandy Hook,
April 18, 1861.

'The Honorable S. Cameron,

'*Secretary of War, Washington, D.C.*

'Sir, — Having defended Fort Sumter for thirty-four hours, until the quarters were entirely burned, the main gates destroyed, the gorge-wall seriously injured, the magazine surrounded by flames, and its door closed from the effects of the heat, four barrels and three cartridges of powder only being available, and no provisions but pork remaining, I accepted terms of evacuation offered by Gen. Beauregard (being the same offered by him on the 11th instant, prior to the commencement of hostilities), and marched out of the fort on Sunday afternoon, the 14th instant, with colors flying and drums beating, bringing away company and private property, and saluting my flag with fifty guns.

'ROBERT ANDERSON,
'*Major First Artillery.*'"*

And so the war began. The news went over the wires, and everywhere met a response in the hearts of the loyal people. On the morning of April 15, 1861, President Lincoln issued a proclamation, — his very first, — calling for patriots to defend the flag. There was but one response amid the echoing hills of the North, and along her resounding shores. "To arms, to arms!" shouted the men; and the women looked up from their needles, and saw their peaceful husbands, fathers, and sons transformed at once into patriots, like the warrior of ancient story springing full-armed into being, as heroes and champions of liberty.

"'COME TO THE RESCUE!' the cry went forth
Through the length and breadth of the loyal North;
For the gun that startled Sumter heard
Wakened the land with its fiery word.
The farmer paused with his work half done,
And snatched from the nail his rusty gun;
And the swart mechanic wiped his brow,
Shouting, 'There's work for my strong arm now!'
And the parson doffed his gown, and said,
'Bring me my right good sword instead;'
And the scholar paused in his eager quest,
And buckled on his belt with the rest;

---

* Greeley's History.

> And each and all to the rescue went
> As unto a loyal tournament:
> For the loyal blood of the nation stirred
> To the gun that startled Sumter heard." *

The Governor of Massachusetts learned before the proclamation arrived the probable necessity of martial resistance to Southern aggression, too long endured; and, as in the days of the Revolution, couriers on horseback rode into towns in the vicinity of Boston, like Paul Revere in those earlier "times which tried men's souls;" while extra trains were run to cities along the railroads, each messenger conveying the intelligence that the war had begun, and the militia must be in readiness to depart. Some towns were aroused at midnight by the alarm-bell; and, early the next morning, the troops of Massachusetts were on their way to defend the capital of the nation, whose capture was threatened by the leaders of the Southern rebels. This was the intention of that double-dyed traitor, Robert E. Lee, whose name has been a terror to loyal hearts in the border States, and will be "a hissing and a byword" in all future generations. A New-England paper thus graphically describes the treasonable intentions of that rebel general, who adroitly slipped his head from the noose he richly deserved: —

"HOW GEN. LEE WENT INTO THE WAR. — On the Sunday when the news arrived of the fall of Sumter, a gentleman of our acquaintance, in whom we place perfect confidence, took the cars at Washington to go to Richmond.

---

* Mrs. Caroline A. Mason.

Upon the train were Alexander A. H. Stuart, William Ballard Preston, and another member of the committee which the Virginia Legislature had sent up to Washington to confer with the Government, or, more properly speaking, to see what manner of man the new President was, and to spy out the land. At one of the stations beyond Alexandria, quite a crowd had collected; and eager demands were made for the news as the train came in. Our informant noticed one well-dressed gentleman, who seemed to be spokesman and chief person in the crowd. He was flourishing up and down the platform with more or less consequence, and, as the train stopped, cried out, —

"'What's the news?'

"'Sumter has fallen,' was the reply.

"'I'll raise an army, and march on Washington!' exclaimed the excited individual, swinging his cane, and walking uneasily about.

"'I'll commence to-morrow morning,' he repeated, 'and raise an army, and take Washington. Hadn't I better do it, Mr. Preston?'

"It was some time before Preston answered, so long that our friend thought he would make no reply; when he said slowly and oracularly, —

"'True courage waits on deliberation.'

"'Was there any bloodshed?' asked the excited man.

"'No.'

"'Wasn't there?' looking down, and speaking as if surprised. As the train moved off, he was heard to repeat, —

"'I shall raise an army, and march on Washington.'

"When the train was under way, our friend asked,—

"'Who is that enthusiastic man?'

"'That is Col. Lee,' said Mr. Preston.

"And that is the man who has since been commander of the rebel forces, and who is represented as having very reluctantly, and only after days of prayer, drawn the sword against the Government that educated and promoted him. And it must be remembered that this occurrence took place before Virginia had passed its bogus ordinance of secession, and five days before Lee's resignation. Lee did raise a force of about three thousand men, and marched them to Harper's Ferry to procure arms. The intention was to march into Maryland, which, it was supposed, would rise at once, and go out of the Union, carrying with it the national capital, which the rebels would at once occupy, and proclaim themselves the Government of the United States. It is evident that they did not intend to go off, and put themselves in the attitude of rebels, but that their plan was to take the capital and the Government machinery, and then let the North 'rebel,' if they didn't like the arrangement." *

Rhode Island was not in the background at this time. As early as January, 1861, she, with other Northern States, offered troops to President Buchanan; but the timid, indecisive President did not accept them. They were offered to Gen. Scott; and, when the proclamation came, they were

* Hartford Press.

allowed to be a part of the seventy-five thousand men for whom President Lincoln called. Ex-Governor Banks, even then, declared the call should have been for seven hundred thousand, in order that the Rebellion be crushed at once; and succeeding events have proved the wisdom of his remark. But the crushing of the viper Secession was not all that was needed: the nest of all the Southern vipers, which was slavery, was to be totally destroyed; and therefore, slowly but surely, the man whom God had appointed to lead the way marched on to freedom and victory.

The Governor of Rhode Island commanded his troops in person; and men of wealth and high social position flocked to his standard. One millionnaire, who had purchased his ticket for a trip to England, destroyed it, and, instead of going, enlisted in his country's service.

Women throughout New England, with the loyal hearts of their fore-mothers of Revolutionary days, lent willing aid in preparing the volunteers for their noble service. Far into the night-hours did some of them, in Massachusetts' ancient town of Beverly, prolong their stay in the old Town Hall, plying the needle with weary eyes, and packing articles of clothing for the soldier-boys, who were already as far as Boston, bivouacking in the old "Cradle of Liberty," on their way to defend Washington and the institutions of liberty and humanity. Doubtless similar scenes occurred in other places. The spirit of many loyal wives is fittingly expressed in the following poem : * —

* By Charles A. Barry.

THE MASSACHUSETTS SOLDIER'S WIFE.

One parting kiss; the time is come
    That severs thee and me :
I hear the rolling of the drum,
    The stars and stripes I see !

My heart leaps up; I catch the cry
    Of freemen, old and young : —
Away, God speed you ! do, or die !
    Be first our foes among !

The Old Bay State will fondly keep
    Her heroes in her sight :
Away ! let slaves and cowards weep ;
    Be bravest in the fight !

Uphold our flag; its Sumter stain
    Avenge with Titan blows ;
Smite down to earth, with leaden rain,
    Columbia's brutal foes !

I mourn not, Richard, that I lose
    The star of all my life ;
Go; and remember that I *choose*
    To *be* a soldier's wife.

I'll teach my boy, " if thou shouldst fall,"
    The GREATNESS of thy fate ;
Thy name shall be his " all-in-all,"
    Thy grave his best estate.

I'll twine around his golden hair
　　The laurel thou mayst earn;
And battle-cry and martial air
　　Our darling boy shall learn.

The gilded eagle on thy breast
　　Against his heart I'll bind;
The crimson sash that keeps thy vest
　　Around *his* waist I'll wind.

And then I'll tell him how you went
　　All grandly to the strife:
Ah, Richard! I was surely meant
　　To be a soldier's wife.

Fear not for us; as strong as oak
　　The arms you gently feel:
Last night I prayed; ere morning broke,
　　My heart was changed to steel.

Go! welcome *any* shape of death!
　　Be my ambition thine;
Fight bravely: every trumpet's breath
　　Proclaims this wish of mine.

Fight bravely, Richard! *fight for me;*
　　Fight bravely, I repeat!
Sustain the flag, or let it be
　　My husband's winding-sheet!

Massachusetts soldiers were the first to fall in this civil war, as Massachusetts blood was the first to be shed in the

Revolution; and it is a remarkable coincidence, that *the nineteenth of April*, 1861, was the day whose deeds paralleled the deeds of the *nineteenth of April*, 1776. Massachusetts was thoroughly aroused. It almost seemed, that, as the eloquent Philips said, " when the South cannonaded Fort Sumter, the bones of Adams stirred in his coffin." He said, too, that Massachusetts " had been sleeping on her arms since '76; and the first cannon-shot brought her to her feet, with the war-cry of the Revolution on her lips." And most impressive was his almost prophetic utterance, " Massachusetts blood has consecrated the pavements of Baltimore, and those stones are now too sacred to be trodden by slaves."

Bayard Taylor tells the tale in his fiery words, the sparks of true genius and patriotism: —

THROUGH BALTIMORE.

THE VOICE OF THE PENNSYLVANIA VOLUNTEERS.

'Twas Friday morn: the train drew near
    The city and the shore:
Far through the sunshine, soft and clear,
We saw the dear old flags appear;
And in our hearts arose a cheer
        For Baltimore.

Across the broad Patapsco's wave,
    Old Fort McHenry bore
The starry banner of the brave,
As when our fathers went to save,
Or in the trenches find a grave
        At Baltimore.

Before us, pillared in the sky,
      We saw the statue soar
Of Washington, serene and high!
Could traitors view that form, nor fly?
Could patriots see, nor gladly die
           For Baltimore?

" O city of our country's song!
      By that swift aid we bore
When sorely pressed, receive the throng
Who go to shield our flag from wrong,
And give us welcome warm and strong
           In Baltimore!"

We had no arms: as friends we came,
      As brothers evermore,
To rally round one sacred name,
The charter of our power and fame:
We never dreamed of guilt and shame
           In Baltimore.

The coward mob upon us fell;
      McHenry's flag they tore:
Surprised, borne backward by the swell,
Beat down with mad, inhuman yell,
Before us yawned a traitorous hell
           In Baltimore!

The streets our soldier-fathers trod
      Blushed with their children's gore:
We saw the craven rulers nod,
And dip in blood the civic rod.
Shall such things be, O righteous God!
           In Baltimore?

No, never! By that outrage black
  A solemn oath we swore,
To bring the Keystone's thousands back,
Strike down the dastards who attack,
And leave a red and fiery track
    Through Baltimore!

Bow down in haste thy guilty head!
  God's wrath is swift and sore;
The sky with gathering bolts is red:
Cleanse from thy skirts the slaughter shed,
Or make thyself an ashen bed,
    O Baltimore!

The story of the tragic events which gave the Sixth Massachusetts a name that will never die is thus told by another [*] in verse: —

A TALE OF 1861.

Come, children, leave your playing; a tale I have to tell,
A tale of woe and sorrow, which long ago befell:
'Twas in the Great Rebellion, in eighteen sixty-one,
Within the streets of Baltimore, the bloody deed was done.

Of gallant Major Anderson I told you yesternight;
Of Moultrie's shattered battlements, and Sumter's bloodless
  fight;
And how the cannon's echo shook the North and East and West,
And woke a flame in loyal hearts which would not be repressed.

---

[*] Edward Sprague Rand, jun.

Oh! 'twas a goodly sight to see the uprising of the people;
To hear the clanging bells ring out from every tower and steeple;
To see our glorious flag flung wide all through the loyal land;
To know at last the North stood up a firm, united band.

A call went forth through all the land: " On, on to Washington!"
On for the Union that we prize, for Right and Freedom, on!
'Twas sunset ere the call was known; but, ere the break of day,
Our brave militia were in arms, and ready for the fray.

They left the plough, forsook the loom; bade hasty, sad farewell
To all they loved, with looks which spoke far more than words
    could tell:
And loving wives and mothers wept, and blessed them on their
    way;
But, 'mid the throng of anxious ones, not one would bid them stay.

As on through loyal towns they went, 'twas one prolonged ovation:
Of all the patriot people did, would weary the narration.
On, on for Washington they pressed; for there the patriot band
For the Union and for Liberty, for Right, must make their stand.

'Twas the nineteenth of April! O most auspicious day!
It ushered in at Lexington the bloody fatal fray;
Baptized our Revolution; and 'twas again to be.
For Massachusetts men to bleed for freedom and the free.

Through Baltimore their pathway led, and boldly on they passed;
But bitter taunts and angry words fell on them thick and fast:
'Twas the low rabble of the town by whom the deed was done;
But men of wealth and rank were there, and urged and cheered
    them on.

Oh! who shall tell of all that chanced, or in that fearful fray
Tell what was done, or truly write the history of that day?
How, not content with scoffs and taunts, the pavement up they tore,
And showered the stones upon our troops, around, behind, before?

"Why did they let them?" Oh, alas! forgetful grows my mind;
The others had passed safely on, a few were left behind:
For thus Secession's chivalry its boldest deeds has done;
And often have they bravely fought, *a hundred against one.*

On, on in close-set ranks they pressed, turned not to left or right:
They all were Massachusetts men; they never thought of flight;
But as the stones came thick and fast, the curses deep and loud,
In self-defence, at bay, they turned, and fired upon the crowd.

Oh! many a taunting traitor fell beneath their deadly fire;
But thicker flew the showers of stones, and fiercer grew their ire.
Enough, — they fought their passage through, and then kept marching on,
Obedient to their country's call, to rescue Washington.

Yet not unscathed: three noble ones fell in the bloody fray;
And many carry scarring wounds in memory of that day;
And high on Honor's scroll are writ the names of those who fell,
First martyrs to maintain the rights of the land we love so well.

Yes, Washington was saved, my boy: another time I'll tell
Of Freedom's armies marshalled there, of all that there befell.
The blood then spilt at Baltimore roused all the loyal land,
And such an army sprung to birth no traitors could withstand.

I mind me when the honored dead in solemn pomp came home;
How our starry banner drooped half-mast on the high State-House
    dome;
How minute-guns spoke sharply out, and sad the bells were toll-
    ing,
And mournfully upon the breeze the funeral dirge was rolling.

Oh! there was that within the looks, within the eyes, of men,
A stern determination I never saw till then:
With hard-pressed lips and swimming eyes they watched the
    funeral train;
With bowed, uncovered heads, they stood amid the falling rain.

In vision yet I seem to see the biers with flags intwined;
The memory of that solemn dirge will never flee my mind:
And Massachusetts lifts her head more proudly at this day
That twice in Freedom's battles her sons have led the way.

O children! guard your heritage; be to your country true;
Be proud of Massachusetts, and let her be proud of you;
Be ready in her cause to fight, and for her sake to fall;
But cherish in your heart of hearts the Union, above all!

Fast in the track of the Sixth came the Eighth Massachusetts and the New-York Seventh. The gallant officer and gifted writer, Theodore Winthrop, wrote a graphic sketch of the short but useful services of the Eighth Massachusetts and New-York Seventh, from which the following extracts are given. Major Winthrop was a member of the New-York regiment, and was killed in the battle of Great Bethel. After describing the departure from New

York, and embarkation on board the "Boston" at Philadelphia, he says, —

"Sunday, the 21st, was a long and somewhat anxious day. While we were bowling along in the sweet sunshine and sweeter moonlight of the halcyon time, Uncle Sam might be dethroned by somebody in buckram, or Baltimore burnt by the boys from Lynn and Marblehead, revenging the massacre of their fellows. Every one begins to comprehend the fiery eagerness of men who live in historic times. 'I wish I had control of chain-lightning for a few minutes,' says O., the droll fellow of our company: 'I'd make it come thick and heavy, and knock spots out of Secession.'

"At early dawn of Monday, 22d, after feeling along slowly all night, we see the harbor of Annapolis. A frigate with sails unbent lies at anchor. She flies the stars and stripes. Hurrah!

"A large steamboat is aground farther in. As soon as we can see any thing, we catch the glitter of bayonets on board.

"By and by boats come off, and we get news that the steamer is the 'Maryland,' a ferry-boat of the Philadelphia and Baltimore Railroad. The Massachusetts Eighth Regiment had been just in time to seize her on the north side of the Chesapeake. They learned that she was to be carried off by the crew, and leave them blockaded; so they shot their Zouaves ahead as skirmishers. The fine fellows rattled on board; and, before the steamboat had time to take a turn or open a valve, she was held by Massachusetts in trust for Uncle Sam. Hurrah for the most important prize thus far in the war! It probably saved the 'Constitution,' 'Old Ironsides,' from capture by the traitors. It probably saved Annapolis, and kept Maryland open without bloodshed.

"As soon as the Massachusetts regiment had made prize of the ferry-boat, a call was made for engineers to run her. Some twenty men at once stepped to the front. We of the New-York Seventh afterwards concluded, that whatever was needed in the way of skill or handicraft could be found among those brother Yankees. They were the men to make armies of. They could tailor for themselves, shoe themselves; do their own blacksmithing, gunsmithing, and all other work that calls for sturdy arms and nimble fingers. In fact, I have such profound confidence in the universal accomplishments of the Massachusetts Eighth, that I have no doubt, if the order were, 'Poets, to the front!' 'Painters, present arms!' 'Sculptors, charge bayonets!' a baker's dozen out of every company would respond.

"Well, to go on with their story: when they had taken their prize, they drove her straight down stream to Annapolis, the nearest point to Washington. There they found the Naval Academy in danger of attack, and 'Old Ironsides' — serving as a practice-ship for the future midshipmen — also exposed. The call was now for seamen to man the old craft, and save her from a worse enemy than her prototpye met in the 'Guerrière.' Seamen? Of course! They were Marblehead men, Gloucester men, Beverly men, seamen all, *par excellence!* They clapped on the frigate to aid the middies, and by and by started her out into the stream. In doing this, their own pilot took the chance to run them purposely on a shoal in the intricate channel. A great error of judgment on his part!—as he perceived, when he found himself in irons and in confinement. 'The days of trifling with traitors are over,' think the Eighth Regiment of Massachusetts.

"But there they were, hard and fast on the shoal, when we came up. Nothing to nibble on but knobs of anthracite. Nothing to sleep on softer or cleaner than coal-dust. Nothing to drink but the brackish water under their keel. 'Rather rough,' as they afterward patiently told us.

"Meantime the 'Constitution' had got hold of a tug, and was making her way to an anchorage where her guns commanded every thing and everybody. Good and true men chuckled greatly over this. The stars and stripes also were still up at the fort at the Naval Academy.

"Our dread, that, while we were off at sea, some great and perhaps fatal harm had been suffered, was greatly lightened by these good omens. If Annapolis was safe, why not Washington safe also? If treachery had got head at the capital, would not treachery have reached out its hand, and snatched this doorway? These were our speculations as we began to discern objects before we heard news.

"But news came presently. Boats pulled off to us. Our officers were put into communication with the shore. The scanty facts of our position became known from man to man. We privates have greatly the advantage in battling with the doubt of such a time. We know that we have nothing to do with rumors. Orders are what we go by; and orders are facts.

"We lay a long, lingering day off Annapolis. The air was full of doubt, and we were eager to be let loose. All this while the 'Maryland' stuck fast on the bar. We could see them half a mile off, making every effort to lighten her. The soldiers tramped forward and aft, danced on her decks, shot overboard a heavy baggage-truck. We saw them start the truck for the stern with a cheer. It crashed down. One end stuck in the mud: the other fell back, and rested on the boat. They went at it with axes, and presently it was clear.

"As the tide rose, we gave our grounded friends a lift with a hawser. No go! The 'Boston' tugged in vain. We got near enough to see the whites of the Massachusetts eyes, and their unlucky faces and uniforms all grimy with their lodgings in the coal-dust. They could not have been blacker if they had been breathing battle-smoke and dust all day. That experience was clear gain to them.

"We staid all next day at Annapolis. The 'Boston' brought the Massachusetts Eighth ashore that night. Poor fellows! what a figure they cut when we found them bivouacked on the Academy grounds next morning! To begin: they had come off in hot, patriotic haste, half-uniformed and half-outfitted. Finding that Baltimore had been taken by its own loafers and traitors, and that the Chesapeake Ferry was impracticable, had obliged them to change line of march. They were out of grub. They were parched dry for want of water on the ferry-boat. Nobody could decipher Caucasian, much less Bunker-Hill Yankee, in their grimy visages.

"But, hungry, thirsty, grimy, these fellows were grit.

"Massachusetts ought to be proud of such hardy, cheerful, faithful sons.

"We of the Seventh are proud, for our part, that it was our privilege to share our rations with them, and to begin a fraternization which grows closer every day, and will be *historical*.

"But I must make a shorter story. We drilled and were reviewed that morning on the Academy parade. In the afternoon, the Naval School paraded their last before they gave up their barracks to the coming soldiery. So ended the 23d of April.

"Midnight, 24th. — We were rattled up by an alarm, — perhaps a sham one, to keep us awake and lively. In a moment, the whole regiment was in order of battle in the moonlight on the parade. It was a most brilliant spectacle, as company after company rushed forward, with rifles glittering, to take their places in the array.

"After this pretty spurt, we were rationed with pork, beef, and bread, for three days; and ordered to be ready to march on the instant.

"Meantime, Gen. Butler's command, the Massachusetts Eighth, had been busy knocking disorder in the head.

"Presently after their landing, and before they were refreshed, they pushed companies out to occupy the railroad-track beyond the town.

"They found it torn up. No doubt the scamps who did

the shabby job fancied that there would be no more travel that way until strawberry-time. They fancied the Yankees would sit down on the fences, and begin to whittle white-oak toothpicks, darning the rebels through their noses meanwhile.

"I know these men of the Eighth can whittle, and I presume they can say 'Darn it,' if occasion requires; but just now track-laying was the business on hand.

"'Wanted, experienced track-layers!' was the word along the files.

"All at once the line of the road became densely populated with experienced track-layers, fresh from Massachusetts.

"'Presto, change!' the rails were relaid, spiked, and the roadway levelled and better ballasted than any road I ever saw south of Mason and Dixon's line. 'We must leave a good job for these folks to model after,' say the Massachusetts Eighth.

"A track without a train is as useless as a gun without a man. Train and engine must be had. 'Uncle Sam's mails and troops cannot be stopped another minute,' our energetic friends conclude. So, the railroad company's people being either frightened or false, in marches Massachusetts to the station. 'We, the people of the United States, want rolling-stock for the use of the Union,' they said, or words to that effect.

"The engine — a frowzy machine at the best — had been purposely disabled.

"Here appeared the *deus ex machina*, Charles Homans,

Beverly Light Guard, Company E, Eighth Massachusetts Regiment.

"That is the man, name and titles in full; and he deserves well of his country.

"He took a quiet squint at the engine (it was as helpless as a boned turkey); and he found 'Charles Homans, his mark,' written all over it.

"The old rattletrap was an old friend. Charles Homans had had a share in building it. The machine and the man said 'How d'ye do?' at once. Homans called for a gang of engine-builders. Of course they swarmed out of the ranks. They passed their hands over the locomotive a few times; and presently it was ready to whistle and wheeze and rumble and gallop, as if no traitor had ever tried to steal the go and the music out of it.

"This had all been done during the afternoon of the 23d. During the night, the renovated engine was kept cruising up and down the track to see all clear. Guards of the Eighth were also posted to protect passage.

"Our commander had, I presume, been co-operating with Gen. Butler in this business. The Naval-Academy authorities had given us every despatch and assistance; and the middies, frank, personal hospitality. The day was halcyon, the grass was green and soft, the apple-trees were just in blossom: it was a day to be remembered.

"Many of us will remember it, and show the marks of it for months, as the day we had our heads cropped. By evening, there was hardly one poll in the Seventh tenable by anybody's grip. Most sat in the shade, and were shorn by a barber. A few were honored with a clip by the artist hand of the *petit caporal* of our Engineer Company.

"While I rattle off these trifling details, let me not fail to call attention to the grave service done by our regiment, by its arrival, at the nick of time, at Annapolis. No clearer special Providence could have happened. The country people of the traitor sort were aroused. Baltimore and its mob were but two hours away. The 'Constitution' had been hauled out of reach of a rush by the Massachusetts men, first on the ground; but was half-manned, and not fully secure. And there lay the 'Maryland,' helpless on the shoal, with six or seven hundred souls on board, so near the shore that the late Capt. Rynders's gun could have sunk her from some ambush.

"Yes, the Seventh Regiment at Annapolis was the right man in the right place!"

At night, Major Winthrop was on guard over a howitzer. He adds, —

"Two of the Massachusetts men come back to the gun while we are standing there. One is my friend Stephen Morris, of Marblehead, Sutton Light Infantry. I had shared my breakfast yesterday with Stephe. So we refraternize.

"His business is, 'I make shoes in winter, and fishin' in summer.' He gives me a few facts, — suspicious persons seen about the track, men on horseback in the distance. One of the Massachusetts guard last night challenged his captain. Captain replied, 'Officer of the night.' Whereupon, says Stephe, 'The recruit let squizzle, and jest missed his ear.' He then related to me the incident of the railroad station. 'The first thing they know'd,' says he, 'we bit right into the depot, and took charge.' 'I don't mind,' Stephe remarked,—' I don't mind life, nor yit death ; but, whenever I see a Massachusetts boy, I stick by him, and if them secessionists attack us to-night, or any other time, they 'll git in debt.'

" Whistle, again ! and the train appears. We are ordered to ship our howitzer on a platform car. The engine pushes us on. This train brings our light baggage and the rearguard.

" A hundred yards farther on is a delicious fresh spring below the bank. While the train halts, Stephe Morris rushes down to fill my canteen. 'This a'n't like Marblehead,' says Stephe, panting up; ' but a man that can shin up *them* rocks can git right over *this* sand.'

" The train goes slowly on, as a rickety train should. At intervals, we see the fresh spots of track just laid by our Yankee friends. Near the sixth mile, we began to overtake hot and uncomfortable squads of our fellows. The unseasonable heat of this most breathless day was too much for many of the younger men, unaccustomed to rough work, and weakened by want of sleep and irregular food in our hurried movements thus far.

" Charles Homans's private carriage was, however, ready to pick up tired men, hot men, thirsty men, men with corns, or men with blisters. They tumbled into the train in considerable numbers.

" An enemy that dared could have made a moderate bag

of stragglers at this time. But they would not have been allowed to straggle if any enemy had been about. By this time, we were convinced that no attack was to be expected in this part of the way.

"The main body of the regiment, under Major Shaler, a tall, soldierly fellow, with a mustache of the fighting-color, tramped on their own pins to the watering-place, eight miles or so from Annapolis. There troops and train came to a halt, with the news that a bridge over a country road was broken a mile farther on.

"It had been distinctly insisted upon, in the usual Southern style, that we were not to be allowed to pass through Maryland, and that we were to be 'welcomed to hospitable graves.' The broken bridge was a capital spot for a skirmish. Why not look for it here?

"We looked, but got nothing. The rascals could skulk about by night, tear up rails, and hide them where they might be found by a man with half an eye, or half destroy a bridge; but there was no shoot in them. They have not faith enough in their cause to risk their lives for it, even behind a tree or from one of these thickets, — choice spots for ambush.

"So we had no battle there but a battle of the elements. The volcanic heat of the morning was followed by a furious storm of wind and a smart shower. The regiment wrapped themselves in their blankets, and took their wetting with more or less satisfaction. They were receiving samples of all the different little miseries of a campaign."

A fine description of a night-march, and the efforts of our citizen soldiers to reach Washington, follows: —

"It was full-moonlight, and the night inexpressibly sweet and serene. The air was cool, and vivified by the gust and shower of the afternoon. Fresh spring was in every breath. Our fellows had forgotten that this morning they were hot and disgusted. Every one hugged his rifle as if it were the arm of the girl of his heart, and stepped out gayly for the promenade. Tired or foot-sore men, or even lazy ones, could mount upon the two freight-cars we were using for artillery-wagons. There were stout arms enough to tow the whole.

. . . . . .

"It was an original kind of march. I suppose a battery of howitzers never before found itself mounted upon cars, ready to open fire at once, and bang away into the offing with shrapnel, or into the bushes with canister. Our line extended a half-mile along the track. It was beautiful to stand on a bank above a cutting, and watch the files strike from the shadow of a wood into a broad flame of moonlight, every rifle sparkling up alert as it came forward; a beautiful sight to see the barrels writing themselves upon the dimness, each a silver flash.

"By and by, 'Halt!' came repeated along from the front, company after company. 'Halt! a rail gone.'

"It was found without difficulty. The imbeciles who took it up probably supposed we would not wish to wet our feet by searching for it in the dewy grass of the next field. With incredible doltishness, they had also left the chairs and spikes beside the track. Bonnell took hold, and in a few minutes had the rail in place, and firm enough to pass the engine. Remember, we were not only hurrying on to succor Washington, but opening the only convenient and practicable route between it and the loyal States.

"A little farther on, we came to a village, — a rare sight in this scantily peopled region. Here Sergeant Keeler of our company, the tallest man in the regiment, and one of the handiest, suggested that we should tear up the rails at a turnout by the station, and so be prepared for chances. So 'Out crowbars!' was the word. We tore up and bagged half a dozen rails, with chairs and spikes complete. Here, too, some of the engineers found a keg of spikes. This was also bagged, and loaded on our cars. We fought the chaps with their own weapons, since they would not meet us with ours.

"These things made delay; and by and by there was a long halt, while the colonel communicated, by orders sounded along the line, with the engine. Homans's drag was hard after us, bringing our knapsacks and traps.

"After I had admired for some time the beauty of our moonlit line, and listened to the orders as they grew or died along the distance, I began to want excitement. Bonnell suggested that he and I should scout up the road, and see if any rails were wanting. We travelled along into the quiet night.

"A mile ahead of the line, we suddenly caught the gleam of a rifle-barrel. 'Who goes there?' one of our own scouts challenged smartly.

"We had arrived at the nick of time. Three rails were up. Two of them were easily found. The third was discovered by beating the bush thoroughly. Bonnell and I ran back for tools, and returned at full trot with crowbar and sledge on our shoulders. There were plenty of willing hands to help, — too many, indeed; and, with the aid of a huge Massachusetts man, we soon had the rail in place.

"From this time on we were constantly interrupted. Not a half-mile passed without a rail up. Bonnell was always at the front, laying track; and I am proud to say that he accepted me as aide-de-camp. Other fellows, unknown to me in the dark, gave hearty help. The Seventh showed that it could do something else than drill.

"At one spot, on a high embankment over standing water, the rail was gone; sunk, probably. Here we tried our rails brought from the turnout. They were too short. We supplemented with a length of plank from our stores. We rolled our cars carefully over. They passed safe; but Homans shook his head. He could not venture a locomotive on that frail stuff. So we lost the society of the 'J. H. Nicholson.' Next day, the Massachusetts commander called for some one to dive in the pool for the lost rail. Plump into the water went a little wiry chap, and grappled the rail. 'When I come up,' says the brave fellow afterwards to me, 'our officer out with a twenty-dollar gold-piece, and wanted me to take it. "That a'n't what I come for," says I. "Take it," says he, "and share with the others." "That a'n't what they come for," says I. But I took a big cold,' the diver continued, 'and I'm condemned hoarse yit;' which was the fact.

"Farther on we found a whole length of track torn up on both sides, sleepers and all; and the same thing repeated with alternations of breaks of single rails. Our howitzer-ropes came into play to hoist and haul. We were not going to be stopped.

"But it was becoming a *noche triste* to some of our comrades. We had now marched some sixteen miles. The distance was trifling; but the men had been on their legs pretty much all day and night. Hardly any one had had any full or substantial sleep or meal since we started from New York. They napped off, standing, leaning on their guns, dropping down in their tracks on the wet ground, at every halt. They were sleepy, but plucky. As we passed through deep cuttings, places, as it were, built for defence, there was a general desire that the tedium of the night should be relieved by a shindy.

"During the whole night I saw our officers moving about the line, doing their duty vigorously, despite exhaustion, hunger, and sleeplessness.

"About midnight, our friends of the Eighth had joined us; and our whole little army struggled on together. I find that I have been rather understating the troubles of the march. It seems impossible that such difficulty could be encountered within twenty miles of the capital of our nation. But we were making a rush to put ourselves in that capital; and we could not proceed in the slow, systematic way of an advancing army. We must take the risk, and stand the suffering, whatever it was. So the Seventh Regiment went through its bloodless *noche triste*.

. . . .

"We put our guns on their own wheels, all dropped into ranks as if on parade, and marched the last two miles to the station. We still had no certain information. Until we actually saw the train awaiting us, and the Washington companies, who had come down to escort us, drawn up, we did not know whether our Uncle Sam was still a resident of the capital.

"We packed into the train, and rolled away to Washington.

"We marched up to the White House, showed ourselves to the President, made our bow to him as our host, and then marched up to the Capitol, our grand lodgings.

"There we are now, quartered in the Representatives' Chamber.

"And here I must hastily end this first sketch of the Great Defence. May it continue to be as firm and faithful as it is this day!

"I have scribbled my story with a thousand men stirring about me. If any of my sentences miss their aim, accuse my comrades and the bewilderment of this martial crowd; for here are four or five thousand others on the same business as ourselves, and drums are beating, guns are clanking, companies are tramping, all the while. Our friends of the Eighth Massachusetts are quartered under the dome, and cheer us whenever we pass.

"Desks marked 'John Covode,' 'John Cochran,' and

'Anson Burlingame,' have allowed me to use them as I wrote."*

We have told at some length the deeds of Massachusetts and other Eastern Regiments, showing the patriotism, valor, and industry of the soldiers in them; and yet "the half has not been told."

In a severe easterly rain-storm, — no slight affair on the Atlantic coast, — the first Massachusetts troops started for Washington. The company from Marblehead, true to the patriotic reputation of their gallant fathers, were the first at the rendezvous. "Among the incidents narrated, it is mentioned, that, while the recruits were forming at Marblehead, one man, calling to mind his deserted store, and his family which he was about to leave, for a moment hesitated; when his wife, in the most emphatic manner, exclaimed, 'If you don't go, I'll never live with you!' and another woman, in the true spirit of '76, said, 'Here are my two sons; and I'm sorry I have not more to go!' A large sum of money was subscribed by liberal citizens for the support of the families of the soldiers during their absence."†

Among the numerous instances of devotion to the country is the following: —

"Gov. Andrew has a letter from a clergyman of an interior society of this State, who asks that the law making him exempt from military duty may be repealed in his case."

Another, showing hearty sympathy, is as follows: —

"While the Massachusetts soldiers were passing down Broadway, amidst the waving of handkerchiefs by the

* Atlantic Monthly, June, 1864. † Salem Register.

ladies and the cheers of the men, there was a group of people in front of a public office, from which the most hearty demonstrations proceeded. That crowd was wholly composed of natives of the Bay State, who felt a just pride in the old Commonwealth. A very prominent citizen of New York joined the group, and was cheering most lustily; when he was pleasantly told by an intimate friend that he could not unite with that crowd, as he was not a native of old Massachusetts. 'I have half a right to be with you,' he replied; 'for, though I am a New-Yorker, I married a Boston lady, and made a first-rate bargain.' We hardly need add that he was allowed to stand among the sons of Massachusetts, and cheer to his heart's content."*

In one of the companies attached to the famous Sixth Regiment, which gave the first martyrs to liberty, was a newly enlisted recruit, the eldest son of a widow in a country town, who followed her son to the city to take a last look of him until he returns from the war. She did not come to urge him to return to his peaceful home and pursuits, but rather to cheer him with a mother's blessing. Fearing that her son might want for money during absence, she raised some by the sale of her cow, and being admitted inside the lines, just before the troops left the State House, pressed the money on her boy, who declined it.

In Gloucester, a woman, with the same spirit as that which animated the Spartan mother, said to her son, "Your country wants you more than I do: GO!"

In Canton, a private in Company H, named Preble, —

* Salem Register.

a name historic and heroic, — went to announce to his betrothed that he was warned to service. She was ill of that siren disease, — consumption. Her mother, who carefully broke the intelligence to her, told her she might prevent her lover from exposing his life; but the loyal-hearted one looked up from her death-bed, and bade her chosen one go with her blessing.

A young girl with all a maiden's love of fine clothing, on receiving a sum of money from her father with which to purchase a silk dress, bought only calico, and gave the rest of the money to the men who were going forth to battle for her safety.

Such are some of the deeds of loyalty and patriotism, which, at the East, inaugurated the war. The Great West joined in this grand uprising of a free people to protect their liberties. Troops came from Michigan to defend Washington; and all through the war the Western States vied with the Eastern in giving tokens of loyalty by a liberal supply of men and means to carry on the war. Volumes could easily be written to show the loyalty, bravery, and patriotism of the North and West. The Atlantic heard the cry, "To arms!" sounded from the Capitol; and the same cry echoed along the shores of the Pacific. Maine gave her choicest sons; and California, stirred by the resistless eloquence of Rev. T. Starr King, did not withhold her jewels. The enthusiasm of the people everywhere was intense; and the civilized world far over the blue waves was soon looking with unwonted interest to behold the result of the grand uprising.

CHAPTER II.

COURAGE, BRAVERY, AND PATRIOTISM ON THE FIELD.

"Shoulder to shoulder ride the brother-bands,
Brave hearts and tender, with undaunted eye,
With manly patience ready to endure,
With gallant daring resolute to die."

HARRIET BEECHER STOWE.

ENTHUSIASM such as was never seen before has been awakened for the American flag during the four years of the Rebellion, and manifested in shout and song wherever the beautiful banner of our country was unfurled. And all along the Atlantic shores, amid the granite hills and village-decked valleys of New England, far over the broad prairies of the West, and on the green Pacific slopes, — everywhere waved the gay stripes and blazed the silver stars of our flag, gorgeous in its beauty, serene in its splendor. Human hearts have thrilled at the sight of its ample folds floating on the air of the free Northern States; human hands have lifted it, rejoicing, to the summit of its staff; human voices have uttered and echoed exultant huzzas as the flag that symbolized Freedom and Union, flung out on the ambient air by loyal hands, cheered and gladdened each sympathetic beholder like an angel presence.*

It is said, that " as one of the brigades of the reserve corps, which came up to the rescue of Gen. Thomas at Chickamauga, was marching through Athens, Ala., a bright-eyed girl of four summers was looking at the sturdy fellows tramping by. When she saw the sun glancing through the stripes of red, and on the golden stars of the flag, she exclaimed, clapping her hands, 'O pa, pa! God made that flag. See the stars!' A shout, deep and loud, went up from that column; and many a bronzed veteran lifted his hat as he passed the

---

* THE FIRST AMERICAN FLAG IN ENGLAND. — We copy from a Memoir of Elkanah Watson, in the last number of the " New-England Historical and Genealogical Register," the following anecdote of Copley the artist, who, it will be recollected, was born in Boston, and was the father of the late Lord Lyndhurst: —

" Soon after Mr. Watson's arrival in England, he dined with Copley, the distinguished painter, a Bostonian by birth; and came to the conclusion to expend a hundred guineas, which he had just easily obtained, for a splendid portrait of himself by that celebrated artist.

"' The painting was finished,' says Mr. Watson in his journal, 'in most admirable style, except the background, which Copley and I designed to represent a ship bearing to America the acknowledgment of independence, with a sun just rising upon the stripes of the Union streaming from her gaff. All was complete, save the flag, which Copley did not deem prudent to hoist under present circumstances, as his gallery was a constant resort of the royal family and the nobility. I dined with the artist on the glorious 5th of December, 1782, after listening with him to the speech of the king formally recognizing the United States of America as in the rank of nations. Previous to dining, and immediately after our return from the House of Lords, he invited me into his studio; and there, with a bold hand, a master's touch, and, I believe, an American heart, attached to the ship the *stars and stripes.* This was, I imagine, *the first American flag hoisted in Old England.*' "

Mrs. Farrar, in her " Recollections of Seventy Years," speaks with commendable pride, at this hour, when the " dear old flag " is dearer than ever, of the fact that a whaleship, the " Maria," belonging to her father, William Rotch, was the first to sail beneath the American flag in English waters.

sunny-haired child, resolving, if his good right arm availed any thing, God's flag should conquer." *

To defend that flag, to save for posterity, as well as for ourselves, all of good and of glory which that dear banner represents, our brave boys went forth to battle. The fairest, bravest of New-England homes, the pride of the young and growing West, the stout-hearted men of the Middle States, all went, as to a gala-feast, or to the mount of sacrifice, with willing hearts and unswerving footsteps. The record of their heroic achievements gilds the lately written pages of our country's history with an undying lustre.

The "New-York Commercial Advertiser" says, " At the depot, an affecting incident occurred. Col. Munroe, of the Eighth, being loudly called for, appeared, surrounded by Gen. Butler, Lieut.-Col. Hinks, and the rest of his staff. A. M. Griswold, Esq., a prominent member of the New-York bar, stepped forward, holding in his hand a magnificent silk flag, mounted on a massive hickory staff. He addressed the colonel of the regiment as follows: ' Col. Munroe, — Sir, you are from Massachusetts, God bless her! Her sons everywhere are proud of her history; and, while her armies are commanded by such officers as are now at their head, we have faith in her future. As a son of Massachusetts, I beg leave to present this standard as a token of my appreciation of the cause in which you are engaged. I confide it to your keeping. Stand by it!'

"Col. Munroe responded, saying, ' As a son of Massachu-

---

* Harper's Weekly.

setts, I receive it from a son of her soil, and will defend it, God helping me.'

"The cheering which followed was deafening. Nine cheers were proposed and given for the flag; and, at that moment, eight hundred hardy soldiers, just arrived from the sacred precincts of Bunker Hill, vowed solemnly to defend that flag with life and honor."

The truthful historian cannot ignore the claims of the domestic champions, the genuine "*Home* Guard," who, without ostentation, bore their part in the struggle for Liberty and Union by aiding and encouraging those who buckled on the armor for a conflict waged before the eyes of an onlooking world. The brave *at home* should not be forgotten.

> "The maid who binds her warrior's sash
>   With smile that well her pain dissembles,
> The while beneath her drooping lash
>   One starry teardrop hangs and trembles,
> Though Heaven alone records the tear,
>   And Fame shall never know her story,
> Her heart shall shed a drop as dear
>   As ever dewed the field of glory.
>
> The wife who girds her husband's sword
>   'Mid little ones who weep or wonder,
> And gravely speaks the cheering word,
>   What though her heart be rent asunder,
> Doomed nightly in her dreams to hear
>   The bolts of war around him rattle,
> Hath shed as sacred blood as e'er
>   Was poured upon a field of battle.

> The mother who conceals her grief
>   When to her breast her son she presses,
> Then breathes a few brave words and brief,
>   Kissing the patriot brow she blesses,
> With no one but her secret God
>   To know the pain that weighs upon her,
> Sheds holy blood as e'er the sod
>   Received on Freedom's field of honor." *

Not of them is it now proposed to speak, though this chapter is one which will unfold a panorama of courage, heroism, and patriotism, such as even Rome herself never rivalled.

That courage which is self-sacrificing, that heroism which does not wait till bullets whistle overhead, that patriotism which is nerved to gallant deeds by the thought of home and loved ones, was often shown by our brave defenders, even before they started for the field of blood. The following story, said to be authentic, and which is, after all, but a type of many similar affecting scenes, illustrates the above assertion:—

"A whole family, mother and five children, led by their stalwart head, the husband and father, presented themselves a few days since to Chairman Blunt, in New York, for the six-hundred-dollars' bounty; he, the husband, having just been examined and mustered in. It was a large family, and a sorrowful one,— all except the little tow-headed fellow in its mother's arms, who was leaping and crowing as though he really thought it was excellent fun, a capital joke. The family

* T. Buchanan Read.

appeared like a respectable one, though the hand of poverty evidently rested heavily upon it; and this, most likely, was the last resort, the last hope, the throwing of one overboard to save the rest.

"As Mr. Blunt counted the money, — one, two, three, four, five, six hundred dollars, — and presented it, a kind of sickly, faint smile was visible through the unbidden tears which were coursing down his checks; for his time, he knew, with his family, its joys and hopes, was now about up. His children were clinging to his legs, begging him not to leave them: his wife, too full to speak, looked unutterable griefs, and clung all the closer to her babe. The money was all right: he held it in his hand, — more than he had owned at once during all his lifetime. 'God bless you, wife and children! we must now part, perhaps forever. This money, wife, is yours: but let me give some to each; it will gratify me, and will go to you whenever you want it. Here, wife, is one hundred dollars for you: may Heaven bless it and you! Here, Billy, is one hundred dollars for you: be good and true to your mother, and, as you are the oldest, watch faithfully over your brothers and sisters. James, here is one hundred dollars for you: give it to your mother whenever she wants it. Mary, take this hundred dollars: be a good girl, and in your prayers remember your father. Come here, my pet Alice: here is one hundred dollars for you to keep until good mamma requires it. And now, my little toad without a name, — yes, let us call him Hope. Do you say so, wife?' It was assented to. 'Then here, you little crowing cock, — bless the little fellow! — I may never see him again. Kiss me, boy! Here, put this hundred dollars in your little hand; and don't eat it, but pass it over to your mother as soon as possible.'

"The noble-hearted fellow's heavy frame seemed to quiver all over as he finished his distribution, and knew that his time had come. He embraced each and all separately, and declared himself ready to go.

"'But,' says Mr. Blunt, 'there is another hundred dollars coming to you,— the band-money. Who brought you here?'—'That wee bit of a babe, your honor: I'd never come in the world had it not been for that dear babe.' 'Well, then, the band-money or premium belongs to him.' 'Bless me! is it so? Wife, put that hundred dollars into the savings bank for Hope, and never touch it, if you can help it,— if you can help it, mind,— until he comes of age. God bless the little fellow! He starts well in the world, after all, and may yet be President.'

"The man stepped upon the platform of the turn-stile, and was whirled in, out of sight of the world and all he loved. The whole scene was a most touching one,— one of true family affection, and long to be remembered by all who witnessed it."

Such scenes often occurred; and though some may have joined the army just to obtain the bounty-money, yet where poverty, or even avarice, drove one man to enlist, unalloyed patriotism induced ten to put on the "army blue." Men thought of their little ones, and enlisted, sometimes, it is true, in order to procure the means of supporting them; but, when they fought, it was for the rights of those children, which were dearer than all. That they fought bravely, all who read aright the records of each terrible conflict know full well. Some "chronicles of the fight" are subjoined, which give evidence of courage and patriotic enthusiasm.

MASSACHUSETTS BRAVERY. — A correspondent of the "New-York Tribune" gives the following statistics and anecdote in evidence of the bravery of Massachusetts troops in battle: —

"Hooker's division, as was expected of them, 'fought like brave men, long and well, and heaped the ground with rebel slain.' This division is known here as the fighting division; and, as an evidence of their work, it may be proper to state that they came on to the Peninsula eleven thousand strong, and now number less than five thousand effective men. Among the regiments of this division which suffered most severely were the Massachusetts First, Eleventh, and Sixteenth. Of the latter regiment, about eighty were either killed or seriously wounded.

"A little incident will show the spirit of the Massachusetts Sixteenth. When the Massachusetts First were ordered to charge, the men of the Sixteenth, addressing the colonel of the First, said, 'May we not charge with you? You are not strong enough to charge that solid column of rebels alone. We have no officers left. Our colonel is dead, and our lieutenant-colonel and adjutant wounded. So, if you will lead us, we would like to charge with you.' They did charge, with an effect that the rebels will be likely to remember for some time. I would say more about the splendid fighting of the Massachusetts troops on this occasion, only for the fact that the Old Bay State has a history which the world knows by heart; and to tell our readers that Massachusetts soldiers are brave, and that they do their duty, is to tell them what they instinctively know. 'God bless the Commonwealth of Massachusetts!'"

INCIDENTS OF THE FIGHT AT BALL'S BLUFF. — Mr. P. H. Hildreth, of Groton, communicates to the "Worcester Spy" some interesting incidents of the battle of Ball's Bluff, narrated to him at Poolesville by the soldiers, after that disastrous struggle. One little Irishman of Company I, belonging in Webster, got six bullet-holes through his coat, but not a scratch on his body. He said he didn't mind the *danger*, but they were *shabby rascals* to spoil his coat; said he should wear it, however, while a rag of it remained. 'Tis a coat of honor to him. Another incident was as follows: —

"One of the privates of Company H had a ball shot through both legs, without, however, injuring the bone. He still kept his place in the ranks, loading and firing wherever he could see a rebel, until another wound in the thigh prostrated him. His comrades were about to bear him from the field; when he came sufficiently near to request them to prop him up against a tree, where he did his duty *nobly*, with his three wounds in *front*, until another shot struck him in the leg, just below the knee, burying itself in the bone. This last was too much for him to stand up under; and he allowed himself to be carried from the field, saying, as he went, to his comrades, 'Give 'em Jessie, boys: I'll be back and help you soon.' He was very low when I left, and I fear he is dead before this; but, if so, his wife and family, while they mourn his loss, may, and I trust will, glory in his fame. A grateful country should remember them substantially."

An officer of Company A, who was in the hospital, when he learned that a detachment of the Fifteenth was ordered across the river, insisted on joining them, declaring to his attendants, who tried to dissuade him, that the thought of a fight with the rebels would give him strength. He went, fought through the day; and the men said the fight seemed to suit him. P. Jorgeson, orderly-sergeant of the same company, saw a rebel aim at him while loading, and hurried to get the first shot; but the rebel was too quick. The bullet of the rebel cut a hole in Jorgeson's tin plate, which was swung under his arm; when he exclaimed in broken English, "Ah! you fire well, you spoil Uncle Sam's crockery, — I pay you for dat," —drew up his gun, shot him through the breast, and dropped him. Just as he fired, another rebel sighted him, and shot him through the arm. This is the third wound he has received in his third war, — once in Germany, once in Mexico, and now at Ball's Bluff.

Charles B. Pratt, Esq., was despatched by Mayor Davis, of Worcester, to the scene of action, with instructions to offer the Massachusetts Fifteenth Regiment, in behalf of the city, any assistance or succor they might require. The duty was promptly performed; and Mr. Pratt returned with this message: "Tell our friends at home that we want immediately *three hundred and ten men* to fill the places of those killed and missing, and a blanket and pair of mittens for each of us. This is all we ask of them for the present."

Massachusetts was not alone in her deeds of valor; though, from a Massachusetts writer, she may possibly have her full share of praise in a volume devoted to incidents of the war.

The green sods of Missouri cover the remains of a gallant Iowa volunteer, whose fame belongs to both New England and the West; for he was born in Massachusetts.*

While taking dinner at a farm-house in Kirksville, Mo., within two miles of the enemy's camp, the little band of only six members of Company C was surrounded by rebels, twenty-five in number, who demanded a surrender.

"The Iowa Third never surrenders!" replied the dauntless young leader, and ordered his men to fire. A severe conflict commenced, which continued for some time. Young Dix, finding it difficult to get a shot at his country's foes, who skulked behind fences and trees, left the house with two of his men, Sergeant Still and Private Schoonover, and engaged them with his revolver, with which he was a crack shot; but the contest was too unequal. He shot down three of the rebels, and wounded another, when he was himself shot by one of the besiegers: the ball passed through his head, killing him instantly. The rebels then fled, leaving six of their number killed, and a seventh mortally wounded. Five others were wounded, but succeeded in getting off.

* Lieut. Hervey Dix, only brother of the late editor of the "Boston Journal,"—James A. Dix, Esq.

On the next day, Lieut. Crawford of the Iowa regiment, with a detachment, visited the scene of this conflict. The wounded rebel had been taken into the farm-house, where he was just dying: with his last breath, he paid a striking tribute to the memory of his conqueror. "Lieut. Dix," said the dying man, "was the bravest, man I ever saw: if the North has many such, we had better give up."

The body of the young and gallant Dix was tenderly prepared for the grave by a noble-hearted Western lady, and interred in the village cemetery, where an appropriate stone is erected to his memory.

Surprise is often expressed that even mere youths exhibit great fearlessness in battle.

The story of the drummer-boy of Marblehead is a case in point. Rev. Mr. Thayer thus narrates it:—

"The name of the drummer-boy was Albert Manson. He had a great desire to do something for his country; and he thought he could drum for it if he could not fight for it. His father consented that he might go as drummer; and afterward the father himself concluded that he would enlist in order to look after his son.

"The father fell wounded in that bold and violent assault upon the enemy's works by the Twenty-third Massachusetts. The son was at his side at the time, using a musket that he had picked up; and he was so intent upon conquering the foe, that he scarcely heeded his father's fall.

"'Look at that child!' exclaimed one officer to another. 'No wonder we conquer, when boys fight so!'

"'Didn't I say that they should run to the old tunes?' shouted the boy as the enemy fled; at the same time seizing a disabled revolver for a drum-stick, and striking up in a defiant way the old strain of 'Yankee Doodle.'

"A rebel heard it, and, turning round, took sure aim at Albert. A soldier by the young patriot's side tried to pull him down: but he stood his ground, beating the tune; and the fatal ball struck him.

"Col. Kurtz lifted the dying lad in his arms. He spoke to him, and the boy's lips moved in reply.

"'What, Albert?'

"'Which beat?—quick, tell me!' said the little hero.

"Tears ran like rain down the blackened faces; and one in a husky voice replied,—

"'We, Albert: the field is ours!'

"His ear caught the sound; but he did not quite understand, dying as he was.

"'What?—tell quick!' he whispered.

"'We beat 'em entirely, me boy!' answered a big Irish sergeant, who was crying like a baby.

"He understood these words, and in a stronger voice than ever said, 'Why don't you go after 'em? Don't mind me: I'll catch up. I'm a little cold; but running will warm me.'

"He never spoke again. His young spirit passed away without a struggle; and many soldiers wept that their brave drummer-boy was no more."

A writer in the "Louisville Journal" thus graphically describes his emotions during a sanguinary struggle:—

"I remember well my feelings during the first battle in which I was engaged. The night before, we received orders to prepare to attack the enemy early on the morrow. All was now bustle, hurry, and anxiety. Guns were cleaned, ammunition inspected, straps adjusted, canteens filled, knapsacks lightened, letters written. We had several in our company who had always boasted of their bravery and prowess; men who had been 'spoiling for a fight,' as they said. These were now as still as mice: they didn't peep. One of them, who had taken a master's degree in all kinds of profanity, now borrowed a Bible, sat down and read it for some time, and intimated to his messmate the propriety of praying before going to sleep that night. It is not your blustering, profane bravado that is the brave man on the field of battle: it is your quiet, patient, retiring man.

"I confess, a feeling of dread and anxiety stole over me. Battle was certain, the enemy was strongly posted, and we had desperate work before us. I wanted to go into battle; yet I dreaded it like death. I slept but little that night. The morning came; and our columns moved quietly and sternly forward through a wood. The first intimation we had of the enemy was the skirmishing between his outposts and our vanguard; the former falling back as the latter advanced. We passed out of the wood, and rapidly deployed into line of battle; a gentle sloping hill hiding the enemy from our view. A part of our force had been sent round to make a flank and rear attack on the enemy; and, while so doing, it was of the utmost importance that we should hold his attention in front. We marched steadily up the hill till the whole line of the enemy burst upon our view: there we halted, and for some minutes not a gun was fired on either side. There stood the two armies, each waiting for the other to begin the work of death. The faces of our men looked pale and determined: some of them stood like statues, others were nervous and uneasy. It was the time to test their courage. A line of cannon was bearing directly upon us. Death to many of us was certain. 'Who will it be?' thought I. A singular feeling came over me: a confused image of a mother and sister appeared flitting and floating before my imagination, like dissolving shadows, while the tremendous reality in front oppressed me with dreadful forebodings.

"A few moments passed like those that intervene between drawing the cap over the criminal's face and letting fall the drop, when a puff of smoke from one of the cannon, followed by a crash and a bomb, went screaming over us. Our men ducked down their heads like geese. Fire was now opened on us along the enemy's entire line. Their first shots were aimed too high: they gradually lowered them. Every discharge brought their balls fearfully nearer. We were impatient to return the fire, but dare not till the command was given. Our colonel passed along in front of the line, and urged us to stand firm till the proper time, and the day would be ours. It is a task to hold men exposed to an enemy's fire without allowing them to return it. They will soon run one way or the other. The enemy's shot now began to howl around us, plough through our ranks, and tear up the earth about our feet. A six-pound ball cut off the bayonet of my messmate on my left: a moment more, and one struck him in the breast, severing him almost in twain. He reeled, and fell like a log. The hot blood from his heart spurted full in my face. Great God, how I felt! A faint, sickening sensation came over me. I stooped down over him. He smiled faintly, spoke my name, gasped, and expired. He was frightfully mangled. I was maddened to desperation. All thought of fear vanished: I could have fought thousands. The command 'Fire!' rang along the line; and a tremendous crash of musketry answered the command. We now loaded and fired for life. Dense volumes of sulphurous smoke hung like a pall over us, and shut out the enemy from our sight. The battle grew warm and bloody. The rattle of musketry, the screaming of shells, the thunders of the artillery, the whistling of bullets, the shouts of command, commingled with curses, prayers, and groans of the wounded and dying, filled all the air. Our men, black with smoke and powder, looked like devils incarnate, as they plied their work of death.

"At length a breeze rolled away the smoke that shrouded us, and disclosed our other columns bearing down upon the enemy's flank. Now was the decisive moment. 'Charge bayonets!' rang out; and with loud shouts we rushed forward to the assault. A storm of grape and canister was hurled against us as we neared the batteries. Like maddened tigers, our men leaped forward with the cold steel. The struggle over the guns was desperate: it was a butchery savage in the extreme. The enemy soon broke and fled, leaving us masters of the field. Since that time, I have not felt the least dread or hesitation on entering a battle. After the first few shots, I fire away as coolly as when hunting squirrels."

In battle-time, the effect of a stirring song or tune is often electrical. The Western armies have one of this character, called "The Battle-cry of Freedom," which is described as of most potent effect:—

"In either Grant's or Rosecrans's army, it only needs to be started to be caught up from camp to camp, till it spreads for miles over the whole army. By order of a general commanding one division of the Army of the Cumberland, the colonel of each regiment is directed to start the 'Battle Cry' whenever the army goes into action; and the effect of thousands of voices united upon the chorus,—

> 'The Union forever! Hurrah, boys! hurrah!
> Down with the traitor! up with the stars!
> While we rally round the flag, boys, rally once again,
> Shouting the battle-cry of Freedom!'—

is described as awakening a frenzied enthusiasm perfectly indescribable.

"It is evident from its effect that this is one of the few songs not written 'to order,' but written because the author could not help it. The great number of thrilling circumstances under which this song has been sung in the army added to its popularity. When Gen. Blair's brigade, that led the assault upon Vicksburg last fall, after being hurled again and again upon the enemy's fortifications, only to see each time a ghastly proportion of their numbers go down in death, were at last ordered to retire, the brave fellows closed up their shattered battalions, and came out of the smoke of that terrible carnage, singing, —

'Yes, we'll rally round the flag, boys, we'll rally once again,
  Shouting the battle-cry of Freedom!'

"We are not surprised that the remembrance of that scene drew tears from the officer who described it to us; and when, after months of hardship, assault, and battle, these same troops ran up the stars and stripes over this same rebel stronghold, Gen. McPherson and staff, on the cupola of the court-house, fittingly started the same song; and we can imagine with what a will it was sung by Grant's entire army."

Here is a glorious record concerning one of our adopted citizens, which may go to the credit of Pennsylvania: —

A BRAVE STANDARD-BEARER. — A correspondent, giving an account of the battle at Winchester, says, "Among the acts of chivalry performed on the field was one by Private Graham, of the Eighty-fourth Pennsylvania. He carried the regimental standard: the left hand, which held it, was shot off; but, before the star-spangled banner fell to the ground, he grasped it in the remaining hand, and held it triumphantly. The right arm was next disabled; but, before the colors fell, he was killed by a third ball. He was a native of the Emerald Isle."

The following anecdote gives proof of a patriotism which many waters cannot quench: —

"ONE LEG MORE FOR HIS COUNTRY.—During the recent visit of Secretary Cameron to New York, a member of the Seventy-ninth Regiment, who was in the battle of Bull Run, and near Col. Cameron when he fell, called upon the secretary. He had been severely wounded and taken prisoner, carried to Richmond, and there suffered an amputation of one of his legs. He came hobbling into the secretary's room on crutches, and begged to be permitted to go to the war again, saying that he thought he could still be of service to the country, even on crutches. Mr. Cameron did not question his capacity, but told him the first preliminary was to get a mate to his remaining extremity. The man said he couldn't afford that luxury, and insisted upon the validity of crutches. Mr. Cameron then told him to go to a limb-seller's, and buy the best leg he could find, and send the bill to him. The wounded soldier went on his way rejoicing."

Read this patriotic answer. Loyal hearts, far and near, respond to it.

When Col. Ripley stepped ashore from the "Persia" at New York, a gentleman said to him, "Your country needs you."—"It can have me," responded the gallant soldier, "and every drop of blood in me."

Here is an instance which should go to the credit of California as well as New England; for the Eldorado country is full of just such emigrants from the Atlantic shores:—

"UNALLOYED PATRIOTISM.—A case of unselfish and persevering patriotism has come to our notice, which we think deserving of public record. Mr. Harvey G. Smith of Boston, who for the last eleven years has been engaged in mining-business at Downieville, Sierra County, Cal., in November last arranged his business so that it could be left in the care of an agent, in order that he might enter upon the service of his country, and contribute his mite towards putting down the Rebellion. Having been for many years a sailor, he proposed to enter the naval service; and, repairing to Washington, he made application for an appointment as sailing-master or master's mate; but, notwithstanding his application was indorsed by the Congress-men from California, it was unsuccessful.

"Mr. Smith then applied to Gov. Andrew for a commission of some sort, but got none. Determined to serve his country in some capacity, he enlisted as a private in the Twenty-ninth Massachusetts Regiment, Col. Pierce. A man who will relinquish his business, and travel three or four thousand miles at his own expense for the purpose of fighting the enemies of his country, is certainly entitled to honorable mention, if not to a commission. Such devoted patriotism is remarkable even in these days, when bright examples of self-sacrifice are numerous." *

Here are a couple of newspaper paragraphs which match each other, and speak well for both East and West. The first is from the " South-Danvers Wizard : " —

" ROCKVILLE, ALL HAIL ! — There is a small village of this town, bordering on Lynn and Lynnfield, comprising a

* Boston Journal.

single school district, and with less than a hundred voters, which has sent seventy-five men to the war! We have not yet heard of the community which has sent such a proportion of its members. None but the old and infirm are left behind. One family named Woodman sends five, being all its male members. One of the last men who enlisted went to Lieut. Warner at Salem yesterday, and begged to be enrolled, as he said he couldn't find a loafer to talk with in all Rockville!

"Mrs. Sarah Larrabee, of Rockville, has now *four sons, seventeen grandsons*, and *one great-grandson*, in the army. The old lady of eighty-five years yesterday walked to Salem to see the last of them depart for the battle-field, and then walked back, about six miles."

The second paragraph is from the pen of Rev. A. V. House, in " The Home Missionary : " —

"IOWA: WESTERN PATRIOTISM. — I have just returned from the meeting of our association; and perhaps some of the particulars of my journey may not be wholly uninteresting to you. To give you an idea of the patriotism of the Western people in these times of war, I will mention that I met more *women* driving teams on the road, and saw more of them at work in the fields, than men. They seem to have said to their husbands, in the language of a favorite song, —

> 'Just take your gun, and go ;
> For Ruth can drive the oxen, John,
> And I can use the hoe.'

" I first went to Clarinda, and the town seemed deserted.

Upon inquiring for former friends, the frequent answer was, 'In the army.' From Hawleyville, almost all the thoroughly loyal male inhabitants have gone; and in one township beyond, where I formerly preached, there are but seven men left; and at Quincy, the county seat of Adams County, but five."

Some of our brave boys met with narrow escapes in battle.

"Sergeant Charles H. Frye, of Salem, Company F, Twenty-first Regiment, son of Mr. James S. Frye, had a very curious and narrow escape from death at the battle of Fredericksburg, which will bear relating. A fragment of shell descended in such a way as to graze his leg from the hip downward, cutting through his pocket, and completely riddling a woollen mitten which was rolled up therein. The mitten is perforated in six or eight places, and the pocket itself, of course, cut through. The wound on the leg was sufficiently severe to detain him in the hospital at Washington till the present time. The fragment of shell and the mitten were sent home to gratify the curiosity of his friends. A companion of Mr. Frye, while assisting him to the rear, was struck by a cannon-ball, and instantly killed." *

The following went the rounds of the press as exhibiting the pluck of a Union soldier. In a speech before the Baltimore Union League, Jos. J. Stewart, of Baltimore County, related the following: —

"The fire which animates the Union soldiers is well illus-

* Salem Observer.

trated by the anecdote related by a chaplain of the army. He says he has regarded it as a part of his Christian duty to attend the dying rebels as well as the Union soldiers; and that, while he has frequently heard rebel soldiers express regret in their last moments for having taken up arms against the good old flag, he has never known a Unionist express doubt or regret for the cause in which he was engaged. One day, the battle raged fiercely: all round him were evidences of awful havoc. A Union soldier was fighting bravely after most of his companions had been shot down. The chaplain watched him. He saw a cannon-ball strike the soldier's left arm, and sever it between the shoulder and elbow. The concussion turned the soldier completely round, his arm falling at the distance of ten feet or more from where he stood. The chaplain still watched him, unconsciously to the soldier, who did not know that he was regarded at that moment by any other than the all-seeing Eye. The soldier looked at his left side, and beheld his bleeding stump; then, turning around, he commenced searching for his dissevered arm. He picked it up, and held it for a moment in its place: he then held it aloft in his right hand, and exultantly exclaiming, 'This is my sacrifice for the Union!' he hurled it with all his might at the retreating foe."

The "Newburyport Herald" furnishes the following bright record of a Harvard boy:—

"Among the wounded soldiers of Williamsburg, returned home for nursing, is Lieut. G. P. Stevens of the First Excelsior Regiment, Hooker's division. He has been at the house of his father, Judge Stevens of Lawrence, for some weeks, severely wounded by a bullet through the thigh. He entered the service six months since, while a member of the junior class of Harvard; and the sword he has so nobly carried was presented by his classmates. He had been wounded prior to the battle of Williamsburg by the accidental discharge of his revolver sending a ball into his foot, which has not yet been extracted. When the cry, 'Forward!' went up from Yorktown, he was in his place, but, on account of his wound, was detailed to look after the baggage, and come on with the trains; but, hearing that a battle was in prospect, he pressed forward eighteen miles on foot through mud and rain, arriving in the midst of the terrific conflict, and sought his regiment, which was at the extreme right. There they fought the enemy at fearful odds, and were outflanked, their colonel wounded and taken prisoner, and a large number of their officers and men either killed or wounded. Several bullets passed through young Stevens's clothes, and one through his thigh; but still he was able to retreat after forty rounds of ammunition had been exhausted, and assisted in forming the men, with empty muskets and fixed bayonets, around the cannon in the woods. Bleeding and exhausted, he still labored and fought; and, having searched the cartridge-boxes of the dead in vain, there was no alternative but to stand the leaden hail with fixed bayonets, till re-enforcements arrived, and victory was won. Then he was carried to the rear, and is now safe at home, though anxious and determined to return as soon as his wound permits."

With emotions of pride that our country can point to such

young men, — heroes, though but beardless boys, — the following testimonial is subjoined : —

ONE OF OUR BRAVES. — The "Worcester Spy" has a touching tribute, from the pen of Henry S. Washburn, to the memory of Lieut. J. William Grout, who was killed at Ball's Bluff. This young and promising officer was only eighteen years old. He was the son of wealthy parents, and early evinced a fondness for military pursuits. When war was declared, he expressed a wish at once to enter the army; but his parents withheld their consent, chiefly on account of his youth. When, however, they yielded to his importunities, his joy knew no bounds; and, with all the ardor of his nature, he engaged in the work of preparation for his new calling. He had received a military education at the Highland Institute, and obtained a commission as second lieutenant in Company D, of the Massachusetts Fifteenth, — an honor rarely bestowed upon so young a person. Of his services at Ball's Bluff, the following account is given : —

"He was there, and nobly did he discharge his duty. It was observed that he displayed great coolness and bravery; and, in one instance at least, his right arm did signal execution. When all hope had fled, and the day was evidently lost, and the order to retreat given, he knew that he and his associates had done all that men could do, and that Massachusetts had reason to be proud of the conduct of her sons on that dreadful field of blood and carnage. Alas that even then his work was done, and his warfare finished!

"He had gained the middle of the stream, and would soon have reached the opposite bank, when a fatal shot pierced him; and he exclaimed, 'Tell Company D I could have reached the shore, but I am shot; I must sink!' and, as the waters closed over him, the spirit took its flight to be forever free from the throes and conflicts of the earth.

"When his death was announced, Col. Devens remarked, with deep emotion, 'Dear little fellow! he came to me at the close of the battle, and said, ' Colonel, is there any thing more that I can do for you?' I replied, 'Nothing but take care of yourself.' Similar testimony to his bravery and fidelity has been received from numerous sources."

Mr. Washburn concludes his touching tribute to the memory of his young friend with the following striking and eloquent remarks: —

"The records of that sad conflict at Ball's Bluff tell the story of the fall of one of the oldest and one of the youngest officers of the Union forces, — one high in political position, and the pride of our Western domain (let the tear of charity forever erase the remembrance of his mistakes, if any he made; for he was a peerless man, and a tower of strength to the nation); the other a fitting representative of the unconquerable pluck and the chivalrous daring of the young men of the oldest Commonwealth in the Union. Thus were united, upon the same altar of patriotism and love of country, the Atlantic and the Pacific, — the blossoms of youth and the frosts of age! Oh! who, in view of such pledges and such consecrations, can despair, whatever may be the reverses of the moment, of the final triumph of the Republic?"

Not only were deeds of noble daring frequent upon the battle-fields of our beloved land in the late contest for liberty and righteousness, but there were not a few scenes exhibiting family affection and the tender ties of friendship, upon which even angels must have looked with admiring interest. Here is one of them: —

FATHER AND SON ON THE BATTLE-FIELD. — A story is told of the veteran Sumner at the battle of Antietam. His son, Capt. Sumner, a youth of twenty-one, was on his staff. The old man calmly stood amidst a storm of shot and shells, and turned to send him through a doubly-raging fire upon a mission of duty. He might never see his boy again: but his country claimed his life; and, as he looked upon his young brow, he grasped his hand, encircled him in his arms, and fondly kissed him. "Good-by, Sammy!"—"Good-by, father!" and the youth, mounting his horse, rode gayly on the message. He returned unharmed; and again his hand was grasped with a cordial "How d'ye do, Sammy?" answered by a grasp of equal affection. The scene was touching to those around.

A Boston paper thus refers to the

DEATH OF A HERO. — Rev. J. F. Mines, chaplain of the Second Maine Regiment, now a prisoner at Richmond, in a letter to a friend in Bangor, gives the following account of the death of William J. Deane, son of Col. B. S. Deane of that city, who was standard-bearer of the Second at the battle of Bull Run: —

"Tell Mr. Deane, the father of William Deane, color-bearer of the Second Maine, who fell in the battle of the 21st, that his son died like a hero. Though sorely wounded, so that he could scarcely whisper, he beckoned me to him; and when I knelt beside him, and put my ear close to his mouth, he hoarsely whispered, 'It's safe.'—'What,' said I, —'what? the flag?' He nodded his head, for he could not speak again, and then closed his eyes. I bathed his head with water, and tried to comfort him; but my own heart was full, and I could not speak for tears. That man was a hero. His father may weep bitterly for his loss; but let him thank God for his glorious death."

A Belfast (Me.) paper thus speaks of

"A PATRIOTIC FAMILY. — *A Father and Six Sons in the Army.* — Mr. James McKinney, of Enfield, in this State, aged fifty-four years, and his six sons, — seven in all, — have enlisted in the service of the country. One son has died in the hospital, and one has returned home sick. The father and two sons enlisted in the Sixth Maine, two sons in the Seventh Maine, one son in the Tenth, and one in the Eleventh. There was still one remaining son, who was prevented from enlisting in consequence of having lost some of his fingers. He was so anxious to go, that he wanted his father and brothers to get him a situation as a teamster; but they declined, urging that he ought to stay at home and take care of the old castle."

Some one truthfully remarks, —

"There are strange scenes in war, mingling the sublime,

the horrible, the fraternal, social, touching. A young Massachusetts volunteer in the battle of Antietam was mortally wounded by a rifle-ball in the abdomen, and fell backward; his lower limbs being entirely paralyzed by the wound. He was, to all appearance, helpless; yet he aided in the fight. Having fallen almost at the beginning of the action, his cartridge-box was nearly full. Having excellent teeth, he handled and tore the cartridges from his box till it was empty, rapidly passing them to his comrades who stood over him; and then, as they found he aided their speed in firing, they took the cartridges from their boxes, and he tore them till their ammunition was expended, when they bore him to the quiet bed of death; he being all the time as calm, deliberate, and earnest as those who remained unhurt."

Prof. Hackett gives in his "Memorials of the War" the following story of an Indiana hero boy, prepared from the "Cincinnati Gazette:" —

"On the cars running from Evansville to Indianapolis, I fell into conversation with a soldier, who, though young in years, carried, as I found, the heart of a man and a hero in his bosom: he was returning home on a discharge furlough. Having found others destitute, I inquired into his condition. He had started without breakfast; had neither food nor money to go to Elkhart, on the Southern Michigan Road, a distance of over three hundred miles, and with the probability before him of being over two days on the way. His voice was gone, and he was obliged to talk in a whisper. On seeing what the prospect before him was, he said to me, with childish simplicity, ' I shall be nearly starved when I reach home; shall I not?' I inquired for his haversack in order to supply him with something to eat when we stopped. He replied that ' it had been stolen from him;' yet he was indifferent about the haversack: it was the Bible contained in it that he felt to be the great loss to him. His parents were religious, as I learned, and had brought him up to habits of rectitude, and in the fear of God.

"He had an impression that he should not live long; and I remarked to him, 'Death is no calamity to a good boy.' His countenance brightened as I said that to him; and he answered with much earnestness, 'No, sir; and I am not afraid to die. I made up my mind that it was my duty to go and fight for my country, and my parents consented. Through exposure, I lost my health early in the winter; and, on the Sunday morning of the battle of Shiloh, I was in my tent sick, and the physician ordered me to remain there. I had been unfit for duty for two months. The physician was very kind to me. The news kept coming back to us near the river, that our army was giving way everywhere; and I thought it my duty to take my gun, and go to their assistance. I went to the front, and, during four hours, loaded and fired as fast as I could; but the exertion was too much for me. My lungs took to bleeding, and I came near dying before the bleeding could be stopped; but I was glad I did what I could. I have never spoken since above a whisper, and I fear I never shall; but it is all right! Our country must be saved at any sacrifice.' At the first eating station, the boy was seated at the table, and his dinner paid for by a stranger; and his thanks were so cordial and heartfelt, that tears filled the stranger's eyes as he turned away, receiving, as he did so, the sick boy's 'God bless you, stranger!'

"Time for supper would bring him to Indianapolis. What would he do there? Who would befriend him there? He was told to go to Gov. Morton, and inform him that he was on his way home from Shiloh with ruined health, and had neither money nor food. He answered that he would do so, if he had strength to walk. He was then told to send him a line: any one would carry it for him. He said he would do so; and added, 'It would not be improper; surely the governor would not let me starve: it seems to me, almost anybody would help a sick soldier.'

"When he arrived at Elkhart, he would still be several miles from home. That occurred to him, and perplexed his thoughts for a moment; and then, smiling, he said, 'Our family physician lives there, and he will take me in his carriage and carry me home; and oh! does not a welcome await me when my mother sees me coming? I shall take her by surprise: she is not prepared for that.' Here the train started with the sick boy, who seemed revived by his food, and the words of encouragement spoken to him, and the thoughts of home."

Another volunteer from the sturdy West has left a shining record: —

"John Henry, of Indiana, is the name of one of the martyr-heroes of the war. Although fifty-six years of age, he enlisted as a volunteer in the Seventy-eighth Indiana Regiment. He was not influenced by ambition, for he went as a private; nor by love of money, for he was not destitute of means, and the soldier's stipend of thirteen dollars a month was little to him; nor yet by patriotism alone, although he loved his country well enough to die for it. He was a teacher in the Sabbath school, and went from love to the members of his class, and from a sense of duty to his Lord and Master, who had committed them to his care. He said 'The great Shepherd will demand them at my hands: I wish to give a good account of my trust. I must care for the souls for whom he cared, and be able, if I can, to present them among the saved in the day when the throne shall be set and the books be opened.' So he enlisted.

"He fell in a skirmish on Monday morning, at Uniontown, Ky., mortally wounded. A ball passed through his face, inflicting a terrible wound. It entered just below the left cheek-bone, and so passed out. He was still able, after this, to make himself understood, and was full of joy in spite of the pains of death. On Sunday, the day before his end, he had spent the forenoon in a neighboring orchard in meditation and prayer. Toward noon, he had this thought impressed deeply upon him: 'Work to-day; for the time is short;' and he did work. He passed from tent to tent, praying, praising, and exhorting, not only during the remainder of the day, but late into the night.

"The next morning, he was among the first to fall; and soon his mutilated tongue was silent in death. Among his last words were these: 'Oh! I am happy; for, when the Master came, he found me at my appointed work!'" *

* Prof. Hackett's Memorials, &c.

Our young braves suffered for dear liberty; but they suffered willingly, and with unrivalled fortitude.

"In a hospital, crowded with the wounded from the bloody field of Antietam, was a mutilated soldier, Charles Warren, from Massachusetts, one of whose limbs required amputation. There was little hope of saving him; but, as no other resource was left, it was thought advisable to make the attempt. The wound was such, that the operation could not be otherwise than painful in the extreme. A clergyman, Rev. Mr. Sloane, who had been useful to the young man in spiritual things, felt that he could not bear the sight of the inevitable suffering, and was about to leave the room; 'but what was our surprise,' he says, ' as they placed him on the table beneath the surgeon's knife, to hear him singing, in a clear and cheerful voice, the familiar words,—

> ' There'll be no more sorrow there:
> In heaven above, where all is love,
> There'll be no more sorrow there!'

"I staid, assured that Charles was calm, trusting in God. The limb was taken off; and he remained in a drowsy state for twenty-four hours, and then gently passed away. We buried him in a quiet spot, with appropriate services, and, as we left the grave, felt that we could think of him as in that heaven of which he so cheerfully sang." *

"Not long ago," said Mr. Gough at a public meeting in Boston, "I was in a hospital, and saw a young man twenty-

---

* Prof. Hackett's Memorials, &c.

six years of age, pale and emaciated, with his shattered arm resting upon an oiled-silk pillow; and there he had been many long and weary weeks, waiting for sufficient strength for an amputation. I knelt by his side, and said, 'Will you answer me one question?'

" 'Yes, sir,' was his reply.

" 'Suppose you were well, at home, in good health, and knew all this would come to you if you enlisted, would you enlist?'

" 'Yes, sir,' he answered in a whisper: 'I would, in a minute! What is my arm or my life compared with the safety of the country?'"

That was patriotism, and the young soldier a hero!

Similar to the above is the testimony of Rev. Mr. Savage, agent for the American Tract Society in the Western department: —

"While I have conversed," he says, "with thousands of our wounded from the battle-fields of Lexington and Pea Ridge and Fort Donelson and Shiloh and Corinth and Iuka, sometimes on the field, sometimes on transports, sometimes in hospitals, I have never found the first wounded man yet that has uttered a single word of complaint, or expressed a regret at having enlisted. It is most wonderful to me. I have seen them armless and legless, pierced through every part of the body, and upon the surgeon's bench undergoing amputation; I have seen them dying, and heard them speak of wife and children and loved ones at home: but I have never heard a word of complaint or regret at having enlisted in the army."

They were patriots, ever faithful to the flag; and not a few of them manifested the spirit which found utterance in the last words of the lamented Gen. James S. Rice, "Let me die with my face to the foe, boys." *

As an example of the kindness of some of our soldiers to their wounded comrades, the following is given from the "Sanitary-Commission Bulletin:"—

"While examining a fearful wound in a young soldier in one of the hospitals the other day, I was astonished at the rapid progress towards recovery, as well as at the patient's unusually vigorous condition, considering the nature of the wound,— a compound fracture in the upper third of the right thigh. The following statement which he gave me accounts for this man's good fortune: He was wounded while in the skirmish line the 3d of June, at Coal Harbor, Va. His comrades had him carefully conveyed to the rear;

---

* James G. Clark, the poet and composer, has written a stirring song suggested by these words, the last stanza of which is,—

> "Let me die with my face to the field, boys,
>   As the shot of the foeman found me:
> I crave no shroud or shield, boys,
>   Save the old flag wrapped around me.
>   Those stars shall gleam forever
>   O'er land and sea and river,
> In Freedom's right and Freedom's light,
>   O'er hearts that will never yield."
>
> CHORUS.
>
> "I hear the shout of the brave ring out
>   Where the land's high hearts lie low:
> Then let me gaze through the cannon's blaze,
>   And die with my face to the foe."

and, as soon as permission could be obtained after the battle, eight of those comrades undertook the task of transporting him on a litter, borne upon their own shoulders, from Coal Harbor to Whitehouse, twenty-two miles by the road they travelled. Carefully they kept step as they went onward to the new base for the transports; and, when they reached the hospital-boat in the Pamunkey River, the field litter and its precious burden were deposited without having been jostled or the wounded parts injured. The physicians promised that the noble object of this tender care should be transported to the hospital-wharf at Washington, and from thence to some general hospital, without being disturbed from the carefully prepared bed upon which he had been brought from the battle-field. The pledge has been fulfilled: and if those affectionate comrades live to reach Jefferson County, N.Y., again, there is reason to believe that they will find there the noble man who was borne upon their shoulders from Coal Harbor to Whitehouse."

Volumes might be written, and yet all the incidents of interest occurring on the battle-field fail to be told. Eye-witnesses of such courage and patriotism have given many sketches of heroic conduct; but only the pen of the recording angel could preserve them all, they were so numerous, so constantly recurring. This is not extravagant language. No words can ever utter our defenders' meed of praise. Only when the Judge of all the earth shall say to each patriot soldier, "Thou hast fought the good fight, henceforth is laid up for thee a crown," and shall place that crown upon the radiant brow of those who were victors though they fell, will their dauntless valor and unfailing patriotism be fully appreciated.

The picket-guard, pacing his lonely beat, should not be forgotten as we call to mind the deeds of daring on the battle-field. It required no little courage to take one's stand, day after day, and night after night, when a bullet from a sharpshooter might at any moment end his earthly career. How many a thought of home and dear ones has crowded upon the mind of the lonely sentinel at such hours! — his eyes bent upon discovering the danger, if lurking foes should reveal themselves; his heart far away with the prattling children, or the anxious wife, longing for peace, it may be, yet willing and ready to stay at his post, or to die in his country's defence.

It should be observed that truthful records of the gallant deeds of the Union army and navy do not mention the officers alone. Excellent, brave, and judicious officers showed wonderful executive ability, and won unfading laurels on many a battle-field; but not the officers alone constituted our patriots. The rank and file won their full share of glory; at least, they exhibited bravery and patriotism enough to deserve it. One who could sneeringly say, as he read the name of a martyred hero, "It was only a private," stamped himself contemptible beyond expression. Our privates were heroes.

> "See! in the battle's fiery track
> Our torn flag falls! — 'tis gone!
> Who leaps to bring the colors back?
> '*Only a private*' born.

A spirit 'mid the sulphurous air,
    Up from '*the ranks*' he came ;
A god-like form, with streaming hair,
    And an immortal name !

No record traced in Spartan blood
    Tells grander victory ;
None with sublimer courage stood
    At dread Thermopylæ." *

Our "boys in blue" were worthy of their noble cause, whether they wore the uniform of privates or officers ; and impartial history will render due praise to the heroic champions of a nation's rights, the noble advocates of liberty and law.

    * Dr. Arthur E. Jenks.

CHAPTER III.

GALLANT EXPLOITS OF OUR NAVY.

" Our country's flag is proudly flung
   With all its stars on every breeze;
And Freedom's voice, with trumpet-tongue,
   Is sounding over land and seas."— G. W. LIGHT.

WHEN the war commenced in 1861, the entire naval force available for the defence of the whole Atlantic coast consisted of the steamer 'Brooklyn,' of twenty-five guns, and the storeship 'Relief,' of two guns. Ships, frigates, &c., belonging to the United States, and mounting in the aggregate eight hundred and seventy-four guns, were in existence; but some of them were lying in port dismantled, and the rest were otherwise rendered unfit for service. The 'Brooklyn' was of too great draught to enter Charleston harbor with safety, except during the high spring-tides; and the 'Relief' was under orders to proceed to Africa with stores for our squadron there.

Including the ships, &c., of our navy abroad, the United States, according to the Navy Secretary's report, could boast of about two thousand four hundred and fifteen guns, and a complement, exclusive of officers and marines, of about seven thousand six hundred men.

These somewhat dry details are mentioned in order to show the state of our navy when the South fired upon the "Star of the West" and Fort Sumter. These pages are not designed to be statistical particularly, nor yet largely historical, but to show, in the graphic language of eye-witnesses whose testimony is gathered from many and authentic sources, the exploits of the almost new navy of the United States while the Rebellion continued. Heavy and efficient blows did this arm of our defence give to the rebel cause; and the soldiers and sailors of those memorable four years of martial strife may clasp hands as brothers in honor. They struggled with equal bravery and success: both are entitled to wear the unwithering bays, and receive a rescued nation's gratitude.

After the war commenced, Congress ordered an addition to the navy, and various gunboats and iron-clad steamers were added to our puny fleet.

Among these floating batteries, as they have been termed, was one whose name is wreathed with immortal honor, and whose commander, Capt. A. H. Worden, received the personal thanks of our martyred President, — the "MONITOR." She was constructed by J. Ericsson, of New York; and being peculiar in build, a *rara avis* in naval architecture, it may be proper to describe her more minutely. Miss Edmonds says,*—

"The first real object of interest which presented itself

---

* Nurse and Spy, p. 67.

was the 'Monitor,' lying off Fortress Monroe. It reminded me of what I once heard a man say to his neighbor about his wife. Said he, 'Neighbor, you might worship your wife without breaking either of the ten commandments.' — 'How is that?' asked the man. 'Because she is not the likeness of any thing in heaven above, or in the earth beneath, or in the waters under the earth.' So thought I of the 'Monitor.'

"There she sat upon the water, a glorious impregnable battery, the wonder of the age, the terror of rebels, and the pride of the North. The 'Monitor' is so novel in structure, that a minute description will be necessary to come to an accurate idea of her character.

"'She has two hulls; the lower one is of iron, five-eighths of an inch thick; the bottom is flat, and six feet six inches in depth; sharp at both ends, the cut-water retreating at an angle of about thirty degrees. The sides, instead of having the ordinary bulge, incline at an angle of about fifty-one degrees. This hull is one hundred and twenty-four feet long, and thirty-four feet broad at the top. Resting on this is the upper hull, flat-bottomed, and both longer and wider than the lower hull, so that it projects over in every direction like the guards of a steamboat. It is one hundred and seventy-four feet long, forty-one feet four inches wide, and five feet deep. These sides constitute the armor of the vessel. In the first place is an inner guard of iron, half an inch thick: to this is fastened a wall of white-oak, placed endways, and thirty inches thick; to which are bolted six plates of iron, each an inch thick,—thus making a solid wall of thirty-six and a half inches of wood and iron. This hull is fastened upon the lower hull, so that the latter is entirely submerged, and the upper one sinks down three feet into the water. Thus but two feet of hull are exposed to a shot: the under hull is so guarded by the projecting upper hull, that a ball, to strike it, would have to pass through twenty-five feet of water. The upper hull is also pointed at both ends. The deck comes flush with the top of the hull, and is made bomb-proof. No railing or bulwark rises above the deck: the projecting ends serve as a protection to the propeller, rudder, and anchor, which cannot be struck. Neither the anchor nor chain is ever exposed. The anchor is peculiar, being very short, but heavy. It is hoisted into a place fitted for it outside of the lower hull, but within the impenetrable shield of the upper one. On the deck are but two structures rising above the surface, — the pilot-house and turret. The pilot-house is forward, made of plates of iron, the whole about ten inches in thickness, and shot-proof. Small slits and holes are cut through to enable the pilot to see his course. The turret, which is apparently the main feature of the battery, is a round cylinder, twenty feet in interior diameter, and nine feet high. It is built entirely of iron plates one inch in thickness, eight of them securely bolted together, one over another. Within this is a lining of one-inch iron, acting as a damper to deaden the effects of a concussion when struck by a ball: thus there is a shield of nine inches of iron. The turret rests on a bed-plate or ring of composition, which is fastened to the deck. To help support the weight, which is about a hundred tons, a vertical shaft, ten inches in diameter, is attached and fastened to the bulk-head. The top is made shot-proof by huge iron beams, and perforated to allow of ventilation. It has two circular port-holes, both on one side of the turret, three feet above the deck, and just large enough for the muzzle of the gun to be run out. The turret is made to revolve, being turned by a special engine: the operator within, by a rod connected with the engine, is enabled to turn it at pleasure. It can be made to revolve at the rate of sixty revolutions a minute, and can be regulated to stop within half a minute of a given point. When the guns are drawn in to load, the port-hole is stopped by a huge iron pendulum, which falls to its place, and makes that part as secure as any, and can be quickly hoisted to one side. The armament consists of two eleven-inch Dahlgren guns. Various improvements in the gun-carriage enable the gunner to secure almost perfect aim. The engine is not of great power, as the vessel was designed as a battery, and not for swift sailing. It being almost entirely under water, the ventilation is secured by blowers, drawing the air in forward, and discharging it aft. A separate engine moves the blowers and fans the fires. There is no chimney; so the draft must be entirely artificial. The smoke passes out of gratings in the deck. Many suppose the "Monitor" to be merely an iron-clad vessel with a turret; but there are, in fact, between thirty and forty patentable inventions upon her, and the turret is by no means the most important one. Very properly, what these inventions are is not proclaimed to the public.'"

Having thus described the little "Monitor," which was then a novelty, and is now a celebrity, it is fitting that the account of the engagement in which she was immortalized should be described also. That engagement was "the greatest naval engagement of the nineteenth century, not only in view of the novelty of the combat and the incalculable issue immediately at stake, but because its result went far to settle the question of foreign intervention. Wooden walls would henceforth avail little in maritime warfare, and ships in the heavy iron armor which would be requisite must incur the utmost hazard in a long voyage over a tempest-breeding sea."*

Among the eye-witnesses of this remarkable conflict was Rev. Arthur B. Fuller, then Chaplain of the Sixteenth Massachusetts Regiment. He furnished for a Northern paper a long and graphic sketch of the memorable event, which is here given. It is written under date of March 15, 1862.

"The past week has indeed been an exciting one here. The dulness and monotony of camp life have been exchanged for the sound of the stirring drum, of men marching in battle array to meet any land force which might second the naval armament arrayed against us, and for the flash and roar of the cannon upon our shores. I have been a witness of the entire naval contest, — our signal defeat at first, our splendid triumph at the last. Never have I known such alternations of feeling as this last week has brought to me. I have seen the proud American flag struck and humbled, and over it the white signal of surrender to a rebel steamer waving; and my heart sank within me for shame;

* R. F. Fuller, Esq.

and then came emotions of stern resentment, and longing to see the affront avenged. I have seen that exultant rebel steamer humbled in her turn before the little 'Monitor,' and the fierce flame-breathing monster towed disabled away to his den; and then came a feeling of exultation, say rather of gratitude to God, whose providence alone sent that deliverance which no language is adequate to express. Let me now briefly recount events of remarkable interest, avoiding the trite details already before the public, and narrating things as I saw them. The like of this naval engagement, in many respects, the world never saw before: the tremendous interests which hung upon the issue have never been exceeded; and each witness is bound to give his testimony, and give it impartially.

"Never has a brighter day smiled upon Old Virginia than last Saturday. The hours crept lazily along, and sea and shore in this region saw nothing to vary the monotony of the scene. Now and then a soldier might be heard complaining that this detachment of the loyal army was having no part in the glorious victories which everywhere else are crowning American valor with such brilliant success; or a sailor might be noted on shipboard, telling how much he hoped the 'Merrimack' would show herself, and how suddenly she would be sunk by our war vessels or land guns if she dared make her appearance. At one o'clock in the afternoon, the scene changed. Two strangely clad steamers appeared above Newport News, coming down the river; and a monster — half-ship, half-house — came slowly steaming from Norfolk. We did not know, but we all felt, that the latter was the 'Merrimack.' Your correspondent at once went to the large seminary building on the shore, about two miles from the Fortress, and so much nearer Newport News, that, with an excellent spy-glass, he could see distinctly every movement made. The engagement was a brief one, and as terrible and disastrous as brief. The 'Merrimack' is a slow sailer. Out she steamed steadily toward Newport News, and at once attacked the 'Cumberland.' There can never be a braver defence than the officers and sailors of that frigate made. They fought long after resistance was hopeless; *they never surrendered*, even when the water was filled with drowning men, and the fast-disappearing decks were slippery with blood: but all was in vain. With terrible and resistless force, the 'Merrimack' steamed at the doomed vessel, and pierced her side with her immense iron beak, at the same time firing her heavy guns directly through her antagonist. The noble 'Cumberland' soon sunk; and her sailors who were yet alive sought safety in the masts yet above water, or by swimming to the shore.

"Meanwhile, the 'Congress' had been fired upon by the rebel steamers 'Yorktown' and 'Jamestown,' and also by the tug-boats which accompanied the 'Merrimack.' She had got as near the shore as possible; but, when the iron monster turned his attention to her, she was soon obliged to surrender. Oh, how bitterly we all felt the humiliation of seeing the white flag rising to the mast-head above the stars and stripes! I am afraid I felt hardly like a Christian for the moment, if indeed a longing for vengeance upon my country's enemies *be* unchristian. I would have given all I possessed to see that accursed tyrant of the seas, with the rebel pennant defiantly flying, sunk beside her victim, the noble 'Cumberland.' But it was not to be. We looked for the 'Minnesota' and 'Roanoke,' our helpers in the strife, the first our main dependence; and, lo! both were aground and helpless in that fearful hour! It was well; for sure as they had floated, and the 'Merrimack' could have come at them, they, too, must have been sunk or captured. The 'Merrimack' draws more water than either of them. It did seem strange, though, that such a mishap should have chanced to both of these steam-frigates, whose pilots ought to have been so familiar with the channel: but the 'Roanoke' for six months had lain in these waters with a broken shaft, which renders her helpless; and the former pilot of the 'Minnesota' had just given way to another and less experienced man. It was all overruled for good.

"The 'Merrimack' now threw her balls thick and fast and heavy upon the camps at Newport News. Strange to say, none of these shot or shell did any material damage; though one of them passed directly through Gen. Mansfield's quarters, made wild work with his room, covered the general with splinters of wood, and, had it exploded, must have killed him. I saw the shell next day, and conversed with the general with reference to it. He has it in his apartment. It weighed forty-two pounds: another by its side, also sent from the 'Merrimack,' weighed ninety-two. The shells were rather badly aimed, and most of them went into the woods, cutting off tops of trees as they fell, but fortunately, nay, providentially, harming no one of the soldiers, or the fleeing women and children and contrabands. A little

tug had been sent meanwhile from the 'Merrimack' to the
'Congress' to take off the prisoners; but this tug was a mark
for the sharpshooters from the shore and from the land
batteries, which had been admirably served under Gen.
Mansfield's skilful direction, and frightened the 'Yorktown'
and 'Jamestown' and the little rebel gunboats from landing
their forces. The officers of the 'Congress,' and most of the
sailors who were not killed, all save twenty-three, escaped to
the shore; and the 'Merrimack,' damaged but not disabled
by the 'Cumberland's' broadsides, with her commander
wounded and several men killed, retired from the conflict,
giving a few passing shots at the 'Minnesota,' but reserving
her case till the morrow, and slowly steaming up to Norfolk,
accompanied by the 'Jamestown,' 'Yorktown,' and the
smaller rebel craft.

"That morrow! How anxiously we waited for it! how
much we feared its results! how anxious our Saturday eve
of preparation! At sundown, there was nothing to dispute
the empire of the seas with the 'Merrimack;' and, had a
land attack been made by Magruder then, God only knows
what our fate would have been. The 'St. Lawrence' and the
'Minnesota' aground and helpless, the 'Roanoke' with a
broken shaft, — these were our defences by sea; while on
land we were doing all possible to resist a night invasion: but
who could hope that would have much efficiency? Oh, what
a night that was! I never can forget it. There was no
fear during its long hours, — danger, I find, does not bring
that; but there was a longing for some interposition of
God, and waiting upon Him, from whom we felt our help

must come, in earnest, fervent prayer, while not neglecting all the means of martial defence he had placed in our hands. Fugitives from Newport News kept arriving: ladies and children had walked the long ten miles from Newport News, feeling that their presence only embarrassed their brave husbands. Sailors from the 'Congress' and 'Cumberland' came, one of them with his ship's flag bound about his waist as he swam with it ashore, determined the enemy should never trail it in dishonor as a trophy. Dusky fugitives, the contrabands, came, mournfully fleeing from a fate worse than death, — slavery. These entered my cabin hungry and weary, or passed it in long, sad procession. The heavens were aflame with the burning 'Congress.' The hotel was crowded with fugitives, and private hospitality was taxed to the utmost. But there were *no soldiers among the flying host:* all in our camps at Newport News and Camp Hamilton were at the post of duty, undismayed, and ready to do all and dare all for their country. The sailors came only to seek another chance at the enemy, since the bold 'Cumberland' had gone down in deep waters, and the 'Congress' had gone upward, as if a chariot of fire, to convey the manly souls, whose bodies had perished in the conflict, upward to heaven. I had lost several friends there: yet not lost; for they are saved who do their duty to their country and their God as these had done. We did not pray in vain.

> 'The heavy night hung dark
> The hills and waters o'er;'

but the night was not half so heavy as our hearts, nor so

dark as our prospects. All at once, a speck of light gleamed on the distant wave: it moved; it came nearer and nearer; and, at ten o'clock at night, the '*Monitor*' appeared! 'When the tale of bricks is doubled, Moses comes.' I never more firmly believed in special providence than at that hour. Even sceptics for the moment were converted, and said, 'God has sent her!' But how insignificant she looked! She was but a speck on the dark-blue sea at night, almost a laughable object by day. The enemy call her 'a cheese-box on a raft;' and the comparison is a good one. Could she meet the 'Merrimack'? The morrow must determine; for, under God, the 'Monitor' is our only hope.

"The morrow came; and with it came the inevitable battle between those strange combatants, the 'Merrimack' and the 'Monitor.' What a lovely Sabbath morning it was! How peaceful and balmy that Southern spring morning! Smiling Nature whispered only 'Peace;' but fierce Treason breathed out threatenings and slaughter, and would have war. Nor would the rebels respect the Sabbath: they know no doctrine but Slavery, no duty but obedience to her bloody behests. War let it be, then, since wicked men so determine, and we have no alternative but shameful surrender of truth and eternal justice. The guilt of violating God's Sabbath be upon the heads of those who will do it: we may not, indeed cannot, shrink from the terrible ordeal of battle. And soon it comes. At nine o'clock, A.M., the 'Merrimack' came out, attended by her consorts the war-steamers 'Jamestown' and 'Yorktown,' and a fleet of little tug-boats, crowded with ladies and gentlemen from Norfolk who were desirous of seeing the 'Minnesota' captured, and perhaps even Fortress Monroe taken; certainly all its outlying vessels, and the houses in its environs, burned.

"The little 'Monitor' lay concealed in the shadow of the 'Minnesota.' The 'Merrimack' opens the conflict, and her guns shake the sea and air as they breathe out shot and flame. Sewall's Point sends from its mortars shell which burst in the air above the doomed 'Minnesota.' The 'Minnesota,' still aground, replies with a bold but ineffectual broadside. All promises an easy victory to the 'Merrimack,' when, lo! the little 'Monitor' steams gently out, and offers the monster 'Merrimack' battle. How puny, how contemptible, she seemed! nothing but that little round tub appearing above the water, and yet flinging down the gauge of defiance to the gigantic 'Merrimack.' 'Twas little David challenging the giant Goliath once again, — the little one the hope of Israel, the giant the pride of the heathen Philistines. Truly our hopes were dim, and our hearts almost faint, for the moment. The few men on the 'Monitor' are sea and storm worn and weary enough; and their little craft is an experiment, with only two guns with which to answer the 'Merrimack's' many. Who can doubt the issue? who believe the 'Monitor' can fail to be defeated? And, if she is, what is to hinder the victorious and unopposed and unopposable 'Merrimack' from opening the blockade of the coast, or shelling Washington, New York, and Boston, after first devastating our camp and destroying its soldiery? That was the issue: such might have been the result, smile now who will. Believe me, there were prayers offered, many and fervent, that

Sabbath, along the shore, and from the Fortress walls, as our regiment watched the battle; and sailors must have prayed, too, as never before.

"The 'Merrimack,' after a few minutes of astounded silence, opened the contest. She tried to sink her puny foe at once by a broadside, and be no longer delayed from the 'Minnesota,' whose capture she had determined upon. After the smoke of the cannonade had cleared away, we looked, fearing, and the crew of the 'Merrimack' looked, hoping, that the 'Monitor' had sunk to rise no more. But she still lived. There she was, with the white wreaths of smoke crowning her tower as if a coronet of glory. And valiantly she returned the fire too; and for five hours, such a lively cannonading as was heard, shaking earth and sea, was never heard before. Literally, I believe that never have ships carrying such heavy guns met till that Sabbath morning. Every manœuvre was exhausted by the enemy. The 'Yorktown' approached to mingle in the fray. One shot was enough to send her quickly back, a lame duck upon the waters, though she, too, is iron-clad. The 'Merrimack' tried to run the 'Monitor' down, and thus sink her: she only got fiercer shots by the opportunity she thus gave her little antagonist. And so it went on, till the proud 'Merrimack,' disabled, was glad to retire, and, making signals of distress, was towed away by her sorrowing consorts. David had conquered Goliath with his smooth stones or wrought-iron balls from his little sling or shot-tower. Israel rejoiced in her deliverance through the power of God, who had sent that little champion of his cause, in our direst extremity, to the battle. Since then, the 'Merrimack' has not shown herself; and the enemy confess her disabled, and her commander, BUCHANAN (ominous name), severely wounded, four of her crew killed, and seventeen wounded. They admit, too, the valor of our seamen, futile though it was. The 'Cumberland's' officers and crew, says the 'Norfolk Day-Book,' 'fought worthy of a better cause;' say, rather, worthy of the best cause in the world; and we who witnessed the fight will agree with them.

"All that night, as well as the previous, and for several succeeding, our regiments were under arms. I will not detail the precautions taken to prevent a defeat by land, as, through the providence of God, an ultimate defeat by sea has been averted. Few of us slept that night; and, had we done so, most of us would have been awakened at midnight by the fearful cries which came to us from the water,—'Ship ahoy! O God, save us! Fire, fire, fire!' and occasionally a heavy cannon mingling its roar with those fearful cries. I rushed to the shore with many others, and there, a little distance from me, beheld the gunboat 'Whitehall' burning, and apparently her crew perishing in the fire, or drowning in the water near. It was terrible; all the more so as we could do nothing to aid, no boat being near our camp. The balls from her shotted guns made even looking on dangerous. One shell struck the United-States hospital at the Fortress, and caused great terror among the inmates, all of whom believed for a while that the 'Merrimack' had come down again, and was shelling the fort. Only four of those poor seamen perished in the flames or water, through the mercy of God. The fire came from a shot from the 'Merrimack,' which had the day before passed through the 'Whitehall,' and left a little spark smouldering unknown within.

"Amid all these events, disastrous or merciful, our soldiers still live, the Fortress yet remains unscathed, and the 'Minnesota' and 'Roanoke' and 'St. Lawrence'—though the first two need repairs—yet fly the old flag at their mainmasts. Above all, the little 'Monitor' floats in triumph,—a sentinel on the waters, and a strict monitor over the rebels. But for the wounding of her noble commander, Lieut. Worden, she would have pursued and sunk the 'Merrimack,' and will probably do so if another encounter occurs. She has now another noble commander, Lieut. T. A. Selfridge of Charlestown, whom I have known from his boyhood, and know to be brave, and worthy of the proud old Bay State. I have visited Newport News, and mourned there the death of the worthy Chaplain Lenhart, and the heroic Capt. Moore, whom I saw but a few days before, and talked with about his intended visit home to Boston. But, while I have mourned, I have also rejoiced over our camps, in which none were killed; and our officers and sailors, so many of whom were rescued. America will never forget that battle. It will mark an era in the history of the navy. It has taught us a useful lesson; and henceforth we have no more wooden walls as our reliance, but first our God, and then plates of steel, and iron-clad frigates and *monitors.*"

These thrilling events are worthy to live in song and story to the end of time. The ill-fated "Cumberland" has thus been mentioned, and the scene painted with a poet's pen: —

"The sun, uprising, gilds the placid bay;
   And, waked to life once more, the bright mists rise:
No breeze to wave the starry ensign folds,
   Where, slumbering on the tide, a stout ship lies.
The sunburnt sailor, from his lookout, marks
   The lazy smoke up-floating from the shore;
In fancy sees his distant cottage home:
   Alas! that home shall never see him more.

Hark! distant booming through the shining calm;
   A signal cannon shakes the silent air:
Then spring to arms the gallant sailor-lads;
   No coward hearts, no blanching lips, are there.
The hurrying footsteps answer with their tread
   The boatswain's whistle, quavering shrill it blows;
The loud drum rolls; the opening ports reveal
   The deep-mouthed cannon ranged in deadly rows.

E'en as the hawk, high-poised in air, surveys
   With cruel eye, then falls, and strikes his prey,
Straight for the fated ship, a monster strange,
   All cased in mail, unerring holds its way.
Swift from the ship's side vivid lightnings flash,
   And peal on peal her cannon shake the main.
Shall not that tempest sweep away the foe?
   Shall all the efforts of the brave be vain?

Ask how the Aztec bared his swarthy breast
   With fearless heart, and, giving blow for blow,
Met the fierce Spaniard, sheathed in glittering steel,
   Safe in his armor, smiling on his foe;

Ask if the breaker, gathering as it rolls,
   And swings with ponderous crash a whelming blow,
Shall harm the gray cliff frowning o'er the tide,
   And heedless of the roaring seas below.

With headlong force, the monster strikes the ship;
   The crashing timbers sound the seamen's knell:
Yet still the spangled flag above them floats,
   As up her sides the blood-stained billows swell.
Yet still defiance thunders in her fires,
   Till surging waters choke the cannon's breath.
She sinks, she sinks! Great Heaven, have mercy now!
   The whirling eddies suck them down to death.

As when in camp the wounded soldier dies,
   He bids good-night, then yields his spirit brave,
His sorrowing comrades lay him down to rest,
   And fire their volleys o'er the new-made grave;
Swift to avenge, the 'Monitor' appears,
   And pays the funeral honors to the dead, —
Their dirge the awful thunder of her guns,
   Her battle-volleys o'er their watery bed.

O gallant sailors! shall we weep for them?
   No: rather let our bosoms swell with pride;
For aged grandsires breathless crowds shall tell
   How fought the 'Cumberland,' — show where they died.
Their names resplendent on the roll of fame,
   Their monument each flag that floats on high:
Why should we weep? No, no! they are not dead;
   A grateful country will not let them die." *

---

* Thomas F. Power.

The "Boston Traveller" thus refers to that scene of heroism:—

"If to deserve success is better than oftentimes to gain it, then Lieut. Maurice and the gallant crew of the ill-fated 'Cumberland' merit the admiration and thanks of the whole loyal country. The sight of such an invulnerable monster as the 'Merrimack' bearing straight down upon a wooden vessel, not in the least affected by a half a dozen heavy broadsides, would have unnerved many a crew; but it had no effect on the gallant sailors of the 'Cumberland.' They kept up their rapid firing till the iron monster crashed her horn into the side of the 'Cumberland,' knocking in a hole as large as the head of a hogshead. Even then, while the water was rushing in like a flood, and the vessel going down, and the 'Merrimack,' at the distance of three hundred yards, was pouring in murderous broadsides, the men fought till the last gun was submerged. The fight continued three-quarters of an hour; and the firing of the 'Cumberland's' guns was so accurate, that, when one of the 'Merrimack's' crew crept out of a port to the outside of her plated roof, a ball instantly cut him in two! We do not believe that there is an action on record which shows more heroic fighting than this hopeless one on the part of the 'Cumberland.' She lies now in fifty-four feet of water, with the stars and stripes still flying from her topmast; but a grateful country will honor her commander and her decimated crew."

THE HEROES OF THE "CUMBERLAND."— The following interesting details of the behavior of the seamen of the

"Cumberland" are from a private letter from Philadelphia: —

"Dr. Martin, who was surgeon on board, passed through here yesterday. He was on board during the fight, and gives a thrilling account of the scene. So far from being a scene of confusion, every man and boy, he says, showed the most astounding courage and coolness. Morris, the first officer in command, fought the ship most gallantly; but after the 'Merrimack' had run her down, and finding that she must soon sink, he told every man to jump overboard, and save himself as he best could. No one left her until the water began to pour over the sills of the ports. Martin did not leave his post below until told that he had not an instant to lose. As he passed up, the men were firing the last guns. He says he looked along the line for a moment, and saw the most magnificent sight of his life. As they fired the last broadside, the men coolly put the sponges in the racks just as they do after drill, and left the ship only at the moment when she was settling under them. The same men, fifteen minutes after they got on shore, were in the water, with rifles, helping to drive the rebel gunboat from the 'Congress.'"

"HEROIC CONDUCT OF A MASSACHUSETTS SOLDIER. — Lieut. Loomis, who commanded the 'Congress,' after firing the last shot at the enemy, when all hope of saving his vessel from destruction had vanished, jumped into the river, and endeavored to swim ashore, about a mile distant. At this time, the shot and shell from the 'Merrimack' were flying in all directions; and escape seemed impossible, even could his strength hold out. At this critical juncture, a soldier of the Twenty-ninth Massachusetts Regiment, Col. E. W. Pierce commanding, sprang into the boat, and made for the half-sinking lieutenant. After prodigious exertion, he succeeded, and brought him safe to shore."

To our lamented President, the news of the David and Goliath encounter was most welcome; and he showed his appreciation of the value of the services then rendered by the "Monitor" and her gallant crew when he visited the wounded commander. A newspaper * correspondent thus describes the visit : —

"That night I left the Fortress, and got Worden safe home in Washington City; when, leaving him to the care of my wife, I went with the Secretary to the President, and gave him the particulars of the engagement. As soon as I had done, Mr. Lincoln said, 'Gentlemen, I'm going to shake hands with that man;' and presently he walked round with me to our little house. I led him up stairs to the room where Worden was lying with fresh bandages over his scorched eyes and face, and said, 'Jack, here's the President, who has come to see you!' He raised himself on his elbow, as Mr. Lincoln took him by the hand, and said, ' You do me great honor, Mr. President; and I am only sorry that I can't see you.' The President was visibly affected, as, with tall frame and earnest gaze, he bent over his wounded subordinate; but after a pause he said, with a quiver

* Advertiser.

in the tone of his voice, 'You have done *me* more honor, sir, than I could do you.' He then sat down, while Worden gave him an account of the battle; and, on leaving, he promised, if he could legally do so, that he would make him a captain."

The services rendered by our brave sailors in subduing the Rebellion were invaluable. Not only did the Chief Magistrate of the nation appreciate them, but the humblest loyal heart throbbed in sympathy with the spirit that would wreathe the names of our naval heroes with immortal honor. A writer in a religious paper* thus expresses his feelings:—

"I was walking up Broadway the other day, when a sailor passed me. He wore the navy blue. His beaming eye bespoke an intelligent patriotism. His stalwart form and sinewy frame must have come from the mountain regions. Perhaps near *Kearsarge* Mountain was his home. Every one noted him as he passed. He seemed to be proud of the national uniform which covered his commanding figure. Just opposite us, as we were side by side, the starry flag was flung from a window. It floated on the air of the free United States. The sailor paused, and looked at the banner: his eye beamed with a new light, and his moving lip breathed afresh its devotion; but his hat was not touched by the ready hand, nor was his arm raised to greet the flag he loved. Both arms had been shot away. Two empty coat-sleeves dangled from his shoulders. They were two coat-sleeves, not empty; full, full of pathos,—a pathos which

* The Home Evangelist.

touched me, which thrilled me. Perhaps he was one of the crew of the 'Kearsarge' when she sent the 'Alabama' to the bottom. Wherever he had been, his duty had been done. Patriotism could ask no more of her noble offspring. It dimmed my eye to look upon the gallant fellow, and think of the sacrifice made by him; but he gazed smilingly upon the flag, and seemed to say, 'What I have given I count no sacrifice, old flag. I'd make my life a rampart to defend you.' Noble fellow! I love him as I love few men. I feel a thrill of pride in thinking of him as my own countryman. The friends who own him, who serve him, who enjoy his companionship, how proud they are to note the heart-heaving gratitude of the thousands who meet the hero! His generosity is known: he gives; he has given his arms to his country."

The allusion to the "Kearsarge" is best explained by the following account of the heroic achievement of that craft and her gallant crew:—

"The 'Kearsarge' was one of the steam war-vessels of the United-States navy, and was ordered to proceed to Cherbourg to watch the movements of the 'Alabama,' one of the privateers of the Southern Confederacy, whose predatory career had been far from agreeable to our Government, or the unfortunate ships which came in her way only to be captured, and sometimes destroyed. On the 15th of June, 1864, the commander of the 'Kearsarge,' Capt. John A. Winslow, received a note from Capt. Semmes, of the 'Alabama,' announcing his intention to fight the 'Kearsarge,' and asking Capt. Winslow not to depart till there had been a trial of strength between them. As this was just what the Federal officer desired, he gladly waited.

"The relative proportions and armaments of the two antagonists were as follows:—

	"ALABAMA."	"KEARSARGE."
Length over all,	220 feet.	214¼ feet.
Length on water line,	210 "	198½ "
Beam,	32 "	33 "
Depth,	17 "	16 "
Horse-power, two engines of	300 each,	400 horse-power.
Tonnage,	1,150 tons.	1,030 tons.

Armament of the "Alabama:" One 7-inch Blakely rifle, one 8-inch smooth-bore 68-pounder, six 32-pounders.

Armament of the "Kearsarge:" Two 11-inch smooth-bore guns, one 30-pounder.rifle, four 32-pounders.

"The 'Kearsarge' had twenty-two officers and one hundred and forty men; and the 'Alabama,' so far as can be ascertained, about one hundred and forty officers and men, the greater part of the ship's company consisting of British subjects. Her gunners were trained artillerists from the British practice-ship 'Excellent.' Availing himself of an ingenious expedient for the protection of his machinery, first adopted by Admiral Farragut in running past the rebel forts on the Mississippi in 1862, Capt. Winslow had hung all his spare anchor-cable over the midship section of the 'Kearsarge,' on either side; and, in order to make the addition less unsightly, the chains were boxed over with inch deal-boards, forming a sort of case, which stood out at right angles to the side of the vessel.

"At twenty minutes past ten on Sunday morning, June 19, the 'Alabama' was seen standing out from Cherbourg Harbor, accompanied by the French iron-clad 'Couronne,' and followed by the steam-yacht 'Deerhound,' whose owner, an Englishman named Lancaster, was on board with his family, ostensibly to witness the engagement, but really, as it subsequently appeared, to act as a tender to the 'Alabama.'

"Upon seeing the 'Alabama' approach, Capt. Winslow kept out to sea a few miles, in order 'that the positions of the ships should be so far off shore, that no questions could be advanced about the line of jurisdiction.' Upon reaching a point about seven miles from the land, the 'Kearsarge' put about, and steered directly for the 'Alabama,' which first opened fire at a range of about a mile. The following account of the fight that ensued is given by Capt. Winslow: —

"'Immediately I ordered more speed; but in two minutes the "Alabama" had again loaded, and fired another broadside, and followed it with a third, without damaging us, except in rigging. We had now arrived within nine hundred yards of her; and I was apprehensive that another broadside, nearly raking as it was, would prove disastrous. Accordingly, I ordered the "Kearsarge" sheered, and opened fire on the "Alabama."

"' The positions of the vessels were now broadside; but it was soon apparent that Capt. Semmes did not seek close action. I became then fearful, lest, after some fighting, he would again make for the shore. To defeat this, I determined to keep full speed on, and, with a port helm, to run under the stern of the "Alabama," and rake, if he did not prevent it by sheering and keeping his broadside to us. He adopted this mode as a preventive; and, as a consequence, the "Alabama" was forced, with a full head of steam, into a circular track during the engagement.

"'The effect of this manœuvre was such, that at the last of the action, when the "Alabama" would have made off, she was near five miles from the shore; and had the action continued from the first in parallel lines, with her head in shore, the line of jurisdiction would no doubt have been reached.

"'The firing of the "Alabama" from the first was rapid and wild: toward the close of the action, her firing became better. Our men, who had been cautioned against rapid firing without direct aim, were much more deliberate; and the instructions given to point the heavy guns below rather than above the water-line, and clear the deck with the lighter ones, were fully observed. I had endeavored with a port helm to close in with the "Alabama;" but it was not until just before the close of the action that we were in a position to use grape: this was avoided, however, by her surrender. The effect of the training of our men was evident: nearly every shot from our guns was telling fearfully on the "Alabama;" and, on the seventh rotation on the circular track, she winded, setting fore-trysail and two jibs, with head in shore.

"'Her speed was now retarded; and, by winding, her port broadside was presented to us with only two guns bearing; not having been able, as I learned afterward, to shift over but one. I saw now that she was at our mercy; and a few more guns, well directed, brought down her flag. I was unable to ascertain whether they had been hauled down or shot away; but a white flag having been displayed over the stern, followed by two guns fired to leeward, our fire was reserved. Two minutes had not more than elapsed before she again opened on us with the two guns on the port side. This drew our fire again; and the "Kearsarge" was immediately steamed ahead, and lay across her bows for raking.

"'The white flag was still flying, and our fire was again reserved. Shortly after this, her boats were seen to be lowering; and an officer in one of them came alongside, and informed us the ship had surrendered and was fast sinking. In twenty minutes from this time, the "Alabama" went down; her mainmast, which had received a shot, breaking near the head as she sunk, and her bow rising high out of the water as her stern rapidly settled. The fire of the "Alabama," although it is stated she discharged three hundred and seventy or more shell and shot, was not of serious damage to the "Kearsarge." Some thirteen or fourteen of these had taken effect in and about the hull, and sixteen or seventeen about the waist and rigging.'

"The boats of the 'Kearsarge' were at once sent to receive the officers and crew of the 'Alabama;' but so rapidly did she go down, that it was impossible to save them all without assistance. Capt. Winslow accordingly requested the 'Deerhound,' which had meanwhile come alongside, to assist in the rescue of his prisoners. The crew of the privateer were by this time struggling for their lives in the water; and many of the wounded men went down. In the confusion of the moment, the 'Deerhound,' after picking up forty-one persons, including Semmes, who was wounded, steamed off toward the English coast; and, when observed, had got too much the start to be overhauled. The total number brought on board the 'Kearsarge' was sixty-nine, of whom seventeen were wounded, and twelve were picked up, and carried into Cherbourg, by two French pilot-boats. Several of the wounded died soon after; and the total number of officers and men belonging to the 'Alabama,' who were landed in France or England, amounted to one hundred and fifteen. The casualties of the 'Kearsarge' amounted to only three wounded. This most remarkable sea-fight between single ships, that has occurred within the century, was witnessed by thousands of spectators on the French shore; and the result produced a profound impression in Europe and America." *

The "Alabama" had been such a terror to the people on the Atlantic coast, and to all who had friends out upon the ocean liable to fall into the hands of her piratical crew, that the news of her capture afforded great joy; and, when the "Kearsarge" returned to the East, her officers and men were received with well-deserved honors.

Many of the navy officers at the commencement of the war ignominiously deserted the flag they were pledged to defend. But there were left a "faithful few," whom loyal hearts should never forget, or cease to honor. The commander of the "Crusader," † at Mobile, when his gunboat was exposed

* Annual Cyclopædia, 1864.   † Lieut. J. N. Muffit.

to the fire of Fort Morgan, which the enemy had seized, was commanded to surrender his vessel to the State of Alabama. His noble reply was, "I may be overpowered; but, in that event, what will be left of the 'Crusader' will not be worth taking."

Capt. Porter, of the ship "St. Mary's," was ordered to surrender to a South-Carolina officer; but he also nobly answered, —

"You, sir, have called upon your brother-officers, not only to become traitors to their country, but to betray their sacred trust, and deliver up the ships under their command. This infamous appeal would, in ordinary times, be treated with the contempt it deserved; but I feel it a duty I owe myself, and brother-officers with whom I am associated, to reply, and state, that all under my command are true and loyal to the stars and stripes and to the Constitution. My duty is plain before me. The Government of the United States has intrusted me with the command of this beautiful ship; and, before I will permit any other flag than the stars and stripes to fly at her peak, I will fire a pistol in her magazine, and blow her up. This is my answer to your infamous letter."

There were sixteen naval engagements during the war. Some of them were gunboat expeditions; but in most of them the large iron-clads took a prominent part. Gen. Frémont is said to have been the originator of the Mississippi gunboat expedition, which proved so efficient in capturing those forts by means of which the enemy hoped to keep a large part of the Mississippi closed to the North.

Many more pages than this volume will contain would be needed if a full and connected history of the gunboat expeditions, which reflect such honor upon American sailors, should be given. Hence there will be presented to the reader only somewhat brief sketches of our naval exploits, and some incidents of interest which occurred in connection with them.

During the naval engagement at Fort Pillow, the Federal gunboat "Cincinnati" was caught in a very critical position by the rebel fleet, being two or three miles farther down the stream than her consorts. She had to sustain the unexpected onset of six huge rebel gunboats, but met them right gallantly, fearful as were the odds. A letter written by a person who was on board the "Cincinnati" during the battle is published in the "Chicago Tribune." It gives a graphic description of the fight. We quote: —

"One glance around showed us how critical was the state of affairs. Fully two miles and a half lay between us and the remainder of the flotilla, who, not anticipating an attack, lay, with steam down, tied securely to the shore, far above us. To attempt to escape up the river, then, were worse than useless. Our only hope was in God and our noble guns. 'Down stream with her!' cried the captain; and, obeying her rudder, the 'Cincinnati' slowly swung round. The first rebel boat, which was now but a few hundred yards from us, divining our intention, sheered out to get a chance at our stern as we came around; the next one came directly on; while the third kept in toward the shore.

"We were thus surrounded on all sides. Turning directly for the largest of our adversaries, we poured into her sides the whole starboard battery at a distance of not over three hundred yards. This huge craft, being now above us, turned, and headed directly for our starboard quarter; her immense hull looming full thirty feet above the surface of the river,—not a man, nor a gun, nor any thing but a huge black mass, to be seen. Down she came, ploughing up the water with her bows. 'Give it to her, boys!' shouted the gunner. A bright flash, a deafening roar, and a whole broadside poured into her hull; but it did not arrest her progress; and the next instant, with a terrible crash, she came into our starboard quarter. We seemed to be lifted bodily out of the water. We surged on to one side, but soon settled back as the rebel boat drew back.

"She turned again on us; when the 'Cincinuati,' even then in a sinking condition, swung a little, and, at a distance of only ten yards, sent a terrible shower of solid shot crashing through the monster's ribs. Smoke and steam came pouring out of her upper works. Quickly loading again, though so near that the balls were with difficulty rammed home, the starboard battery belched forth another broadside. Through and through the black hulk the balls tore their way. The monster's vitals are touched; his head swings off several points; and slowly the huge mass drifts down stream. During this time, another craft, painted a dirty mud-color, of the same build, but not quite so large, as our first adversary, came steaming down on our port-quarter; but, on our sheering, she fell astern, and, crowding on all steam, came fairly flying at us. Our stern-battery only got two shots at her; when, about three minutes after the first shot struck, the second came into our stern with a crash that took nearly every one off their feet.

"The water poured into our hull in two unbroken streams. Capt. Stembel had been shot while giving orders on the spar-deck; and, about the same time, the fourth master, while gallantly working his division, was shot down in his footsteps by a shot through the port-hole. The boat was gradually settling; and a deep gloom overspread the crew as our appalling situation became evident. A cheer reaches our ears; and joy comes to every heart as our eyes greet the 'Benton,' 'Carondelet,' 'Mound City,' 'Pittsburg,' and 'St. Louis' sweeping like an avalanche into the rebel fleet. Now came a naval engagement, the like of which has been seldom seen,— the rams trying to run our boats down while we poured broadside after broadside into their huge hulls. They were not done with us yet.

"Our last adversary drew back from us some hundred yards, and, cracking on steam, came rushing along at a fearful rate. The port stern gun was trained on her; and a solid 32-pounder ball entered her bow, and raked the entire length of the boat. 'Haul down your flag, Yanks, and we'll save you!' shouted some one. Another 32 was the only response; and the next instant she struck just inside the starboard rudder. The water was now rising in the boat at a fearful rate: the engineers were up to their waists in water: a few inches more would put out the fires. Under the impression that it was useless to attempt to save her, the first master came down the companion-way, and said, '*Boys, fight while you can: our flag will not go down until we do.*'

"The men cheered, and with renewed alacrity sprang to their guns; those at the starboard battery had two broadsides at a rebel craft which was trying to run the 'Carondelet;' but the 'Benton' came between us, and engaged it. She gave first her bow-guns; wheeling, she delivered a whole broadside, and last her stern battery. The rebel craft, having an immense hole in her bow, hauled down her flag; when the 'Benton' ceased firing, and left for another: but she was no sooner away than the cowardly, dastardly rebels ran it up again.

"Three of the rebel boats were now drifting helplessly down stream; one, the 'Mexico,' was laboring heavily, while another was on fire: but our own condition was too critical to pay much attention to any thing else. We were slowly drifting down stream, and would soon be in range of the fort. Our rudders smashed, the fires out, our case did indeed look hopeless. But the gallant old 'Cincinnati' was not destined to be another 'Cumberland:' her days, glorious as they have been, were not over yet. The powerful little tugs 'Jessie Benton' and 'Dauntless' made fast to her bow, and succeeded in running the boat quarterwise across the river, just in time to get her on the bank, when she sunk."

"Carleton," of the "Boston Journal,"* thus graphically pictures the destruction of a rebel gunboat: —

"DESTRUCTION OF THE 'NASHVILLE.'— The rebel steamer 'Nashville,' which began piratical depredations by burning

---

* C. C. Coffin, Esq.

the ship 'Harvey Birch,' has been cooped up at Savannah for several months. Several times we have had reports of her running the blockade, and escaping seaward, — fabricated, doubtless, to mislead our blockading fleet, — but our lookouts along the coast have seen her quite often inside. She had a choice of three channels in her endeavor to escape, — by the Savannah River, past Pulaski, by the Wilmington River, or by the Ogeechee; the two last named being connected with Savannah at high water by creeks. For several weeks past, she has been seen in the Ogeechee above Fort McAllister. By contrabands who have come in, we learn that the commander at Fort McAllister had high words with the captain of the 'Nashville,' accusing him of cowardice in not attempting to run the blockade.

"On Saturday morning, the last day of February, a dense fog hung over the marshes, islands, and inlets of Ossabaw Sound. The 'Montauk' lay at her anchorage, at the junction of the Great and Little Ogeechee Rivers: just below her, toward the sea, were the 'Seneca,' 'Flambeau,' 'Dawn,' 'Sebago,' and 'Wisahickon.' The fog lifted about seven o'clock, and disclosed the 'Nashville' aground above Fort McAllister. The 'Montauk' up with her anchor, and steamed up stream. As she came within range of the fort, she received a furious fire, to which she paid no heed. Taking a position fifteen hundred yards, or about three-fourths of a mile, distant from the 'Nashville,' and about half a mile from the fort, she opened upon the 'Nashville' with both her guns. The 'Nashville' replied with her hundred-pound rifle-gun. At the fifth shot, black smoke was seen issuing from the 'Nashville,' which increased in volume. The 'Montauk' still kept up her fire, throwing six fifteen-inch and eight eleven-inch shells; nearly all of which struck the fated steamer, which was soon in flames from stem to stern. She burned till the fire reached her magazine, when a terrific explosion tore her to pieces. By the negroes who have come in, we learn that she had about five hundred bales of cotton and a large amount of turpentine on board. The blackness of the smoke, and the rapidity with which the flames spread, make it a probable story.

"Capt. Worden was strongly tempted to engage the fort: and his crew, elated with what had been accomplished in so short a time, desired to continue the work; but, knowing that the 'Passaic' was on her way from Wilmington River to join in an attack, he quietly withdrew, paying no more attention to the shot falling around the 'Montauk,' and rattling against her sides, than if they were so many peas blown from a pop-gun. So the 'Nashville' received her retribution."

One after another, the gunboats and iron-clads of the rebels disappeared; in many cases committing suicide, as it were, as did the monster "Merrimack," which was blown up in Norfolk Harbor by her owners, or rather the thieves who had her in possession. Thus did the "Diana," the "Queen of the West," and "Nashville" disappear. The following is Carleton's account of the destruction of two of these vessels: —

"A short time after the battle of the morning had ceased, the famous 'Diana' came puffing up the Têche, and, laying in sight of our skirmishers, began to shell the woods in which our skirmishers lay. She was provided with good ammunition, because, forsooth, she was so lately stolen from Uncle Sam. Her firing was kept up continuously for several hours; but, so far as heard from, only one man was injured by it, though her shells came in uncomfortable proximity to several impromptu hospitals in the edge of the woods. The skirmishers were hid behind the massive trunks of the live-oaks by the banks of the river, with orders to pick off the gunners if the vessel advanced farther up the bayou; but the precaution was useless. Already her doom was written in the book of fate. A louder report than any of the rest startled us;. but no shell came crashing through the trees. The 'Diana'— the prize over which so much Confederate joy had been wasted — was no more. Close pressed behind by Gen. Banks, and fearful of falling into Gen. Grover's trap by advancing, the rebels had applied the match; and the explosion we heard was of her magazine, as her splintered planks and timbers littered the bayou and the adjacent shores, and

> 'Down her black hulk did reel
> Through the black water.'

"A NAVAL VICTORY. — The most brilliant thing of the whole campaign, or at least that on which most rejoicing is based, was the encounter between the 'Queen of the West' and her comrades, and our fleet in Grand Gulf. I have the facts from one of the officers of the 'Arizona,' and give you his plain statement: 'Shortly after daybreak on Monday morning, the "Queen of the West," with the "General Quitman" and the "Lizzie Emmons," steamed down from Butte la Rose, on the Gulf, and showed signs of attempting to sink the "Arizona" and other vessels of our fleet. In the contest, a shot from the "Arizona" struck the rebel amidships, setting her on fire; and, shortly after, she exploded. In the neighborhood of a hundred of the poor fellows on board were either drowned, or burned to death; and some thirty were taken prisoners, including Capt. Jewett, whom the rebels take pride in styling "the Paul Jones of the Southern waters;" and Lieut. Semmes, second officer (supposed to be a son of the pirate). The engineer is a prisoner, but shockingly scalded. On witnessing this mishap, the other boats retreated as fast as possible, while the "Arizona" started in pursuit, but, fearing an ambuscade, wisely returned.' Thus it will be seen Providence has not prospered the stealers of steamboats."

Another rebel vessel met with like fate, near Baton Rouge. Gen. Butler, in thanking the Union troops, says, "To complete the victory, the iron-clad steamer 'Arkansas,' the last naval hope of the Rebellion, hardly awaited the gallant attack of the 'Essex,' but followed the example of her sisters, the 'Merrimack,' the 'Manassas,' the 'Mississippi,' and the Louisiana,' by her own destruction."

The following is Admiral Farragut's own report: —

"As soon as the enemy [on shore] was repulsed, Commander Porter, with the gunboats, went up stream after the ram 'Arkansas,' which was lying about five miles above, apparently afraid to take her share in the conflict.

"According to a preconcerted plan, as he came within gunshot, he opened on her, and probably soon disabled some of her machinery or steering apparatus; for she became unmanageable, continuing, however, to fire guns at the 'Essex.'

"Commander Porter says he took advantage of her presenting a weak point towards him, and loaded his guns with incendiary shells. After his first discharge of this projectile, a gush of fire came out of her side; and from that moment it was discovered that she was on fire, and he continued his exertions to prevent it from being extinguished.

"They backed her ashore, and made a line fast, which soon burnt, and she swung off into the river, where she continued to burn, until she blew up with a tremendous explosion; thus ending the career of the last iron-clad ram of the Mississippi.

"There were many persons on the banks of the river witnessing the fight, in which they anticipated a triumph for Secessia; but, on the return of the 'Essex,' not a soul was to be seen.

"I will leave a sufficient force of gunboats to support the army, and will return to New Orleans, and depart immediately for Ship Island, with a light heart that I have left no bugbear to torment the communities of the Mississippi in my absence. "D. G. FARRAGUT."

The admiral just mentioned is a moral as well as military hero. The following from a religious paper,* gives us

* Parish Visitor.

a delightful picture of one who has earned many laurels for his country: —

"Admiral Farragut, in his recent successful attack on the forts in Mobile Bay, did a very heroic thing, and the nation rings with his praises. We delight to tell, and you delight to hear, how he lashed himself to the mast aloft. There, with his glass, did he study out his course of action, and from thence did he send down to the deck his orders. Not every man would have thought of such a post of observation. The commander's place is usually upon the quarter-deck. The thought of the admiral which took him to the masthead was a very happy one. It was an ingenious and fertile expedient, and conduced much, undoubtedly, to his subsequent victory.

"But he did another thing before he went to the masthead to look sharp after the rebels, which was even more to his credit. We have one version of the action from the lips of the Secretary of State. This honorable gentleman recently made an address to his fellow-citizens in the interior of New York. He places this anecdote of Admiral Farragut among the first of his remarks. In view of the impending conflict, some of the officers of the fleet asked whether some rations of grog should not be served out to the men, — not enough to make them drunk, but some to enliven their spirits, and make them fight better. The admiral's reply was as quick and sharp and forcible as one of his broadsides: 'No, sir! I never found that drinking spirits was necessary to a faithful discharge of duty. You may tell the men they shall have two cups of good coffee each at two o'clock to-morrow morning, just as we go into action; and at eight o'clock we will breakfast in Mobile Bay, when they shall have more.'"

The description, by "Carleton," of the naval battle which resulted in the recapture of Galveston, is of such interest as to justify quotation. Though the rebels gained a brief victory on this occasion, yet the display of heroism and valor on the part of our loyal sailors was as great as if their efforts had been crowned with victory.

"ATTACK ON THE 'HARRIET LANE.'—About two o'clock, the foremost of the rebel gunboats turned, and seemed inclined to go into Bolivar Channel, but did not do so; probably being intimidated by the appearance of the transports, of whose true character the enemy were ignorant. The enemy's boats increased: one after another they hove in sight through the mist that overhung the harbor, till finally appeared two rams and three lofty river boats, their sides walled up with three tiers of cotton-bales; behind which, on each boat, were between two and three hundred blood-thirsty rebels, each man armed with two revolvers, a rifle, and a bowie-knife. They had been plied with liquor, and were more like demons than men, going about their bloody work. Three of the steamers, a ram, and two river boats, bore down upon the 'Harriet Lane,' which was now throwing shot and shell upon the rebel artillerymen on shore. The other two boats, on one of which was Gen. Magruder in person, lay off and on at the upper end of Pelican Island, watching the course of events below; while away in the distance, up the bay, rolled a turgid column of ominous smoke, a certain indication that another rebel steamer was approaching.

"The moon, which had all this time shed its pale rays over land and sea, rendering visible the steamers as they approached, went down; and a Cimmerian darkness enshrouded the scene. From out the blackness flashed the bright-red glare of the guns of the 'Harriet Lane,' the 'Sachem,' and 'Owasco,' and the rebel artillery; while the air resounded with a continuous cannonade, and reports of musketry flashed from the windows of buildings in which the rebel infantry and sharpshooters were concealed.

"Now a simultaneous attack was made upon the little pet steamer 'Lane' from the town and rebel boats. The former showed fight, and driving, stem on, into one of the large river boats, cracked her like a nut-shell. The rebel boats closed upon her; and the infuriated soldiers poured a deadly fire of musketry upon decks, involving officers and men in the general slaughter. Her brave sailors were shot down at the guns by the rebels, who, rendered desperate by famine and whiskey, leaped on board; when a scene of carnage and bloodshed ensued, which is without a parallel in the history of modern warface. Unable to cope with such superior numbers, — the enemy had at *least three* thousand men afloat, — the small remnant of the gallant crew were driven below, to be again forced on deck and butchered by the rebels, who, with bowie-knife and revolver, cut down all before them. The gallant and accomplished Wainwright was shot through the knee: he rallied, and with his revolver despatched two rebel soldiers. He encouraged his men to fight, and shouted, 'Stand up to it, boys!' when a Confederate officer approached, and blew out his brains. The young and intrepid Lee was shot through the bowels, and fell mortally wounded. He cried out to his men, 'The enemy will give you no quarter: see that you give them none!' But what can men do against such fearful odds? Right and left the horrible butchery went on; and the rebel officers, scarcely more human than their cut-throat minions, with difficulty prevented their men from setting up the few survivors as targets."

"THE 'CLIFTON' TO THE RESCUE. — While this bloody business was going on on board the 'Lane,' the other Union gunboats were not idle. The 'Owasco' hurled her iron missiles from her eleven-inch 'growler;' and the 'Sachem' blazed away with her long 32's at the rebel steamers, which were on the other side and astern of the 'Lane.' The latter had disabled one of her adversaries, which sunk alongside: another got her head-gear entangled in the wheel of the 'Lane.'

"The 'Clifton,' unable to extricate the 'Westfield' from her situation, steamed down the channel on her way to the scene of attack. While she had been tugging at the 'Westfield,' the rebels, crossing the island above the town, with heavy cannon drawn by ten-mule teams, had placed several guns in position behind an earthwork at Fort Point. Nothing was seen there when the 'Clifton' passed the point on her way down; but, as she neared it on her way up, the rebels opened fire from two heavy guns, to which she replied with energy. The men worked like heroes, surprising even Commander Law by the rapidity of their fire: they kept a shell in the air all the time, and dropped them into the rebel work with such precision as to effectually silence the rebel battery. The rebels are reported to have had forty pieces of artillery, which they brought to bear upon our gunboats and the barracks. The shore of Galveston Island flashed with their fire from the gas-works above the town down to Fort Point, and kept up an incessant fire; while, from buildings on shore, the rebel sharpshooters poured a galling fire upon the decks of our gunboats.

"Those who were spectators of the engagement waited with intense anxiety for daylight. The guns of the 'Harriet Lane' had long been silent. The rebel steamers still lay alongside; but no one outside of the ill-fated vessel knew whether she had captured them, or they had taken her. The rebel steamers above Pelican Island still lay smoking, evidently waiting to learn the result of the fighting."

"DAYLIGHT AND A TRUCE: DEMAND FOR A SURRENDER. — In the gray of dawn, the 'Owasco' ran up her ensign: the 'Clifton' and 'Sachem' did the same. The 'Westfield' displayed the commander's pennon. This was a moment of doubt and fear, and all watched to see what reply came from the 'Harriet Lane.' The first faint streaks of light discovered to the anxious and now despondent spectators a white flag flying from the 'Lane,' and the small remnant of her crew who had survived the fearful slaughter placed by the rebels in such a position that the fire from any of our vessels must have been fatal to them.

"A boat put off from the 'Lane,' in which were a rebel officer, Capt. Lovereux, and Acting Master Hannam, who, with eleven, were the sole survivors of her devoted officers and crew. They proceeded to the 'Clifton,' where the rebel officer, informing Capt. Law that the 'Harriet Lane' had been captured, her commander killed, her executive officer mortally wounded, and her second officer severely wounded, demanded the surrender of all the Federal vessels in port, with the exception of one to be selected by the vanquished, and in which they were to depart with all their people, and leave the entire coast of Texas. The rebel officer further stated, that the 'Harriet Lane' and three other steamers were ready to move against the Federal ships, provided they were not surrendered.

"Capt. Law proceeded to the 'Westfield' to refer the matter to Commander Renshaw, who, as may be supposed, scorned to accept the terms, and refused to surrender to the enemy."

"PREPARATIONS TO EVACUATE. — Soon after the above interview, Commander Renshaw sent a boat to the 'Mary Boardman,' requesting the privilege of transferring his officers and crew, and a portion of the ship's furniture, personal effects, and such other articles as could be easily moved, on board of that vessel; at the same time informing Capt. Weir of the 'Boardman' that he intended to blow up his ship, which was still aground, and could not be got off till the next flood-tide, if then, to prevent her from falling into the hands of the enemy, who were now preparing to advance in full force upon them. The request was granted; and the crew and baggage were transferred to the 'Boardman,' which was all the while under way, lying near the 'Westfield.' In the mean time, the rebel steamers up the bay, confident of their victory, steamed down to the scene of the engagement. The Federal boats at the same time commenced to drop down the channel; seeing which, the rebels re-opened their batteries upon them. The battery at Fort Point fired into the bark 'Cavallo,' and sunk her at her anchors.

"Soon after ten o'clock in the morning, the rebel rams began to move down toward Fort Point, and Commander Renshaw immediately sent word to the 'Boardman' to be ready to leave the harbor as soon as the 'Westfield's' men were all on board. The 'Sachem' fought her way past the shore-batteries in splendid style: the coolness and bravery of her commander, Acting Master Amos Johnson, excited the admiration of all who witnessed the affair, if we may except the rebels themselves, who could not have failed to appreciate the intrepidity which he displayed. The 'Clifton' proceeded down the channel as far as Fort Point, where Capt. Law slowed down for the purpose of drawing the fire of the enemy, if he showed any disposition to attack the transports as they passed out."

"BLOWING-UP OF THE 'WESTFIELD.' — As soon as it had been decided to blow up the 'Westfield,' Commander Renshaw gave the order to clear the ship, and a scene of confusion followed. The men hastily collected their clothing and other articles, and, thrusting them into bags, tossed bags, hammocks, small arms, furniture, and various personal effects, into the boats, which went back and forth between the 'Westfield' and 'Boardman.' The 'Saxon' took off some forty odd officers and men; and the remainder of the crew that succeeded in getting clear of the 'Westfield' went on board the 'Boardman.' Among the latter was Acting Master Smalley, who deserves great credit for the skill and coolness he displayed in bringing the 'Boardman' out of the harbor.

"The decks of the 'Westfield' were covered with turpentine, trains were laid to the magazine, which were opened, and the safety-valves of the boilers were chained down, to make the total destruction of the vessel more certain. The magazines were full of powder: there were one hundred loaded shells on deck; and the guns were loaded for action. A fire was lighted on the gun-deck forward, and the ship abandoned. The captain's gig was alongside, containing Lieut. Zimmerman, Chief Engineer Green, Kellihan, the quarter-gunner, and the gig's crew, waiting for Commander Renshaw, who had been once in the gig, but had just set foot on the ladder as if to go back, when the vessel blew up with a tremendous explosion. Fragments of shot and shell, splinters of timber, were hurled to an immense height; and what remained of the shattered hull settled as if forced down by an enormous weight. A vast column of flame and smoke shot up, and hid the ill-fated vessel from sight. When the smoke cleared away, no vestige was seen of the boat, which, but a moment before, had been freighted with so many brave men. Officers and men had found a common grave with their beloved vessel. Their fate was involved with that of their noble ship.

"It is plain that the explosion of the after-magazine was premature, and not apprehended by any of those who were lost. The scene on board the transports was sad in the extreme. The sailors from the ill-starred gunboat lamented the loss of their officers and comrades, exclaiming, 'Poor Zimmerman, poor Zimmerman!—and the captain too!' One old boatswain's mate, who had grown gray in the service of his country, while the tears coursed down his cheeks, cried out, 'I had rather have spilt my blood and left my bones on board the "Westfield" with the old man, than got off in this way.' The 'Westfield' blew up at thirteen minutes of nine, A.M.; a sorrowful *finale* to the tragic performances with которых the rebels ushered in the new year."

VICTORY IN SOUTH CAROLINA.—To offset this account of a Union defeat, a graphic description of the Union victory at Port Royal, S.C., is here given, from the pen of one who was on board the United-States steamer "Pocahontas" at the time of the engagement:—

"PORT ROYAL, S.C., Nov. 9, 1861.
"*To the Editor of the 'Boston Journal,'* —

"Our expedition left Old Point on the morning of the 29th ult.,—a beautiful morning; and, though we had quite a severe gale on the 30th, the fleet kept together until the 1st inst., when we experienced a very severe gale, which scattered the fleet, or at least scattered us from the fleet; and we saw no more of our companions, with the exception of one or two transports, till the morning of the 7th. At daylight, off Savannah, we chased away a secession steamer which seemed to have a fell design upon the schooner 'Western Star' of Boston, which we took in tow, and coaled ship from her, till, as we neared Port-Royal entrance, we heard the boom of heavy ordnance, and soon saw the white smoke as it curled up in the still morning air. It is needless to say that the schooner was dropped. We put on all steam, not even hoisting our boats, and were soon up to the entrance, which we found buoyed temporarily on each side the channel: so we stood directly in.

"We could distinguish the 'Wabash,' our flag-ship, pouring in a most deadly fire, also the 'Susquehanna,' 'Mohican,' and several other gunboats.

"The forts were firing rapidly from both sides; but the ships did not appear to be much injured, none of them having lost their masts. We passed the transports lying at anchor, well clear of the contest, outside; and, as we dashed by at full speed, we received the cheers of thousands eager for the fray, but unable to participate.

"Forward we went, our men at quarters all eager to get their first pop at South Carolina; and, as soon as our long ten-inch pivot-gun could be brought to bear, we sent our first compliment to Fort Walker. They held their fire on both sides till we got midway between both forts; and then for ten or fifteen minutes they rained grape, rifle-shot, and hollow shot upon us in a manner very romantic indeed, but more agreeable to think about afterward than when one is under it. We had no white feathers on board, though, to show; and our captain is brave as a lion and full of spirit when under fire. Capt. Drayton is a South-Carolinian, as true as steel; and we pelted away at them from both sides in a most gratifying manner to ourselves at least. After the capture of the forts, we found that Gen. Drayton, in command of this district, was our captain's own brother, and that he had, besides, two other relatives engaged in the secession cause at this place. Such patriotism as this is soul-cheering in these times, and a stinging reproach to a Northern *peace man*. Our ship received three shots aloft, one of which ruined the mainmast; but they first rained shot over our heads as we ran the gantlet of the forts.

"Once inside, we hauled in under Fort Walker, out of near range of the guns on Bay Point, leaving us but one side to fight; and in about half an hour, during which time a perfect storm of shell was thrown into every part of the fort, they left their guns, and ran quicker than our tired men did at Bull Run. They *can run* some, even in a South-Carolina morass; but they looked very ridiculous, and as if they had no stomach for a Yankee hunt, in which they are said to delight so much. A naval officer from the 'Wabash' landed with a flag of truce; and the sailors scrambled to a house-top, and flung the glorious old flag to the breeze. Cheer on cheer went up from the thousands on ship-board; and a portion of South Carolina was again redeemed from its disgrace by being covered by an honorable flag and an honorable people."

The brilliant descriptions which " Carleton " gives of the Union attack on Sumter in 1863, and of the capture of Beaufort, S.C., cannot be omitted; for they display the seamanship and valor of our brave navy boys in a style to awaken hearty praise. The following is the description of the taking of Beaufort:—

"At five minutes before ten o'clock, the Hilton-Head battery opened fire on the 'Wabash:' in three minutes after, another shot from the battery. Still the ships stood on, and did not, apparently, notice the efforts of the rebels, until the 'Wabash' came in good range with the face of the battery; when she fired a shell at them, which struck close to the battery. In a few minutes, the 'Wabash' opened a smart fire, throwing her shells into the woods, where the rebels were encamped in some force. After firing a few guns to ascertain the range, she opened a broadside fire on both batteries, which was one of the finest sights ever witnessed in this country. How the troops did cheer! It was hearty and long. The other vessels now opened their fire, and the shells fell thick and fast into the battery.

"The rebel steamers now opened a smart fire, and it was the subject of general remark,—the fine shots they made. The small gunboats now steamed rapidly ahead, and opened on them with their ten and eleven inch pivot-guns. At fifteen minutes past ten o'clock, the fire was so hot, that they up helm, and started for Broad River; the gunboats chasing them. By this time, the shells were bursting in the Bay-Point battery at the rate of about two a minute, to which the rebels replied with rapidity and great execution.

"The flag-ship and her division were rapidly drawing up to the point around which they were to turn, so that they could come down along the shore, and engage the Hilton-Head battery; while the small gunboats took up independent positions, and battered away at Bay Point and the rebel naval vessels. As the 'Wabash' turned, so that her broadside could bear upon the rebel fleet, she opened upon them, and soon sent them up the river for a time at least. About this time, the 'Vandalia' came up in range; and she delivered a splendid broadside to the Bay-Point rebels, several of her shells making the sand fly inside of the works. She kept up a galling fire upon them until out of reach, when she devoted her attention to the rebel navy. During this time, the 'Wabash,' 'Susquehanna,' and 'Bienville' had come around, and were close upon the Hilton-Head battery. All eyes were upon these vessels, especially as we saw plainly that they were steering so as to come within six hundred yards of the rebels' guns, some of which we knew were excellent rifled pieces of the most approved patterns.

"At about twenty minutes before eleven o'clock, the 'Wabash' commenced operations on the Hilton-Head battery in good earnest, delivering a broadside at one command. All her gun-deck armament is nine-inch shell guns; while on her spar-deck they are eight-inch shell guns, with a ten-inch pivot aft, and a sixty-eight rifled Dahlgren gun on the forecastle. The noise was terrific, while the bursting of the shells was as terrible as it was destructive. I counted no less than forty shells bursting at one time, and that right in the battery and in the woods, where about eight hundred rebels lay. In addition to this, the 'Susquehanna,' with her tremendous battery, aided by the 'Bienville,' the 'Pawnee,' and half a dozen smaller gunboats, was making the air brown with the sand, while the blue smoke of the explosions went to make up a most magnificent sight.

"The troops were wild with enthusiasm; and with deafening cheers they applauded the boldness and courage of the gallant naval officer. A moment or two elapsed,—just time enough to load the guns,—and again the scene was enacted afresh. The rebels replied with seven guns, which were worked splendidly; and from appearances they did considerable execution. After the second broadside, the firing became less concerted; and it seemed as if each division on all the vessels were endeavoring to outvie each other in the rapidity with which they worked their guns.

"The tide drifted the vessels quite fast by the battery; but they backed them considerably, so as to remain as long as possible: and at eleven o'clock they had reached as near to the reef as it was safe to go; and they were obliged to haul off to again take up their position, but giving them another broadside as they turned. To do this, a track, circular in form, and extending nearly five miles, must be sailed over. The Bay-Point battery must again be passed, where there were several fine rifled cannon, which were well served; and the navy of the Confederates must receive their due share of the shells which were destined to be expended on the day's work. To this duty they undauntedly steamed up, while the little gunboats fought the steamers.

"About this time, the firing on both sides materially diminished. Occasionally the rebels fired from either battery, which was replied to by the gunboats. As the 'Wabash' and her consorts rounded to, to come down again and pitch into the battery where they had made such a beautiful display of their skill, the troops again gave vent to their feelings in tones not to be mistaken. It appeared that with such a terrible fire poured in upon them they could not stand, and in the course of a few hours the stars and stripes must wave on the 'sacred soil' of South Carolina.

"At half-past eleven, they drew near to the Hilton-Head battery again; the rebels keeping up a brisk fire upon them as they approached. Occasionally the pivot-guns of the 'Wabash' and the 'Susquehanna' threw a shell into the battery; but the grand affair was yet to come. At ten minutes before twelve o'clock, again the ships were enveloped in a dense cloud of white smoke; and, in a few seconds after, the shells were bursting into the battery in a splendid manner. The sand was flying in every direction; and it seemed impossible that any one could be saved from death who was within the walls of the battery. The rebels now worked only two guns; but I will give them the credit of working them beautifully. This style of fighting lasted just twenty minutes; and in that time over two hundred shells had burst over their heads and in the works. At ten minutes past twelve, again the ships hauled off, firing a parting round as they left.

"At twenty minutes past twelve, the Bay-Point battery opened fire on the 'Wabash' as she passed up to take her position. Five minutes afterwards, the gunboats opened a terrible volley of shells on Hilton Head, breaching it in several places, and dismounting one of the guns. This display of gunnery was a grand sight, and was only second to the broadside firing of the other ships. The gunboats kept up this kind of work several minutes, when they eased down, and fired at intervals, so that there was a shell striking about once a minute.

"At ten minutes of one, not a rebel boat was to be seen; and from appearances they had gone behind the Point to take on board the troops, who could not stand another round of broadside-firing. The battery was badly damaged, and the houses and tents bore the marks of shells; and it looked as if there was a stampede in the rebel camp. At five minutes of two o'clock, the 'Wabash' and her consorts were in position to advance; but they remained quiet, and let the gunboats pepper away at the battery, which only replied with one gun, which looked as if they were only firing to deceive us while they embarked their forces. At two o'clock we weighed anchor, and got still closer in, feeling assured that they had become pretty well used up, and would not or could not injure us.

"The transports now launched their surf-boats, nearly one hundred in number, and placed the crews in them, all ready to commence disembarking the troops.

"At twenty minutes of three o'clock, a boat — the whaleboat of the 'Wabash' — was manned, and with a white flag flying over the bow, and Commander John Rodgers in the stern, started for the shore. I can assure you that every stroke of the oars was watched by thousands of anxious people. She strikes the beach. Capt. Rodgers, borne on the backs of true and trusty tars, with the stars and stripes floating over his head, and a large ensign, goes on shore; and, at *three o'clock precisely, the stars and stripes wave in triumph over South-Carolina soil and a deserted rebel battery.* A glorious and brilliant naval victory has been won. All honor to the gallant seamen of the United-States Navy!

"As soon as the good old flag was seen from on shipboard, our boys gave nine rousing cheers, and they were taken up from ship to ship; and the band saluted the flag with the 'Star-spangled Banner' and 'Hail Columbia,' &c. For an hour, the cheers of the patriotic soldiers made the air resound. Again we got under way, and proceeded to within a half-mile of the shore, and anchored; and the debarkation was commenced, and until long after dark the work went on."

The following is a description of the attack on Sumter: —

"At half-past one, P.M., the signal for sailing was displayed from the flag-ship. The 'Weehawken,' with a raft at her prow, immediately got under way, and moved rapidly up the main channel, followed by the others, which maintained their respective positions, distant from each other about one-third or half of a mile. There are no clouds of canvas, no beautiful models of marine architecture, none of the stateliness and majesty which has marked hundreds of great naval engagements. There is but little to the sight calculated to excite enthusiasm. There are eight black specks and one oblong block gliding along the water, like so many bugs. There are no human beings in sight, no propelling power visible.

"Sumter has discovered them, and discharges in quick succession nine signal-guns to announce to all Rebeldom that the attack is to be made. Morris Island is mysteriously silent as the 'Weehawken' advances, although she is within range. Past Fort Wagner, straight on toward Moultrie, the 'Weehawken' moves. The silence is prolonged. It is almost painful, the calm before the storm, the hushed stillness before the burst of the tornado.

"There comes a single puff of smoke from Moultrie, one deep reverberation. The silence is broken: the moments, the long months of waiting, are over. The shot flies across the water, skipping from wave to wave, tossing up fountains, hopping over the deck of the 'Weehawken,' and rolling along the surface with a diminishing ricochet, sinking at last close upon the Morris-Island Beach. Fort Wagner continues the story, sending a shot at the 'Weehawken:' it also trips lightly over the deck, and tosses up a waterspout far toward Moultrie. The 'Weehawken,' unmindful of this play, opened its ports, and sent a fifteen-inch solid shot toward Sumter, which, like those which have been hurled toward her, takes a half-dozen steps, making for a moment its footprints on the water, and crashes against the south-west face of the fort, followed a moment later by its eleven-inch companion. The vessel is for a moment enveloped in the smoke of its guns. Bravely done! There comes an answer. Moultrie, the tremendous batteries on either side by the hotel and east of it, and toward the inner harbor, burst in an instant into sheets of flame, and clouds of sulphurous smoke. There is one long roll of thunder, peal on peal; deep, heavy reverberations and sharp concussions rattling the windows of our steamers, and striking us at the heart like hammer-strokes.

"The ocean boils. Columns of spray are tossed high in air, as if a hundred submarine fountains were let instantly on, or a school of whales were trying which could spout highest. There is a screaming in the air, a buzzing and humming never before so loud.

"At five minutes before three, Moultrie began the fire. Ten minutes have passed. The thunder has rolled incessantly from Sullivan's Island. Thus far, Sumter has been silent; but now it is crowned with a cloud. In an instant it is hid from view; first a line of light along its parapet, and thick folds of smoke unrolling like fleeces of wool. Other flashes burst from the casemates; and the clouds creep down the wall to the water, then slowly float away to mingle with that rising from the furnaces in the sand along the shore of Sullivan's Island.

"You almost think the earth's crust has ruptured, and the volcanic fires, long pent, have suddenly found vent.

"It was the first grand round. Then comes a calm, a momentary cessation. The rebel gunners wait for the breeze to clear away the cloud, that they may obtain a view of the monitor to see if it has not been punched into a sieve, and is disappearing beneath the waves. But the 'Weehawken' is there moving straight on up the channel, turned now toward

Moultrie. Nothing has happened. To her it has been only
a handful of peas or gravel-stones or pebbles. Some
have rattled against her turret, some upon her deck, some
against her sides. Instead of going to the bottom, she revolves her turret, and speaks two words to Moultrie, moving
on the while to gain the south-eastern wall of Sumter.

"Again the forts and batteries begin, joined now by Cummings Point and long ranges from Fort Johnson. All
round the 'Weehawken' the shot flash, plunge, hop, skip,
falling like the rain-drops of a summer shower. How quickly
the 'Wabash,' the 'Minnesota,' or any one of the wooden ships
of the navy, would be bored through and through from port
to port, from bow to stern, from deck to keel, by the point-blank and plunging shot, converging from more than ninety
degrees of the circle, — be made into kindlings, sent sky-high
by a shell in boiler or magazine, or to the bottom of the
channel, by the opening of barn-doors in the hull! Unarmed, undaunted, she moves straight on, feeling her way,
moving slowly, with grappling-irons dragging from the raft
in front to catch up torpedoes. It is for the 'Weehawken' to
clear the channel, and make smooth sailing for the remainder of the fleet. Two torpedoes explode, — so much
wasted powder, nothing more!·

"To get the position of the 'Weehawken' at this moment,
spread out your map of Charleston Harbor, draw a line from
Cummings Point to Moultrie, and stick a pin on the line a
little nearer Moultrie than to Morris Island. It is about
one-half a mile from Moultrie, about one-third of a mile

"There she is, — the target of probably two hundred and fifty or three hundred guns at close range, of the heaviest caliber, rifled cannon throwing forged bolts and steel-pointed shot, turned and polished to a hair in the lathes of English workshops, — advancing still, undergoing her first ordeal, a trial unparalleled in history!

"For fifteen minutes, she meets the ordeal alone: but, the channel found to be clear, the 'Passaic,' the 'Montauk,' and 'Patapsco' follow, closing up the line; each coming in range, and delivering their fire upon Sumter. At twenty minutes past three, the four monitors composing the right wing of the fleet are all engaged, each pressing on to reach the northeastern face of the fort, where the wall is weakest; each receiving, as they arrive at particular points, a terrible fire, seemingly from all points of the compass, — points selected by trial and practice indicated by buoys. They pass the destructive latitudes unharmed. Seventy guns a minute are counted, followed by moments of calm and scattering shots, but only to break out again in a prolonged roar of thunder. They press on, making nearer and nearer to Sumter, narrowing the distance to one thousand yards, eight hundred, six, five, four hundred yards, and send their fifteen-inch shot crashing against the fort with slow, sure, deliberate, effective fire.

"At first the fort and the batteries and Moultrie seem to redouble their efforts in increasing the fire; but after an hour there is a perceptible diminution of the discharges from the fort. After each shot from the iron-clads, clouds of dust can be discerned rising above the fort, and mingling with the moke. Steadying my glass in the lulls of the strife, watching where the south-west breeze whiffs away the smoke, I can see increasing pock-marks and discolorations upon the walls, as if there had been a sudden breaking-out of cutaneous disease.

"The flag-ship, drawing seventeen feet of water, was obliged to move cautiously, feeling her way up the channel. Just as she came within range of Moultrie, her keel touched bottom on the east side of the channel. Fearing that she would run aground, the anchor was let go. Finding the vessel was clear, the admiral again moved on, signalling the left wing to press forward to the aid of the four already engaged. The 'Ironsides' kept the main channel, which brought her within about one thousand yards of Moultrie and Sumter. She fired four guns at Moultrie, and received in return a heavy fire. Again she touched bottom, and then turned her bow across the channel toward Sumter, firing two guns at Cummings Point. After this weak and ineffectual effort, the tide rapidly ebbing the while, she again got clear, but gave up the attempt to advance. The 'Catskill,' 'Nantucket,' 'Nahant,' and 'Keokuk' pressed up with all possible speed to aid the four, which were receiving a tremendous hammering.

"See them sweep past the convergent points and radial lines! See the bubbling of the water, the straight columns thrown up in the sunlight, the flashes, the furrows along the waves, as if a plough, driven with lightning speed, was turning up the water! They are all close up to Sumter, within four or five hundred yards. Behind them is Moultrie and Fort Ripley and Fort Beauregard, flashing, smoking, bellowing; in front is Sumter; and in the background, Fort Wagner and Cummings Point. Across the shallow waters is Fort Johnson; still farther off to the right is Castle Pickney, too far away to do damage, but, as you have seen curs at a grand fight of bull-dogs, harmlessly snarling, growling, and yelping, and making believe they are doing something. From all sides, the balls fall around the fleet. The din of uproar is nearly all on one side. Calmly and deliberately the fire is returned, — a deliberation which must command the admiration of the enemy.

"The 'Keokuk' presents a fair mark with her sloping sides and double turrets. She comes to the ordeal bravely. Her commander, Capt. Rhind, although not having entire confidence in her invulnerability, is determined to come to close quarters. She is not to be outdone by those who are in advance. Swifter than they, drawing less water, she makes all haste to get up with the 'Weehawken.' The guns which have been trained upon the others are brought to bear upon her. Where she sails, there the shower is hardest, the fire fiercest. Her plating is but pine-wood to the steel projectiles, flying with almost the swiftness of a Minie bullet. Shot which glance harmlessly from the others penetrate her angled sides. Her after-turret is pierced in a twinkling, and a two-hundred-pound projectile dropped inside. A heavy shot crashes into the surgeon's dispensary, and mixes emetics, cathartics, pill, and powders, not according to prescriptions. The enemy notices the effect of his shot, and increases his fire. Capt. Rhind is not easily daunted. He opens his forward turret, and gives three shot in return for the three or four hundred rained around him. The sea with every passing wave sweeps through the shot-holes; and he must retire, or go to the bottom with all on board.

"Meanwhile the signal has been displayed from the flag-ship for the retirement of the fleet. It comes seemingly at an inopportune moment; for the fire of the fort is evidently on the wane. Moultrie and all the guns of Sullivan Island are still bellowing; but Sumter has few flashes, a cloud of smoke less dense than an hour ago. Capt. Ammen is confident that he has sent a shot clear through the wall; that a gun is silenced. There is but little diminution of the fire of the fleet. It is, as it has been, slow and steady; but the 'Keokuk' is moving out of range: the 'Ironsides' has not been in. It is past five o'clock,—almost sunset. Never in the history of the world has there been such a two and a half hours' hammering of iron. There is the imperative order flying above the flag-ship 'Retire.' They obey. It is twenty minutes past five o'clock when the last guns are fired, —an exchange of shots with Cummings Point.

"The uproar has ceased. The fleet is at anchor. The monitors of the right swing within range of Fort Wagner. On Sullivan's Island, the sulphurous clouds still linger. The red sun sinks behind the sand-hills, and we who have watched every changing feature of the attack welcome the coming-on of silence."

Some of the gallant exploits of our navy have not been mentioned; but again it must be said, "The half has not been told." Our brave tars have "covered themselves with honor" on every sea where they fought.

It may be well to add a few words in regard to some of the leaders in our navy. The following has been published concerning two of them. The anecdotes are characteristic, and probably correct.

Admiral Farragut is a native of Tennessee. The "Louisville Journal" gives the following notice of his career:—

"In childhood he was adopted by the late Commodore David Porter, receiving his baptismal name; and is thus the brother adoptive of Capt. J. D. Porter, of the 'Essex,' in our flotilla, and of Lieut. Porter, in command of the mortar-fleet at the mouth of the Mississippi. Though only twelve years of age, he was on the 'Essex,' at Valparaiso, in 1814, in that most gallant naval fight, and was specially commended to the department for his brave deportment. An anecdote told of him, though trifling, indicates character. After the surrender, a pig which he claimed was carried off by a midshipman of the British frigate 'Phebe.' Young Farragut appealed to the British captain for restitution, and received for reply, that he could do nothing about it, but that he might go and whip the middy. 'Is that all?' said the lad; and, acting on the leave given, instantly whipped the aggressor, and carried off his pig.

"He has been almost constantly in active service. During the years 1821–4, he was employed in cruising after pirates in the Caribbean Sea, and distinguished himself by most efficient service and gallantry. He was for some time in command of the 'Brooklyn' at the Vera-Cruz station, at the time of the mission of Mr. McLean to Mexico. He was twice married in Norfolk, Va., and is the owner of a large property in that rebel city; but before the outbreak, and to avoid entanglements, he removed his family from Norfolk to a cottage on the Hudson, whence he was called to active duty in putting down the Rebellion. He is a most accomplished officer, versed in every point of his profession, and most energetic in all naval duties. He speaks with fluency five or six modern languages; and, sailor as he is, is a gentleman of fine scholarly taste and acquirements.*

"Commander Charles S. Boggs, of the United-States gunboat 'Varuna,' which was sunk in the recent engagement with the enemy at New Orleans, where he attacked thirteen gunboats of the rebels, and sunk six of them, and his last shot, fired when his deck was under water, sunk a gunboat of the rebels, is a native of New Brunswick, N. J. When a lad, he told his father he wished to go into the navy. His father said to him, 'You are too clumsy: you would fall into the water from the deck.' The next morning his father saw him on the roof of the house: he had climbed

---

* "Vice-Admiral Farragut has his headquarters at the Navy Yard in Brooklyn. He is chiefly now employed on court-martials, of which he is President. He suffers greatly from an affection of the eyes, resulting from a sunstroke received on the coast of Africa when he was quite young. His immense correspondence has to be carried on by other hands, he being unable to write. The glare of public audience-rooms is very painful to him. He is bored almost to death by applications for his presence at public meetings where a crowd is needed. Although both travel and gaslight are exceedingly distressing to him, yet such is his kindness of heart, that he rarely refuses an invitation to a meeting that has a beneficent aim. He left the city to-day for Philadelphia to meet Gen. Grant, and with him inaugurate an institution for the benefit of disabled soldiers and sailors." — *Boston-Journal correspondent.*

the lightning-rod, going up hand over hand. His mother was a sister of the gallant Lawrence, of the 'Chesapeake.'

"It will be observed that both of these officers have had ancestors which might account for their fighting qualities; one being a member of the family of the elder Porter, and the other a relative of the heroic Lawrence."

Admiral Foote was another hero: he has gone up higher. The following is the official order concerning the late Admiral Foote:—

General Orders, No. 19.

WASHINGTON, June 27, 1863.

A gallant and distinguished naval officer is lost to the country. The hero of Fort Henry and Fort Donelson; the daring and indomitable spirit that created and led to successive victories the Mississippi flotilla; the heroic Christian sailor, who, in the China seas and on the coast of Africa, as well as the great interior rivers of our country, sustained with unfaltering fidelity and devotion the honor of our flag and the cause of the Union; Rear-Admiral Andrew Hull Foote, — is no more.

On his way to take the command of the South-Atlantic squadron, a position to which he had been recently assigned, and the duties of which were commanding the earnest energies of a mind of no ordinary character, he was suddenly prostrated by disease, and, after a brief illness, breathed his last at the Astor House, in New York, on the evening of the 26th instant.

Among the noble and honored dead whose names have added lustre to our naval renown, and must ever adorn our national annals, few will stand more prominent than that of the gallant and self-sacrificing Christian sailor and gentleman whose loss we now deplore.

Appreciating his virtues and his services, a grateful country had rendered him, while living, its willing honors, and will mourn his death. As a mark of respect, it is hereby ordered that the flags at the several navy-yards, naval-stations, and on the flag-ships of the squadrons, be hoisted at half-mast, and that thirteen guns be fired at meridian, on the day after the receipt of this order.

(Signed) GIDEON WELLES,
Secretary of the Navy.

Admiral Foote was as eminent in piety as in arms. This incident is related of him: —

"On the Sabbath after the capture of Fort Henry, quite a large congregation had assembled at the little Presbyterian Church in Cairo. They waited a long time for the regular preacher to come and open the services, but waited in vain; and it soon became apparent that they were to go home sermonless. Just then, the old flag-officer, as he was then, appeared, went forward to the sacred desk, and opened the service with prayer. It was very hard for the audience to restrain their applause when he appeared in the aisle, coming as he did from the scene of strife, and the winner of a victory whose merits were upon every tongue; but, the first buzz of wondering over, the congregation bowed in silence and awe, the more marked because of the strangeness of the coincidence. Hardly forty-eight hours before, the old veteran was hotly engaged in dealing death and destruction to the enemy at Fort Henry: now he stood before the people in the character of a preacher of the gospel of peace. But the prayer was not all. After the hymn, he took his text from Acts xiv. 1, and preached such a sermon as had not been heard before for years. Clear, calm, logical, he proved, in truly eloquent diction, that the happiness of man depended upon the condition of the heart, and not upon worldly prosperity or adversity. After the sermon, the congregation vied with each other in endeavors to reach him to congratulate him upon his success in the late action; but the old veteran met them with a peculiar look, as much as to say, 'This is the Sabbath Day, and this is God's house, and no time or place to glory over the downfall of an enemy.'

"Some days before his death, he stated that he had but little time to live, and felt that he was gradually sinking. He was anxious that Admiral Dupont should be informed that he had not intrigued to obtain command of the squadron. The two were warm friends. He bore his painful sickness with Christian fortitude and meekness, and felt that he was going to a better land, and to scenes more delightful than he had enjoyed; and, in that faith, he who never sacrificed a life needlessly, and had no blood on his hands, who never went to battle without having his soul prepared by prayer, sank quietly and peacefully to his rest."

Of Dupont the "Philadelphia North-American" says,—

"No one was as well qualified for the head of the great

expedition as Commodore Dupont. His whole heart is in his country's troubles; and he would cheerfully die, as the gallant Lyon did, to promote her welfare. He entered the navy as a midshipman when just twelve years of age, and he is now in the prime of his physical life. With more than forty years' experience in his profession, and a well-disciplined and cultivated mind, he unites every quality which can distinguish a great naval captain. It does not, in our estimation, detract from his abilities that he walks humbly before his God as a Christian soldier and gentleman. No one has ever sailed with him who does not honor and love him, while no ships ever exhibited better discipline than those which he commanded. He was always firm, but kind; rigid, but lenient. No profanity ever polluted his lips, and no carelessness of living ever set a bad example to younger men who were serving under him."

There is another American sailor, who, though not in the navy, deserves to be mentioned for his bravery, and determined resistance to rebel piracy: —

"THE MAN WHO DEFIED WADDELL THE PIRATE. — The 'San-Francisco Bulletin' gives the following account of the circumstances of the defence and capture of the whaling-ship 'Favorite,' of Fairhaven, Mass., on the 28th of last June. Capt. Young, the master of the 'Favorite,' is described to be between sixty and seventy years old, and belongs to the John Brown stamp of mortals, who believe in fighting the wrong under all circumstances, and never letting right back down to it, however great may be the odds. Accordingly, when he found himself cornered by the rebel pirate, with no chance of escape, he proceeded to make preparations for the coming conflict with such means as were at hand; and, had it not been for what was done by his officers as described below, somebody would have been hurt.

"Seeing a boat shove off from the 'Shenandoah' toward his bark, Capt. Young ordered the old blunderbuss used for shooting whales to be brought up from below, together with his revolver and ammunition. Having carefully loaded the weapons, the old salt took his position on the cabin-roof, and awaited the approach of the pirate's boat. As he came near the side of the vessel, Capt. Young pointed his blunderbuss at the officer in charge, and shouted to him to 'stand off!' The pirate was greatly astonished at such a reception, and at first was inclined to think that the old man was playing a 'goak' on him; but, seeing his determined look and the unerring aim of the blunderbuss, he came to the conclusion that discretion was the better part of valor, and ordered his men to paddle back with all due despatch to the 'Shenandoah.'

"By this time, Capt. Young's fellow-officers began to get shaky in the knees; and, fearing that matters would come to a serious pass, they took the precaution to steal away the old man's ammunition, and even took the caps off the weapons already loaded. Having done this, they, with all the crew, crawled into the boats, lowered themselves into the water, and left Capt. Young alone in his glory, sole occupant of the vessel. The captain thinks this was a shabby trick: it was hard enough for him to fight the rebels alone anyhow; but to leave him with nothing but a bomb-gun, and a revolver uncapped, to answer the broadside of the 'Shenandoah,' was putting the odds altogether too heavy against him. He did not back down, however, but kept his position on the cabin-roof, and awaited the flash of the enemy's guns. He had had some experience of the uncertainties of cannon-balls and shells, having run a schooner with supplies up the Potomac in the earlier part of the Rebellion. 'Besides,' said he, 'I have only four or five years more to live, anyway; and I might as well die now as any time, especially as all I have is invested in my vessel; and if I lose that I will have to go home penniless, and die a pauper.'

"While thus reasoning to himself, he heard the officer of the 'Shenandoah' give the order to 'fire, but fire low.' Without deigning to rise from his reclining position, he coolly awaited the result of the order; but no fire came. Soon he saw another boat pushing off toward him from the 'Shenandoah.' It seems, that, after the order to 'fire' was given, some one on board the pirate discovered that one of the 'Shenandoah's' boats was in range, and hence the order was countermanded. When the pirate's boat came alongside the second time, the officer in charge ordered Capt. Young to haul down his colors. 'I'll see you d—d first!' replied the captain. 'If you don't do it, I will shoot you!' said the officer. 'Shoot, and be d—d!' said the captain. Hereupon the officer dropped his gun that he had raised to shoot the captain, and ordered his men to board the whaler.

Capt. Young had by this time discovered that the caps had been removed from his weapon; and, being without means of defence, he could offer no resistance, and was therefore obliged to allow himself to be taken.

"They conveyed him on board the 'Shenandoah,' and immediately ordered him to be put in irons, and sent to the topgallant forecastle; at the same time telling him, that, if he was anyway saucy, they would gag him. A sentry was placed over him; and he was kept there four hours, or until he was put aboard the 'Nile' to be brought to San Francisco. He was robbed of every thing, including a hundred and twenty dollars in money, a gold watch, and even his shirt-studs. He also had a library of two hundred and twenty volumes, which was stolen from the 'Favorite' before she was committed to the flames."

To this account may properly be added an anecdote, which illustrates the patriotism of Young America. It is from the "Plymouth Rock:"—

"A Boy Hero.—Our readers will remember the incident, at the capture of the United-States steamship 'Harriet Lane' in Galveston Harbor, of a boy coming on deck, when she was boarded by the rebels, with a revolver in each hand, and after firing every barrel, finding the vessel surrendered, threw his pistols overboard to keep them out of the hands of the rebels. His life was in danger from the act, as a rebel soldier had a sword uplifted to cut him down for throwing away his pistols, but was stopped by an officer.

"All loyal citizens will rejoice to know that a boy of

such a fearless and lofty spirit has been rewarded, and placed in a position where these qualities will have a full chance of development. By a letter to his son, from our townsman Capt. Phineas Leach, who is acting-master on board the receiving ship 'North Carolina,' stationed in New-York Harbor, where this young hero was placed when released, we learn, that, upon the act of this boy hero coming to the notice of the Secretary of the Navy, that officer issued a warrant of midshipman to the boy, and gave orders for his admission to the Naval School at Newport.

"By the kindness of Capt. Leach's son, we are enabled to give the following information of this young hero: 'His name is Robert Cummings. He was born in Scotland, from which country he came, with his father and mother, when he was five years old. His father died about three years after coming to this country; and young Robert was obliged to help support the family. He had not been at school since he was ten years old. He went on board the "Harriet Lane" when thirteen years old (being now but fourteen), leaving a half-pay ticket of five dollars per month to his mother, who lives in Philadelphia.'

"Capt. Leach enclosed a photograph of young Cummings, which we saw. He is a light-built youth, small of his age, with a handsome, determined face, and good head. If he lives, and has an opportunity, we doubt not that Robert Cummings will again be heard from to his credit."

With such naval heroes, can any thing but supremacy on the seas be predicted for the American navy? Can any banner float above the stars and stripes?

"Flag of the seas! on ocean wave
    Thy stars shall glitter o'er the grave :
When Death, careering on the gale,
    Sweeps darkly round the belted sail,
And frighted waves rush wildly back
    Before the broadside's reeling rack,
Each dying wanderer of the sea
    Shall look at once to heaven and thee,
And smile to see thy splendors fly
    In triumph o'er his closing eye.

Flag of the free heart's hope and home!
    By angel hands to valor given,
The stars have lit the welkin dome,
    And all thy hues were born in heaven.
Forever float that standard sheet!
    Where breathes the foe but falls before us,
With Freedom's soil beneath our feet,
    And Freedom's banner streaming o'er us?" *

---

* Joseph Rodman Drake.

CHAPTER IV.

BATTLE-SCENES.—ARMY OF THE POTOMAC.

"Strike till the last armed foe expires,
Strike for your altars and your fires,
Strike for the green graves of your sires,
God and your native land!"

THE Army of the Potomac!—green are the bays that twine around that name, unfading forever the laurels it has won under Sherman and Sheridan and Grant! To present all its history would require volumes. The reader of these pages can be furnished only with pictures of its valor and glory, sketched, it may be, with a feeble hand sometimes, but, it is hoped, always truthfully.

"At the time of the attack on Fort Sumter, the entire military force at the disposal of the Government was sixteen thousand and six regulars. They were principally employed in the West to hold in check marauding Indians. It has always been the policy of the Government to maintain the army at the lowest number of privates which was practicable with the interests of the country, and to rely upon volunteers whenever any emergency should arise. . . . The nucleus of our army was always preserved by the education of officers at West Point. . . . The call of the President for troops for three months, in his proclamation of April 15, asked for seventy-five thousand men. This call amounted, in the aggregate, to ninety-four regiments, making seventy-three thousand three hundred and ninety-one officers and men. Of the States called upon, the governors of Virginia, North Carolina, Tennessee, Arkansas, Kentucky, and Mississippi, peremptorily refused to comply with the requirements made by the War Department. All the other non-seceding States promptly furnished the number required of them, except Maryland, whose governor was prevented from so doing by the outbreak at Baltimore. . . . The remainder, to constitute the seventy-five thousand men, was composed of troops in the District of Columbia." *

The soldiers who fought in Virginia, North and South Carolina, and Maryland, are included under the general term of the Army of the Potomac. Their victory at Bull Run, or Manassas, led the rebels to regard themselves as greatly the superiors of the Northern people in battle: hence they became enthusiastic for continuing the war; and, before the autumn of 1861, they had a large army in front of Washington. The Union army was increased also, and Gen. McClellan called to the command. "The people wanted a leader. Gen. Scott, who had fought at Niagara and Lundy's Lane, who had captured the city of Mexico, was too old and infirm to take the field. Gen. McDowell, although his plan of attack at Bull Run was approved, had failed of victory. Gen. McClellan had been successful in

* Annual Cyclopædia, 1861.

the skirmishes at Philippi and at Rich Mountain. He was known to be a good engineer. He had been a visitor to Russia during the Crimean War, and had written a book upon that war, which was published by Congress. He was a native of Pennsylvania and a resident of Ohio when the war broke out. The governors of both of these States sent him a commission as a brigadier-general, because he had military experience in Mexico, because he was known as a military man, and because they were in great need of experienced men to command the troops. Having all these things in his favor, he was called to Washington, and made commander of the Army of the Potomac, on the 27th of July." *

The principal events in connection with this army during a long period of inactivity, in 1861, were the disaster at Ball's Bluff and a victory at Drainsville.

It is not designed to present a history of army operations in any part of the country, but only incidents of the conflicts. The following is one of war's terrible scenes in connection with the Ball's-Bluff defeat, describing the scene of crossing the river after the battle : —

"We got down the Bluff to the water's edge. Of the two boats that brought us over, one was departing laden with wounded; one returning, also full of men. But, as they neared either shore, the eagerness of the occupants embarrassed the men who were in charge. The frail craft oscillated to and fro; then, half full of water, and almost at the same time, they both swamped. Seeing no chance of escape, the

---

* Following the Flag, by Carleton.

men plunged by dozens into the river, some naked, some with all their clothes on. Our second lieutenant and some eight or ten of the company had collected on the shore: our first lieutenant joined, and both prepared to swim across. This was the last seen of them. Many were drowned. As you stood and watched them swimming across, you would see here and there one throw up his hands and utter a cry, then slowly disappear, then rise again with outstretched hands, then sink again, and rise no more."

REMARKABLE ESCAPE AT BALL'S BLUFF.—The "Albany Journal" prints an extract from a letter written by Corporal P. Young, of Company D, Fifteenth Massachusetts Regiment, to his brother in that city, in which he gives the following account of his escape from the rebels after the battle of Ball's Bluff: —

"The dread alternative of surrendering and becoming a prisoner of Jeff. Davis, or swim across the Potomac, or make my grave at its dark and murky bottom, presented itself; and I chose to swim, with all my uniform on, after thinking the matter all over fully in a cleft of the rock, where I hid myself about sundown, when the friendly darkness covered my escape, and put an end to the awful conflict.

"The rebels came all around me, passed by and over me. The cleft was about twenty feet perpendicular height where I was concealed from view. When it became dark, I ventured forth, and crept the whole length of an oak-tree lying out into the river. Then another difficulty presented itself. The moon just began to cast its silver light from the eastern horizon, — a dreaded light; for it made all a conspicuous mark on the prostrated tree. I found that it would not do to stay there long: so, as I passed by one man and another, I put my hand on a stick, which was loose, and I took it in my hand to steady myself; and I thought it would do to use to push a raft over to the island, in case they made one.

"But I soon concluded, that, if they made a raft, it would be swamped by the rush of desperate men for their lives, just as the boats had been before. Before I got to the end of the tree, a man asked me in piteous tones to give him the stick. I hesitated, and he asked me several times: finally I consented; when, for some unaccountable reason, he did not accept of it, neither did he even thank me for the offer. I then stepped into the mud and water up to my breast, and put the stick crossways of my shoulders, and commenced to make motions like a fish; when, finding that others behind me who were undressed would be likely to take hold of my stick, gaining upon me, I turned it parallel with my body; and, strange as it may seem, I was pleased with the idea that I somewhat resembled, with the stick projecting from my head, the sword-fish. And, just at this time, a little dark cloud shut down before the moon, preventing rebel riflemen from seeing me in the water, and firing upon me as they did upon scores of others, even after they had crossed to the island. I made no noise, not opening my mouth as many did, attracting the attention of the rebels.

"While I was in the water, I gave myself up to my Saviour in prayer, using the same prayer which had availed on another occasion: 'Lord, save, or I perish!' I did not even feel cold or uncomfortable or unhappy, but could see the ripple at the end of my sword (if you call my stick a sword-fish), by which I knew that I was making headway, the heavy current taking me away down stream a long distance. But at length I reached the island, and went to the building where the wounded had been carried during the day, where I found so many so much worse than myself, that I did not speak to anybody, the floors being all covered with dead and wounded.

"I found I was getting cold, and immediately went out for exercise, and met a man who was waiting on the wounded, carrying them blankets, overcoats, &c. He asked me if I did not want something to put on. I replied, 'Yes,' thankfully; and he took off his own coat, as I supposed; but, to my perfect surprise and astonishment, he had given me my own overcoat, taken from an outhouse in which hundreds had been thrown before the battle, and carried off during the day without any regard to who the owner was. I made my way home to camp, and did not feel exhausted after all the almost superhuman labors and trials and sufferings of that bloody day."

The following lines were penned by a Greenfield soldier soon after the battle:—

THE HEROES OF BALL'S BLUFF.

> Above them, dark and stormy clouds;
> Before them, forests thick with foes;
> Behind them, yon steep precipice;
> Beneath, a rapid river flows.

Thus compassed is our gallant band;
  'Tis not for them to question why:
Though ten to one the foe advance,
  'Tis theirs to charge, to fight, to die.

Come ye who deem that valor's fled,
  That ancient knighthood's gone for aye,
And weep with us who mourn our dead
  As on the battle-field they lie.

With pale, cold faces upward turned,
  See the strong man, the tender youth,
Who nobly fought and nobly fell
  For God, for country, and for truth.

Their mission done, their work fulfilled,
  They're gone with God in peace to dwell;
And now, perchance, are watching o'er
  The country they have loved so well.

O country! to our sons so dear,
  That their life-blood they freely give,
Enshrine those heroes in thy heart,
  And let their names forever live.

Among the battles fought by the Army of the Potomac was that of Antietam, in which the Union forces lost so heavily, that it could hardly be determined whether we gained a victory or suffered a defeat. The following extract from a private letter gives the impression of the hour upon the mind of a young soldier[*] who left the

---

[*] John Groves Smith, jun., of Beverly, Mass.

student haunts of Andover to defend his country's life and honor: —

"Within a week, I have been an actor among scenes which God grant may not be enacted over again, at least many times in my life. I will tell you as well as I can what I have seen since last Sabbath morning. At that time, our brigade was in Middletown, Md., from whence troops in advance of us had driven the enemy. At this place, I ate the last substantial meal, a good breakfast, which I got by paying twenty-five cents. About noon, we took our line of march onward, and, about five o'clock, reached the scene of action. As we neared it, wounded men, supported by comrades and borne in ambulances, were met, being conveyed to hospitals, and places of safety. Our regiment first formed in line of battle in a cornfield, and directly advanced through a piece of woods, acting as deployers or skirmishers. Here the regiment broke badly; and it is wonderful that it was not either surrounded, or taken prisoners, or used up, as the enemy were in strong force all around us. Soon we came together in a lane as well as we could, and, advancing, turned into another lane running at right angles with this, and, jumping over a fence, took position on one side of it. We remained here but a moment; when order was given to fall back into the lane whence we had first come. We did so, and, advancing down about forty rods, crossed the fence into an open field on the right, and had hardly done so, when, from the other side, the enemy, under cover of our flag, poured upon us a volley of musketry which caused every man to drop *instanter:* had we not done so, the loss of life would have been terrible; as it was, we had some fifty wounded during this fire. Our general (Reno) was killed, and our colonel (Wild) was shot through the arm.

"As soon as it was deemed safe, we fell back into a piece of woods, under cover of the darkness, and came together again in the lane a little below where we had received the volley. We remained here some two hours perfectly quiet, the balls of the enemy meantime whistling over our heads incessantly: had their range been lower, you can imagine the result. About ten o'clock, the firing ceased; when we passed into an open field, and rested as well as we could. In the morning, I, at my leisure, went over the battle-field. The lane I have spoken of, and the piece of woods through which we skirmished, were thickly strewn with dead bodies, mostly of the enemy. As I looked upon them, I felt very solemn; then I thought of my God and my country, and felt strong and resolute, and prayed that I might be prepared for whatever an all-wise Providence might have in store for me. I needed to think and pray; for in a little time my strength, resolution, and resignation were to be tested. Come with me now to the battle-field of Wednesday, which was three miles from here, and eight from the action of Sunday. Early in the forenoon, our brigade marched forward gradually, and about noon came to the bridge at which the tremendous battle was going on. The enemy were across the bridge, and, aided by almost every natural advantage, were contesting our passage.

"Our regiment lay on the left slope of a hill, and for more

than an hour listened to the play of the artillery above and the infantry below us: and it was effective; for, at the expiration of that time, our troops, cheering loudly, commenced the passage of the bridge. The Thirty-fifth was the second regiment to cross. As soon as we were over, we charged up the hill, although encumbered with our ammunition, blankets, overcoats, and rations, right into the face of a rebel battery of five or six guns. Falling back, we lay motionless under shelter of the hill for two hours or more; and a more dangerous position when we first took it can scarcely be conceived. We had nothing in front of us, not even a skirmisher; and had the enemy, backed by their battery, advanced upon us, God only knows the consequence. But after a while, upon our extreme right, several regiments sent out skirmishers, and gradually advanced; and two regiments came right on over us into the position whence we had fallen back. Directly came the order, 'Forward, Thirty-fifth!' and, advancing to the left, we formed in line of battle on both sides of a lane. While doing so, a shell which exploded struck a poor fellow two files front of me, and killed him instantly. Directly we were at it, and the slaughter on both sides was terrible. Five of Company C were killed, and twenty wounded; among the latter your brother,—thank God! not seriously. The Thirty-fifth was awfully cut up: three companies had every commissioned officer badly wounded; one company numbered fifty-seven killed and wounded; and the whole regiment at the close of the fight mustered but about three hundred effective men out of over seven hundred."

An extract from another private letter * gives a graphic picture of scenes just after the battle: —

"The dead lay just as they fell; but they were terribly swollen, and all turned black in the face, with their eyes almost out of their heads: it was an awful sight. They all looked just alike in the face: they lay in long rows just as they had stood in line of battle. At one place, where they had formed behind a fence, they lay two and three deep. I saw several officers among them. William Warren was shot in the right arm, taken prisoner, and paroled by the rebels: he got back the same day, and joined the regiment. He went to a hospital near by, and I sat up with him all night. It was a hard night for me: we were in a very large barn, filled with wounded men, mostly rebels; and there were only two stewards to attend to about two hundred men: so I was up all night. First I would turn over one man, then I would prop up the arm or leg of another, then pour water on their wounds, or give them some to drink. We had to take one man out into the yard to die. I stood by and saw two or three men die. It was a very eventful night for me. The man who lay next to Warren was a very gentlemanly fellow: he belonged to the Fifth South-Carolina Regiment; he said he had been in the battles of Savage Station and Malvern Hill. It seemed queer to be feeding with a spoon the man, who, a little while before, had been trying to kill me. It is queer any way to talk to men, who, you know, would kill you if they had the means."

* Written by Lieut. Charles P. Abbott, son of Rev. Joseph Abbott, D.D., of Beverly, Mass.

The following letter from a well-known war-correspondent gives some interesting incidents of the battle of Antietam : —

SHARPSBURG, MD., Sept. 19, 1862.

To the Editor of the " Boston Journal," —

The village of Sharpsburg suffered severely from our shells during the battle. Burnside's, Richardson's, Franklin's, and Sumner's batteries were at times playing upon the rebels in the direction of the town. I remember especially the vigor with which Ayer's battery was worked, pouring an incessant fire into the cornfield west of Roulet's house, and upon the hills above it, where the Washington artillery of New Orleans was in position.

Many of the houses of Sharpsburg are of wood, lined with brick. In one house, a shell had burst in the second story, tearing out the side and a portion of the end, throwing the clapboards and brick into the street, making a hole through which you might drive a four-wheeled coach. A large and substantial brick house had several shots pass through it. A twelve-pound shot passed through a wooden house, tearing out a large oak post, and fell upon the back of a horse in the street, killing him instantly. A large barn was set on fire near the town, and consumed. Several houses and barns north of the town, in range of Sumner's batteries, were burned, but whether by our shells or by the rebels, I have not been able to ascertain.

The inhabitants fled when the shock of battle began. They were returning when our army reached the place. They were very kind to our soldiers. They have been stripped of nearly all their provisions, their pigs, and poultry: their gardens are destroyed, their apples and fruit taken, their cornfields trampled down, and potatoes stolen. Yet, with their own losses so heavy, they distributed freely of what they had to our suffering soldiers. They are large-hearted, kind, benevolent, and will be remembered with gratitude by many a soldier.

Although I saw thousands of wounded men, I heard but few complaints. I cannot tell why it is that wounded men make so little ado upon the battle-field. Possibly it may be their systems are benumbed, possibly because the excitement of the hour acts as an anæsthetic, producing partial insensibility to pain, but probably from a consideration that thousands are suffering with them, and that it is childish to make complaint over that which cannot be helped. Their heroism sustains them.

I noticed it after the battle of Pittsburg Landing, where I passed twenty-four hours on a steamboat with five hundred wounded. I noticed it yesterday in a hospital containing some of the wounded of the New-Hampshire Ninth, the Massachusetts Twenty-first. Lieut.-Col. Titus of the New-Hampshire Ninth, and several of his officers, were there; and, although severely wounded, they were very cheerful.

Passing by a large straw stack, where several hundred privates were lying, I found them equally cheerful. I heard but few groans.

One of the most affecting incidents occurred during the night. I was finding forage for my horse at a house near Keitiesville, which was filled with those slightly wounded, —

those who had received balls in their feet, hands, and arms. They had had supper, hard-bread and coffee, and were happy. They were singing, not rollicking songs, but "Our Flag is there."

Then there came thoughts of home, of loved ones, of past scenes and pleasant memories, and expressed in that old familiar song: —

> "Do they miss me at home? do they miss me
>   At morning, at noon, or at night?
> And lingers a gloomy shade round them
>   That only my presence can light?
> Are joys less invitingly welcome,
>   And pleasure less hale, than before,
> Because one is missed from the circle,
>   Because I am with them no more?"

There was a shade of sadness in the tones of those who sang, not of discouragement; but it was the welling-up of affection, the return of sweet recollections, which neither hardship, suffering, privation, or long absence, could efface.

Missed at home? — ah, how sadly! CARLETON.

It was on this sanguinary battle-field that the gallant young Capt. Richard Derby fell, while cheering his men, and nobly leading them on to the conflict.*

One aged father was called to mourn the loss of three sons at Antietam.

The following paragraph will show how the venerable patriot gave all to his country, and, like many another noble soul, did not regret the terrible sacrifice: —

* See Memoir published by Degen & Estes, Boston.

"An old gray-headed man, upwards of eighty years of age, came in from the East this morning by the train, on his way home to Michigan. He had a sad story to tell of the sorrows caused by this unholy Rebellion. The old gentleman, whose name is Crane, residing in Wayne County, Mich., had three sons. Two of them joined one of the Michigan regiments, and have done good service in several of the battles in Eastern Virginia. The third, not much more than a lad, was also anxious to join his brothers, but was for some time dissuaded from the step by his father and mother; the latter having been for years a confirmed invalid. At last, the urgent entreaties of the lad prevailed; and but a short time since he passed through Cleveland on his way to join the regiment to which his brothers belonged. The bloody struggle at Antietam soon followed after; and in that battle the three brothers fell, fighting bravely. Information was sent home to the bereaved parents; and the shock of the news was so great, that the mother, enfeebled by long sickness, died in a few days. As soon as she was laid in the grave, the old man set out for the battle-field, with the hope of finding the bodies of his three sons, and bringing them home to rest beside that of their mother. The search was long and thorough, but was unsuccessful. They had been probably buried on the field, with nothing to mark where they lay. Mr. Crane returns home bent down with years and with his great sorrow. He says that he has now no relatives left, and nothing to live for. Yet he does not regret the sacrifice made on the altar of his country, and only laments that he has not strength to shoulder his musket, and go himself to fight against this wicked Rebellion." *

The "Boston Journal" says, "One of our correspondents, who was with the division of Gen. Sturgis at the battle of Antietam, gives the following account of the part taken by that division in the contest. It will be seen that the New-Hampshire Ninth and Massachusetts Thirty-fifth, new regiments, won much credit by their bravery: —

"'Our division, under Gen. Sturgis, were on the extreme left, and were not placed in line until about five, P.M., when a double-quick movement took place, and the whole division started like Bengal tigers let loose for prey. They run through a galling fire of shot and shell until they were within reach of the enemy's musketry, when a heavy fire opened on us, which Gen. Naglee, commanding our brigade, saw at once would decimate the brigade; and so the order came to charge bayonets. Promptly the glistening steel was placed in position, and here one of the most brilliant bayonet charges took place that has been seen during the war. The brigade had to charge up hill, over stone walls and other obstructions, and met the enemy at a great disadvantage. The Massachusetts Thirty-fifth Regiment was put in order of battle, and did great execution at the first onset. In Gen. Naglee's brigade and Sturgis's division was also the Ninth Regiment New-Hampshire volunteers, Col. Fellows, one of the most experienced colonels in the army. It was a handsome sight to see him put his regiment into action. When the clear, sonorous order came from Col. Fel-

* Cleveland Herald.

lows, " Charge, bayonets!" every eye gleamed in the "Bloody Ninth," as the brigade now call the regiment. Every man threw away his knapsack, blanket, and haversack, and leaped over a stone wall six feet high, with a yell that fairly sent terror through the rebel ranks opposite. With eyes gleaming with joy and determination, and every bayonet fixed, they charged up the hill and through the cornfield at double-quick, with a perfect yell of triumph. Col. Fellows and Lieut.-Col. Titus astonished the old veterans in the service by the manner in which they brought the Ninth New-Hampshire volunteers into the action. It was a grand and magnificent sight, and one seldom seen in battle. The rebels fled before them, and every rebel regiment broke and run. Gen. Reno fell beside the Ninth New-Hampshire volunteers and Thirty-fifth Massachusetts about dark, just in the moment of victory.'"

One more incident illustrating the bravery of our men may be given, and then other battles in which the Potomac Army was engaged may be mentioned.

AN INCIDENT OF THE BATTLE OF ANTIETAM. — Mr. Thomas Drew, of this city, has received from eye-witnesses an account of the death of his brother, Herbert M. Drew, of the Haverhill Company, Thirty-fifth Massachusetts Regiment. The letter giving the account says, —

"You remember, in reading the accounts of the battle of Antietam, that there was a certain hill that Gen. McClellan wished Burnside to hold at all hazards, and that Burnside sent word that he could not hold it half an hour. Upon the holding of that hill depended the fate of the whole of Burnside's corps.

"The Thirty-fifth Massachusetts Regiment was stationed on the top to defend it; but the fire was so severe, that they fell back and retreated down the hill, with the exception of twenty-five determined men, who remained and held the hill, without a single commissioned officer to lead them. Gen. Burnside said those noble twenty-five men saved him the day.

"Herbert was conspicious among these, fighting with the most determined bravery; and, although the rebels charged up the hill to within two rods of the devoted band, they were repulsed. It was at this charge that Herbert was killed, receiving two full charges of buck and ball near the heart. He died almost instantly, without a word or a struggle. Out of this little band of heroes, fifteen were killed outright; and they were buried on the very spot they had bought so dearly for a resting-place."*

While the memory of such bravery and patriotism exists, each loyal heart must rejoice, and have hope for our country's future. Our flag, the emblem of liberty to all, is destined to wave in triumph to the end of time.

> "Washed in the blood of the brave and the blooming,
> Snatched from the altars of insolent foes,
> Burning with star-fires, but never consuming,
> Flash its broad ribbons of lily and rose.

---

* Boston Journal.

Vainly the prophets of Baal would rend it,
   Vainly his worshippers pray for its fall :
Thousands have died for it, millions defend it,
   Emblem of justice and mercy to all, —

Justice that reddens the sky with her terrors,
   Mercy that comes with her white-handed train, —
Soothing all passions, redeeming all errors,
   Sheathing the sabre, and breaking the chain.

Borne on the deluge of old usurpations,
   Drifted our ark o'er the desolate seas :
This was the rainbow of hope to the nations,
   Torn from the storm-cloud, and flung to the breeze !

God bless the flag and its loyal defenders
   While its broad folds o'er the battle-field wave,
Till the dim star-wreath rekindle its splendors,
   Washed from its stains in the blood of the brave ! "*

From a letter to the " Baltimore American " by its editor, C. C. Fulton, Esq., some of the battle-scenes in connection with the great battle before Richmond in 1862, when McClellan commanded and was defeated, are here given : —

"About seven o'clock on Friday evening, numbers of the wounded commenced to arrive from the front of the lines, with a few of the most intelligent of whom I had an opportunity of conversing. Those engaged in the repulse of Stonewall Jackson represent his rout to be most quick and disastrous. He came down on them, expecting a surprise, but found them all momentarily expecting his approach,

---

* Dr. O. W. Holmes.

having been informed by Gen. McClellan, two days previous, that he was coming upon them. Instead of a surprise, the enemy received the first shot, and, after two hours' fight, retreated in confusion.

"The wounded from the fight which immediately ensued represented it to have been a most terrific encounter; the enemy coming out from Richmond upon them in such dense masses, that the shell and grape poured into them as they advanced made great gaps in their lines, which were immediately filled up, and they moved forward most determinedly. Their artillery was so poorly served, that the damage to our ranks was light in proportion. They still moved on, and exchanged showers of Minie balls, which were destructive on both sides; but, when Gen. Porter ordered a bayonet charge, they retreated in double-quick, though Gen. Porter pursued them but a short distance.

"The enemy again rallied, and approached our lines a second time, when the same terrible slaughter ensued: this time, their artillery, being better served, was more effective in the ranks of our men. On coming to close quarters, they were again repulsed, and driven back a still greater distance; this twice fought over battle-ground being literally strewn with the dead and dying. Gen. Porter then a second time fell back to his position, and waited nearly an hour for the enemy to renew the assault. They, however, finally came on in increased numbers, having been largely re-enforced, and were again received with shell and grape, causing great chasms in their ranks; and one poor fellow who had lost his arm assured me that he saw the loose arms and portions of the bodies of the enemy making gyrations through the air. A third time the enemy bore down most bravely and determinedly on our lines, and this conflict was the most severely contested of the whole; but, when the bayonet was brought to bear, he fell back, and was pressed toward Richmond fully a mile beyond our original lines.

"Again, for the fourth time, Gen. Porter fell back to his first position; when an order was received from Gen. McClellan to continue his retrograde movement slowly and in order. So soon as it became apparent to the enemy that it was the purpose of Gen. Porter to retire, the enemy again pushed forward most boldly and bravely; when their advance was checked by the entire reserve force, consisting of the New-York Fifth, Lieut.-Col. Duryea, the New-York Tenth, Col. Bendix, and two other regiments, under command of Col. Warren, acting brigadier-general, and the entire force of regulars under Major-Gen. Sykes. This fresh force held the enemy in check, while the force which had previously borne the brunt of the battle moved steadily back and in good order, carrying with them their wounded and dead.

"The enemy made a fierce attack on the reserve; but cannon were posted at various points of the route by which they were retiring toward the Chickahominy, which occasionally poured in shot and shell upon them, and checked their movements, and enabled the troops to move back in the most admirable order. At one time in this retrograde movement, the reserve force of Gen. Sykes charged on the enemy with the bayonet, and drove him back nearly a mile. In this charge, the gallant New-York Fifth, and Col. Bendix's New-

York Tenth, drew forth the plaudits of the army by their steadiness and bravery, in which they, however, lost about a hundred of their numbers, whose bodies it was necessary to leave on the field. Cheers went up along our whole lines at this gallant repulse, which was at three o'clock in the afternoon; and the enemy did not again renew the attack during the balance of the evening, but turned his columns down toward Whitehouse, which seemed to be the haven of all his hopes."

The Nineteenth Massachusetts Regiment, under Col. Hinks, won fadeless laurels in that battle.

"In order that the reader may be fully informed of the gallant conduct of the officers and men of this command, it is necessary to go back to the opening fight of Wednesday, the 25th of April. The regiment was attached to Sedgwick's division, and constituted a part of the reserve at the battle of Fair Oaks, where they went into action at the close of the last day's fighting, and came out with the loss of only one man. On Wednesday morning, Col. Hinks received orders to advance his regiment, from the intrenchments where they had lain for two weeks without shelter of any kind, to the front of Fair-oaks Station, to extend Hooker's lines to the right.

"Col. Hinks was compelled to advance his regiment through a swamp which was filled with dense underwood. He commenced moving his command at eight o'clock by throwing out Company K, the Boston Fire Zouaves, as skirmishers. Col. Hinks speaks in praiseworthy terms of the conduct of this company. The company pressed on about two-thirds of the way through the swamp; when Col. Hinks extended his skirmishers to the right of the regiment, and advanced his whole command in line, in face of two regiments of rebel infantry, who opened a fire on our troops. Our skirmishers engaged those of a rebel brigade on their extreme right, and bore down steadily upon them, forcing them to retreat.

"In this manner the Nineteenth advanced through the woods to the extreme edge of the swamp; and, entering a clear field, they opened fire on one rebel column advancing, and another which opposed them in line. After an engagement which lasted fifteen minutes, during which the Nineteenth lost forty-five officers and men killed and wounded, the rebel columns broke and fled. Our troops no sooner observed the 'skedaddle' movement of the rebels than they burst out with hearty cheers. The Fire Zouaves had three or four men wounded, and three cut off and taken prisoners, in the skirmish.

"Immediately after the dispersion of the enemy in front, the rebel column on the right broke, turned about, and fled before the steady fire of the Massachusetts troops, who were never in better spirits, or more desirous of engaging the enemy. Col. Hinks immediately obliqued his ranks, and prepared to charge upon the retiring foe; when orders came for him to retire. He did not stop to question, but marched his regiment back to the intrenchments, which he reached at eleven o'clock. During this engagement, the First Massachusetts Regiment was the second regiment on the right of the Nineteenth; and the line was composed mainly of Massachusetts troops.

"On the afternoon of Wednesday, the line was again ordered to advance, and regain the ground which they had been ordered to abandon after taking it in the morning. The Nineteenth advanced again in the same spirited manner as before, but found the woods filled with rebels, who had in the mean time got a battery in position to rake our troops. The position was finally retaken; but, in view of the great sacrifice of life which would follow an attempt of the rebels to regain it, the Nineteenth, in obedience to orders, fell back to their bivouac. Col. Hinks was complimented by Gens. Sedgwick and Dana for the gallant conduct of himself, his officers, and men, their steadiness under fire, and the success of the undertaking.

"The regiment remained in quarters till Friday, when they commenced throwing out traverses to prevent the enemy from shelling them out of the works; evidences warranting the belief that he was planting a battery on their flank. On Saturday afternoon, orders were unexpectedly received to load the ambulance and wagon trains; and all the sick and wounded, as well as the supplies, were promptly loaded, and the trains started for White-oak Swamp Bridge about six o'clock in the evening. Most of the ordnance was also removed; some light guns being retained to defend the position against the enemy.

"Saturday night was one of the most distressing ever passed by the officers and men of the Nineteenth. A deathly and ominous stillness reigned in front of the Confederate lines. Gen. Dana and Col. Hinks, not content to trust the tried sentries on duty, and apprehensive of impending danger, went the rounds of the earthworks all night.

"At three o'clock Sunday morning, Col. Hinks received orders from Gen. McClellan, through Gen. Sumner, to retreat; and in five minutes the regiment was on the march, leaving nothing of value behind. All the spare muskets were broken to prevent them from falling into the hands of the enemy; and all the property that had not been previously removed was destroyed. The regiment marched out of the works, and joined Gen. Sedgwick's division, which was also joined by Richardson's division; the two corps constituting the rearguard of the centre of McClellan's army. The Nineteenth retired to Orchard Station, on the Richmond and York-River Railroad, where they came into line of battle to resist the rebels who were in pursuit. Near Orchard Station were collected all the spare gun-carriages and arms, ten days' rations for forty thousand troops, worth at least one million of dollars, which were destroyed by pouring upon them several hundred barrels of commissary whiskey, and setting it on fire as the army retreated.

"At about nine o'clock Sunday morning, the rebels appeared with strong force of infantry and artillery, who were first engaged by French's brigade on the right of the new line of battle. The enemy came down the road leading to Sumner's Grape-vine Bridge, and received the fire of our artillery along the entire length of the line. French's division at the same time engaged the enemy, and repulsed them with fearful slaughter. The Nineteenth were in the front line of battle, exposed to the rebel artillery; but, throwing themselves on the ground, the regiment escaped with few slight casualties. No sooner were the rebels repulsed than orders were given by Gen. Sumner for the troops to resume their retreat, and each regiment to make the best of its way to Savage's Station.

"The Nineteenth marched all day Sunday, most of the time at double-quick. The heat was oppressive; and fifty men fell out of the ranks, and into the hands of the rebels, who, pressing close upon the retreating army, appeared in their rear about four o'clock, opening fire with two thirty-two pounders. Our artillery replied with terrific effect; and the heaviest cannonading ever heard on the Peninsula ensued. The rebel artillery was silenced; but the enemy shortly after appeared with two guns on the Williamsburg Turnpike, from which they again opened fire on our troops. Simultaneously with the appearance of the artillery, an immense force of infantry opened fire along the entire line of the wood in front of the Federal position. Here occurred the most desperate fight of the retreat. Brooks's Vermont brigade engaged the rebels in a succession of splendid charges, capturing the guns on the turnpike, and driving the rebels back at the point of the bayonet.

"Immediately after this, our army resumed their retreat, leaving their dead and wounded on the field. All who could walk crawled along with the retreating army; many fell into the hands of the rebels, and many more struggled into the White-oak Swamp, where they doubtless perished.

The Federal army crossed the swamp, blowing up the bridge, and reached the south side on Monday morning. From this point, they marched two and a half miles to Charles City Cross Roads, where they halted for wagon and ambulance trains to pass on.

"At five o'clock Monday afternoon, heavy musketry firing was heard on the direct route of the Federal army to Turkey Bend, giving evidence that the enemy had intercepted their line of retreat. The troops, weary from continued fighting and from long and forced marches, were in no condition to meet the foe as they desired. They were not, however, dismayed, but determined to stand boldly up to the work of driving back the rebels, who commenced an attack on the whole line. Brigade after brigade, and division after division, of McClellan's army went in, until almost the entire force was engaged. The fighting was mostly against rebel infantry. Upon the return of Dana's brigade from supporting Franklin's division, the Nineteenth was intercepted by a rebel battery, which dashed through the column from a cross-road; and, before it reached the body of the brigade, the other regiments were more or less engaged.

"Col. Hinks advanced his command at double-quick across an open field, and into a dense wood, up a steep hill, some hundred and fifty yards, against a murderous fire from the rebel regiments, one a North-Carolina regiment. Reserving their fire till they came face to face with the enemy upon the crest of the hill (not ten yards distant), his troops delivered a volley into the breasts of the rebels, who fell back disordered, and fled. At the moment they delivered their fire, the Nineteenth received a volley from our own lines, from the rear, through the two left companies. At the same time, the regiment was attacked by the other rebel corps, which, from the rear of his right flank, was cutting them down by a cross-fire. Col. Hinks ordered his men to fall back to the margin of the wood, changed front, and advanced against the enemy. After advancing fifty yards, he was met by a heavy fire, which he returned with effect. It was here that the colonel received his wound; and here Major Howe fell mortally wounded. Capt. Wass was disabled by a wound; and, Lieut.-Col. Devereux being sick in the hospital, the command of the regiment devolved upon Capt. Edmund Rice. Col. Hinks is unable to give a correct estimate of the casualties of his regiment, but thinks that he lost, in killed, wounded, and missing, three hundred and six men.

"He had but six hundred men when he left Fair Oaks; and the regiment now numbered from two hundred and fifty to three hundred effectives. He fought his regiment till he had fewer officers than companies, made two bayonet charges, and led on his troops till he was wounded, and borne from the field. He was saved from capture by the heroic conduct of Sergeant McGinnis, Corporal Young, and several privates of Company A, who carried him on a litter seven miles, through the woods, to a place of safety. His deeds and that of his gallant regiment carry their own praise with them."

That our men fought bravely, we of the North do not

doubt; that they deserve praise as soldiers, in every particular, Gen. Cluseret, a French officer in the United-States service, thought; for he wrote to the Paris "Pays" as follows : —

"After two months of campaign and sufferings such as I never endured even in the Crimean War, where we never were in want of food, nor exhausted by long marches, I can speak to you knowingly of the American soldier. During all that time, we have been marching night and day, oftentimes without bread, with half of our men shoeless, exposed to a chilly rain, without shelter, tent, or village. We have thus walked between one hundred and fifty and two hundred miles. But that which, in my estimation, makes the American soldier the first in the world, the equal of the French soldier, is, that I never heard him utter a complaint or grumble. I never was compelled to inflict a punishment upon him. When I ordered a straggler to fall in, he used to show me his naked feet, and hurry on as much as he could. I have but a word to express my opinion of the American soldier: he is an admirable soldier. He adds to the qualities of the French a patience and a resignation which I did not think it possible for a soldier to acquire."

So long was the Army of the Potomac at one time in a state of quiescence, that the phrase, "all quiet along the Potomac," became stereotyped, as it were. Yet though no decisive battles, or skirmishes worthy the name, occurred, the faithful pickets were often shot at their posts. Some poet has thus immortalized —

THE PICKET-GUARD.

"All quiet along the Potomac," they say,
   Except now and then a stray picket
Is shot, as he walks on his beat to and fro,
   By a rifleman hid in the thicket.
'Tis nothing: a private or two now and then
   Will not count in the news of the battle;
Not an officer lost,— only one of the men
   Moaning out all alone the death-rattle.

All quiet along the Potomac to-night
   Where the soldiers lie peacefully dreaming;
Their tents in the rays of the clear autumn moon,
   Or the light of the watch-fire, gleaming.
A tremulous sigh, as the gentle night-wind
   Through the forest-leaves softly is creeping;
While stars up above, with their glittering eyes,
   Keep guard; for the army is sleeping.

There's only the sound of the lone sentry's tread
   As he tramps from the rock to the fountain,
And thinks of the two, in the low trundle-bed,
   Far away in the cot on the mountain.
His musket falls slack; his face, dark and grim,
   Grows gentle with memories tender;
And he mutters a prayer for the children asleep,
   For their mother,— may Heaven defend her!

The moon seems to shine just as brightly as then,
   That night, when the love yet unspoken
Leaped up to his lips, when love-murmured vows
   Were pledged to be ever unbroken.

Then, drawing his sleeves roughly over his eyes,
  He dashes off tears that are welling,
And gathers his gun closer up to its place,
  As if to keep down the heart-swelling.

He passes the fountain, the blasted pine-tree;
  The footstep is lagging and weary:
Yet onward he goes, through the broad belt of light,
  Toward the shade of the forest so dreary.
Hark! was it the night-wind that rustled the leaves?
  Was it moonlight so wondrously flashing?
It looked like a rifle! "Ha! Mary, good-by!"
  And the life-blood is ebbing and plashing.

All quiet along the Potomac to-night;
  No sound save the rush of the river;
While soft falls the dew on the face of the dead:
  The picket's off duty forever.

During the advance of the Army of the Potomac south of the Rapidan, on those very cold nights, the troops and guards suffered terribly. Several had limbs frost-bitten, and one man in the second corps froze to death while on picket-duty. Capt. G. S. Burnham thus wrote of the incident, entitling his poem —

DEAD, — EN BIVOUAC.

By the margin of the river,
  'Midst the plunging snow and sleet,
On the picket-post they shiver,
  As they pace their lonely beat.

Of the loved one calmly sleeping,
  Safe from cold, alarm, or fight,
They are thinking, whilst they're keeping
  "Watch-in-watch" this bitter night.

Near the Rapid Ann we rested,
  After weeks and months of toil,
(Faith and valor meanwhile tested,)
  On Virginia's "sacred soil."
By the lonely weird camp-fire,
  Hard upon the foeman's track,
Mid the gloom and dampness dire,
  We lay down *en bivouac*.

All is well!" the sentry uttered
  Far away upon the right;
' All is well!" the centre muttered;
  Then the left. 'Twas dead of night.
Still the storm was fiercely raging;
  Bitter blasts came down the vale
And the elements were waging
  Ruthless war amid that gale.

But the sentinels kept pacing, —
  Pacing up and down their track;
While the Storm-King still kept tracing
  Snowy ridges front and back.
Ah! that air was deathly frigid,
  And the sleet came tempest-tost;
But the orders out were rigid, —
  "Not a man must quit his post."

For in front (we'd had the warning),
   Massed in force, the rebels lay;
Yet we looked for, *prayed for*, morning,
   Though 't should prove our final day!
Hours passed. *One* watcher, weary,
   Faltered, halted, breathed a moan;
Then, amidst the darkness dreary,
   Failed, and sank to earth, alone.

When the gray light broke at dawning,
   Calm, beneath a friendly tree,
Blanched and still lay Harry Corning!
   Sleeping on his post was he?
Surely *no!* A soldier braver
   Never met or charged the foe:
Such true hearts are few; and never
   Could *he* fail in duty so!

"*Forward!*" came the word. We lifted
   Quickly up his stiffened form:
Round it wreaths of snow had drifted;
   But his heart no more was warm.
He had frozen dead on picket:
   Dreadful fate was this, alack!
And we laid him 'neath the thicket
   Where he died *en bivouac*.

Hear "Carleton's" testimony to the bravery of our men in that great battle before Richmond: —

"MASSACHUSETTS TROOPS. — Gentlemen testify to the bravery and valor of the Massachusetts troops. The Nineteenth, Col. Hinks, in the fight on Monday, behaved with unparalleled bravery. Col. Hinks and Lieut.-Col. Devereux were wounded, and Major Howe killed; also a large number of captains and lieutenants were either killed or wounded. Notwithstanding this terrible decimation, it never wavered, never flinched, but stood to the last, and joined in that last onset which sent the rebels back to Richmond, defeated, routed. The same may be said of the Sixteenth, Col. Wyman; and of the Ninth, Col. Cass. The Ninth. was terribly cut up on Friday; but on Monday it was as ready as ever to engage in the conflict. I have no high-sounding panegyric for their bravery, their cool, steady conduct, their unswerving obedience to orders. Simple words are best. They covered themselves with glory; they sustained their mother's honor. The living and the lost alike did their duty.

"And so the sons of Maine, New Hampshire, Vermont, and Rhode Island. Connecticut, I believe, had not the honor of being there. It was Vermont, under Gen. Smith, which poured upon the enemy's flank with such terrible effect on Sunday.

"Waterloo nor Borodino saw no braver fighting. The men of this generation are not degenerated in physical vigor, heroism, or courage. Civilization, long years of prosperity, of commercial transactions, have not dwarfed us. After a half-century of peace, we are still great-hearted in war, not for love of glory, not for conquest, — we are not intermeddlers in the affairs of other nations, like the foreign monarchies, — but to preserve the garnered wealth of ages; to save liberty; to hand down to all who shall follow us a priceless boon, bought with blood, like the gift of the Son of God. It is this which makes men great in this strife; which makes this a holy war; and which, through all coming time, will keep forever green the graves of the fallen, and forever blessed their memory."

The following is an extract from "Carleton's" description of one of the days of the battle, when victory, for the moment, hovered over our beloved banner:—

"Early in the afternoon, the enemy in strong force appeared, opening with artillery, and advancing division after division of infantry in solid masses. We resisted bravely, but were compelled to fall back to a new position. The enemy followed, employing his old tactics of hurling masses of men, now upon the right, now upon the left, and now suddenly in the centre. We held our ground unaided till six o'clock. Our ranks were terribly thinned, and we were compelled to bring up McCall once more. Our division had been in nearly all the fights; it was worn out: but, with hearts as true as steel, we responded to the order. Simultaneously upon our advance came fresh troops from Richmond; and loud and terrific as at any time during the six-days' fighting roared the contest. But the masses of the enemy rolled along the road. Their leaders had no care for saving life. This was war,—a strife for mastery. It was their determination to win, no matter what it cost. They rushed on impetuously, charged upon our batteries, captured Bendall's, and took a large number of prisoners.

Here the brave and efficient commander of the corps, Gen. McCall, went down at the head of his troops, supposed to be badly wounded. A score of officers fell; the lines gave way: it was a critical moment. Now or never was brave work to be done; now or never was the army to be saved. All hearts felt it; all hands were ready. Men lived ages in those moments. Oh! you who live far away among peaceful valleys, on sunny hillsides, with smiling children at your feet, reading this tame account, cannot know the thrill which brave men feel when the heart wells up from its inmost depths to dare all, to do all that God has given, to save defeat. Untutored men look with clearest visions in such moments down the future ages. They see, they feel, that uncounted millions are beckoning them to do their duty now. They are great moments!

"Sedgwick came; Hooker and Kearney came, — Hooker with the Second New-Hampshire, and First and Eleventh Massachusetts; Kearney with the life-blood of New Jersey: brave men, all of them. They rallied for a desperate charge; one which has determination in it; when every man feels that he stands at the gateway of centuries, as Leonidas stood at Thermopylæ. Twenty-four cannon additional were brought up. The united divisions, firm and unyielding as the granite of their native mountains, moved to the charge, 'Onward, right onward!' unheeding death or life. They came upon the enemy like a thunderbolt; bore down the living masses in front as if they were automatons; sent them flying over the field; and captured twelve pieces of artillery, one brigade, including three regiments; also Col. Pendleton of the Louisiana battalion, and Ex-Congressman Lamar of the First Georgia Regiment.

"It was the finale. The enemy was defeated at last. He had come on with high hopes: he retired discomfited. It was a brilliant victory: it inspired our troops. Here let me speak of the influence of music. While the fight was going on, Gen. Morell ordered the bands to play. For a month they have been silent, under orders. They gave 'Yankee Doodle,' the 'Star-spangled Banner,' and 'Hail Columbia.' It was like bread to a hungry man. The troops felt the soul-stirring strains, and forgot that they were tired, hungry, exhausted, and ready to faint."

But these chapters cannot contain a complete record of all the battles fought, nor even allusions to them all. It is said that "the number of battles fought during the late war is two hundred and fifty-two. Of these the soil of Virginia drank the blood of eighty-nine; Tennessee witnessed thirty-seven; Missouri, twenty-five; Georgia, twelve; South Carolina, ten; North Carolina, eleven; Alabama, seven; Florida, five; Kentucky, fourteen; the Indian Territory and New Mexico, one each. Once the wave of war rolled into a Northern State, and broke in the great billow of Gettysburg. Of the battles enumerated, sixteen were naval achievements."

Of one of these, fought in 1864, the following is an incident which was narrated by a correspondent of the "New-York Tribune," and versified by George H. Boker: —

IN THE WILDERNESS,

May 7, 1864.

Mangled, uncared for, suffering, through the night,
   With heavenly patience the poor boy had lain:
Under the dreary shadows, left and right,
    Groaned on the wounded, stiffened out the slain.
       What faith sustained his lone
       Brave heart to make no moan,
To send no cry from that blood-sprinkled sod,
Is a close mystery with him and God.

But when the light came, and the morning dew
   Glittered around him like a golden lake,
And every dripping flower with deepened hue
    Looked through its tears for very pity's sake,
       He moved his aching head
       Upon its rugged bed,
And smiled, as a blue violet, virgin meek,
Laid her pure kiss upon his withered cheek.

At once there circled in his waking heart
   A thousand memories of distant home, —
Of how those same blue violets would start
    Along his native fields; and some would roam
       Down his dear humming brooks,
       To hide in secret nooks,
And, shyly met, in nodding circles swing,
Like gossips murmuring at belated Spring.

And then he thought of the beloved hands
  That with his own had plucked the modest flower;
The blue-eyed maiden, crowned with golden bands,
  Who ruled as sovereign of that sunny hour, —
    She at whose soft command
    He joined the mustering band;
She for whose sake he lay so firm and still,
Despite his pangs, nor questioned then her will.

So, lost in thought, scarce conscious of the deed,
  Culling the violets, here and there he crept
Slowly, ah! slowly; for his wound would bleed:
And the sweet flowers themselves half smiled, half wept,
    To be thus gathered in
    By hands so pale and thin,
By fingers trembling as they neatly laid
Stem upon stem, and bound them in a braid.

The strangest posy ever fashioned yet
  Was clasped against the bosom of the lad,
As we, the seekers for the wounded, set
  His form upon our shoulders, bowed and sad;
    Though he but seemed to think
    How violets nod and wink:
And as we cheered him, for the path was wild,
He only looked upon his flowers, and smiled.

One of the brilliant exploits of the war was the cavalry reconnoissance of Fredericksburg by Capt. Dahlgren and fifty-seven men of the First Indiana and a portion of the Third Ohio Regiments. The following is an extract from "Carleton's" letter describing the exploit: —

"The enemy was partly in saddle. There was a hurrying to and fro, mounting of steeds, confusion, and fright among the people. The rebel cavalry were in every street. Capt. Dahlgren resolved to fall upon them like a thunderbolt. Increasing his trot to a gallop, the fifty-seven dauntless men dashed into town, cheering, with sabres glittering in the sun, riding recklessly upon the enemy, who waited but a moment in the main street, then ignominiously fled. Having cleared the main thoroughfare, Capt. Dahlgren swept through a cross-street upon another squadron with the same success. There was a trampling of hoofs, a clattering of scabbards, and the sharp ringing cut of the sabres, the pistol flash, the going-down of horsemen and rider, the gory gashes of the sabre-stroke, a cheering and hurrahing, and screaming of frightened women and children, a short, sharp, decisive contest, and the town was in the possession of the gallant men. Once the rebels attempted to recover what they had lost: but a second impetuous charge drove them back again, and Capt. Dahlgren gathered the fruits of the victory, — thirty-one prisoners, horses, accoutrements, sabres; held possession of the town for three hours; and retired, losing but one of his glorious band killed and two wounded, leaving a dozen of the enemy killed and wounded. I would like to give the names of these heroes if I had them. The one brave fellow who lost his life had fought through all the conflict; but, seeing a large rebel flag waving from a building, he secured it, wrapped it around his body, and was returning to his command, when a fatal shot was fired from a window, probably by a citizen. He was brought to the northern shore, and there buried by his fellow-soldiers beneath the forest pines. Capt. Carr, of Company B, encountered a rebel officer, and ran his sabre through the body of his enemy. Orderly Fitter had a hand-to-hand struggle with a rebel soldier, and, by a dexterous blow, struck him from his horse, inflicting a severe wound upon the head. He seized the fellow's horse, a splendid animal, his carabine and sabre. His own sabre still bears the blood-stains, — not a pleasant sight, but yet in keeping with war.

"It thrills one to look at it, to hear the story, to picture the encounter, — the wild dash, the sweep like a whirlwind, the cheers, the rout of the enemy, their confusion, the victory! — victory not for personal glory nor for ambition, but for a beloved country; for that which is dearer than life, — the thanks of the living, the gratitude of unnumbered millions yet to be! Brave sons of the West, this is your glory; this your reward! No exploit of the war equals it. It will go down to history as one of the bravest achievements on record."

In the battle of Cedar Creek, the Thirty-fourth Massachusetts behaved gallantly. It was the only regiment which did not break in the panic with which the day opened. Gen. Sheridan honored the regiment by calling for three cheers in their behalf.

The following lines * commemorate their valor. Allusions are made to their general, Wells, who fell at the head of his regiment, which he had himself organized. When he was at the first battle of Bull Run, he was lieutenant-

* By Mary Webb, in the Salem Gazette.

colonel of the First Massachusetts. He approached the batteries, and took up the musket of a disabled soldier. At the second battle, his regiment covered the retreat.

THE MASSACHUSETTS THIRTY-FOURTH.

They're standing firm in swerveless lines
    That meet the battle shock,
As ocean's furious charge is met
    By the resisting rock.

Two hundred men!—the ranks around
    Breaking in wild dismay,—
Two hundred men, alone, to quell
    Lee's ruffian chivalry!

Two hundred men against the odds
    Of that disastrous fray,
Before our untamed eagle looks
    Into the eye of day!

Around the regimental flag,
    Where thickest volleys pour,
The loyal-hearted closer press,
    As if *he* rode before,

The echo of whose rallying cheer,
    Scarce yet a vanished tone,
Haunts the proud-battle steeps from whence
    " His soul is marching on."

> White as the plume crest of Navarre
>   Flashes his beckoning fame;
> While, side by side, they're keeping step
>   To the music of his name.
>
> O Mother State! behold with pride
>   The line that will not break;
> Braid chaplets not unwet with tears,
>   For their late leader's sake, —
>
> He who, in earlier, *darker* days,
>   At once was sword and shield;
> Who even now, in shadowy form,
>   Seems master of the field.
>
> So was our challenged honor held,
>   'Till through the valley rang
> The bugle-blast which sounded out
>   The charge of Sheridan!

There were raids of pluck, dash, and romantic incidents, in connection with the Army of the Potomac, which deserve to live in song and story along with the charge of Balaklava, when

> "Into the mouth of hell
> Rode the six hundred."

Gen. Stoneman's, Col. Kilpatrick's, and other raids, were made with great success. The rebels in their advance often met with patriotic resistance, even from loyal men " single-handed and alone."

"Near Hancock, an old farmer had some fine horses. The rebels undertook to seize them. He loved the animals he had raised as he did his life. He was determined not to be robbed. He informed the rebels that he would shoot the man who should attempt to take them. Laughing at his bold words, the attempt was made. The heroic old man was true to his word. He killed two and wounded three others before they killed him."

But the limits of this chapter forbid allusion to other raids or battles than those of Fredericksburg and Gettysburg, and brief sketches of the closing scenes of war in our land, when Richmond at last fell into the hands of its lawful owners, and *negro* soldiers bore the banner of our country in triumph along its streets.

It was determined that the army should cross the river, and occupy Fredericksburg. Pontoon-bridges were accordingly commenced. But this did not please the rebels; and their sharpshooters picked off the engineers so fast, that finally it was deemed necessary to shell the town.

"At ten o'clock, Gen. Burnside gives the order, 'Concentrate the fire of all your guns on the city, and batter it down!' The artillery of the right, eight batteries, was commanded by Col. Hays; Col. Tompkins, right centre, eleven batteries; Col. Tyler, left centre, seven batteries; Capt. de Russy, left, nine batteries. In a few moments, these thirty-five batteries, forming a total of one hundred and seventy-nine guns, ranging from ten-pounder Parrotts to four and a half inch siege-guns, posted along the convex side of the arc of the circle formed by the bend of the river and land opposite Fredericksburg, opened on the doomed city. For a time, the roar is indescribably awful. The city from its walls of brick hurls back a thousand echoes, which beat up against the Falmouth Bluff, roll back again beyond the town, and then, from the distant hills, once more swell over to us, as though the heavens were rent asunder. At Gen. Sumner's headquarters, half a mile distant, it becomes difficult to converse in a low tone; while, at the batteries, orders must be signalled. By and by the firing ceases, and one is almost awe-stricken with the profound silence. The mist still clings to the river, the sun struggles up red and fiery, and the air is suffocating with the odor of gunpowder. Presently the bank of fog begins to lift a little; the glistening roofs gleam faintly through the veil: then the sunbeams scatter the clouds that intervene; and Fredericksburg, utterly desolate, stands out before. A huge column of dense black smoke towers like a monument above the livid flames that leap and hiss and crackle, licking up the snow upon the roofs with lambent tongues, and stretching like a giant. The guns renew their roar; and we see the solid shot plunge through the masonry as though it were pasteboard. Other buildings are fired; and before sundown a score of houses are in ashes, while not one seems to have escaped the pitiless storm of iron. A less number have been fired than was anticipated; but the damage done by solid shot is terrible, and will require years to repair.

"During the thick of the bombardment, a fresh attempt had been made to complete the bridge. It failed; and evidently nothing could be done till a party could be thrown over to clean out the rebels and cover the bridge head. For this mission, Gen. Burnside called for volunteers; and Col. Hall, of Fort-Sumter fame, immediately responded, that he had a brigade that would do the business. Accordingly, the Seventh Michigan and Nineteenth and Twentieth Massachusetts, two small regiments, numbering in all about four hundred men, were selected for the purpose.

"The plan was, that they should take the pontoon-boats of the first bridge, of which there were ten lying on the bank of the river, waiting to be added to the half-finished bridge, cross over in them, and, landing, drive out the rebels.

"Nothing could be more admirable or more gallant than the execution of this daring feat. Rushing down the steep banks of the river, the party found temporary shelter behind the pontoon-boats lying scattered on the bank, and behind piles of planking destined for the covering of the bridge, behind rocks, &c. In this situation, they acted some fifteen or twenty minutes as sharpshooters; they and the rebels observing each other. In the mean time, new and vigorous artillery firing was commenced on our part; and, just as soon as this was fairly developed, the Seventh Michigan arose from their crouching-places, rushed for the pontoon-boats, and, pushing them into the water, rapidly filled them with twenty-five or thirty each.

"The first boat pushes off. Now, if ever, is the rebels' opportunity. Crack, crack, crack, from fifty lurking places, go rebel rifles at the gallant fellows, who, stooping low in the boat, seek to avoid the fire. The murderous work was well done. Lustily, however, pull the oarsmen; and presently, having passed the middle of the stream, the boat and its gallant freight come under cover of the opposite bluffs.

"Another and another boat follows. Now is their opportunity. Nothing could be more amusing in its way than the result. Instantly they see a new turn of affairs. The rebels pop up by the hundred, like so many rats, from every cellar, rifle-pit, and stone wall, and scamper off up the streets of the town. With all their fleetness, however, many of them were much too slow. With incredible rapidity, the Michigan and Massachusetts boys sweep up the hill, making a rush for the lurking-places occupied by the rebels, and gaining them; each man capturing his two or three prisoners. The pontoon-boats, on their return trip, took over more than a hundred of these fellows.

"You can imagine with what intense interest the crossing of the first boat-load of our men was watched by the numerous spectators on the shore, and with what enthusiastic shouts their landing on the opposite side was greeted. It was an authentic piece of human heroism, which moves men as nothing else can. The problem was solved. This flash of bravery had done what scores of batteries and tons of metal had failed to accomplish. The country will not forget that little band.

"The party once across, and the rebels cleaned out, it took the engineers but a brief period to complete the bridge. They laid hold with a will, plunging waist-deep into the water, and working as men work who are under inspiration.

In less than half an hour, the bridge was completed; and the head of the column of the right grand division, consisting of Gen. Howard's command, was moving upon it over the Rappahannock. A feeble attempt from the rebel batteries was made to shell the troops in crossing; but it failed completely."

"Carleton" thus describes the bombardment and street-fight:—

"I am informed, that, when Sumner made his demand two weeks ago for its surrender, the ladies of the place begged Lee not to surrender it. If so, they have met with a terrible retribution. The place is sacked, completely gutted. I do not believe there is a house which has not been ransacked from cellar to attic by the soldiers. The tremendous storm of iron hurled upon it has knocked it pretty nearly to pieces. Four or five buildings were burned; and the rest will need a great deal of joiners' and plasterers' work to restore them to their former excellence. One hundred and seventy pieces of artillery were at one time playing upon the town; and, strange to say, there were but two or three casualties, although there were a large number of women and children in the place who sought refuge in the cellars. One citizen displayed great bravery when the bombardment was heaviest, and his house in danger of being burned. He drew water from a well, and saved his dwelling, though hit several times by pieces of brick torn from the walls by passing shot.

"It was about dark before Gen. Howard was ready to push his troops into the streets. The rebel sharpshooters were concealed in the houses, and poured rattling volleys upon the advancing columns. The Twentieth Massachusetts went up the principal street from the bridge, and met with great opposition. The houses blazed with musketry; but nothing could withstand their impetuosity. They advanced to the houses, broke open the doors, and bayonetted all who resisted. The Fifty-ninth New York joined them. The Nineteenth Massachusetts went up another street; and for two hours there was a continuous crack of rifles and muskets. The brigade cleared three or four streets, and then rested for the night, — Gen. Howard establishing his quarters in the splendid residence of Douglas Gordon, one of the richest men in Virginia, and a red-hot rebel.

"The shot made ugly holes in the house; and the soldiers, before the arrival of Gen. Howard, sacked it. Could its proprietor, who is worth two millions, see it, he would probably dislike the Yankees quite as much as ever.

"I have been watching the closing scene. I cannot picture it truly. The sun has gone down. The sky is without a cloud. The western horizon is dyed with richest hues, — such as fill the souls of poets and artists with strange delight. The shadows deepen: the growing darkness shuts out the masses of men upon the hills; but, looking into the west, I see in profile, along the hills, the cannoneers manipulating at their pieces. Then come a flash and a white cloud. There is a screaming in the air; and far over the river you see a second flash, — a little handful of cloud, which dissolves into thin vapor, and floats away. You see it all along the hills, — the flashes, the clouds; you hear a continued pounding, rolling, like grumbling of angry thunder reverberating along the stream.

"In the town are blood-red flames illuminating the ruins of dwellings. You see that brick walls are standing; for the flames shine through the windows. It is not in me to exult at the sight. I pity the houseless, homeless wanderers; but so falls the chastisement, — a just retribution to the guilty. On pitying the sufferings of the innocent children, I cannot forget the thousands of mourners, throughout the land, mourning for those who have been murdered by the Rebellion.

"The cannon cease; but now the musketry begins. All day long, there has been a deafening fire, — single shots from the pickets, like stray rain-drops upon the roof.

"The fire increases; the drops become a shower. It is like pouring peas into a pan, like hemlock upon the fire, like thunder growling between the clouds. The air is full of hissings, sharp cutting sounds, as the leaden rain sweeps in deadly gusts. The battle-smoke is settling along the valley so densely, that the flashes are indistinctly seen. You see only a continual glimmering, like heat-lightning on a summer's night. So, till the last of daylight fades, the combat continues."

The threatened invasion of Pennsylvania by the rebel Gen. Lee, brought on, in July, 1863, the decisive battle of Gettysburg. Our gallant heroes went into the fight with the spirit of Holmes's —

TRUMPET-SONG.

The battle-drum's loud rattle is rending the air;
The troopers all are mounted, their sabres are bare;
The guns are unlimbered, the bayonets shine:
Hark, hark! 'tis the trumpet-call! Wheel into line!
      Ta ra! ta ta ta!
      Trum trum, tra ra ra ra!
      Beat drums and blow trumpets!
      Hurrah, boys, hurrah!

March onward, soldiers, onward! the strife is begun;
Loud bellowing rolls the boom of the black-throated gun;
The rifles are cracking, the torn banners toss,
The sabres are clashing, the bayonets cross.
      Ta ra!

Down with the leaguing liars, the traitors to their trust,
Who trampled the fair charter of Freedom in dust!
They falter, they waver, they scatter, they run!
The field is our own, and the battle is won!
      Ta ra!

God save our mighty people, and prosper our cause!
We're fighting for our nation, our land, and our laws!
Though tyrants may hate us, their threats we defy;
And drum-beat and trumpet shall peal our reply!
      Ta ra! ta ta ta!
      Beat drums and blow trumpets!
      Trum trum, tra ra ra!
      Hurrah, boys, hurrah!

Mr. Samuel Wilkeson of the "New-York Times," whose son was mortally wounded at Gettysburg, thus describes the battle-scenes: —

"The battle of Gettysburg, — I am told that it commenced on the 1st of July, a mile north of the town, between two weak brigades of infantry and some doomed artillery, and the whole force of the rebel army. Among other costs of this error was the death of Reynolds. Its value was priceless, however; though priceless was the young and the old blood with which it was bought. The error put us on the defensive, and gave us the choice of position. From the moment that our artillery and infantry rolled back through the main street of Gettysburg, and rolled out of the town to the circle of eminence south of it, we were not to attack, but to be attacked. The risks and the disadvantages of the coming battle were the enemy's. Ours were the heights for artillery; ours the short inside lines for manœuvring and re-enforcing; ours the covers of stone walls, fences, and the crests of hills. The ground upon which we were driven to accept battle was wonderfully favorable to us. A popular description of it would be to say that it was in form an elongated and somewhat sharpened horse-shoe, with the toe to Gettysburg, and the heel to the south.

"Lee's plan of battle was simple. He massed his troops upon the east side of this shoe of position, and thundered on it obstinately to break it. The shelling of our batteries from the nearest overlooking hill, and the unflinching courage and complete discipline of the Army of the Potomac, repelled the attack. It was renewed at the point of the shoe; renewed desperately at the south-west heel; renewed on the western side with an effort consecrated to success by Ewell's earnest oaths, and on which the fate of the invasion of Pennsylvania was fully put at stake. Only a perfect infantry, and an artillery educated in the midst of charges of hostile brigades, could possibly have sustained this assault.

"Hancock's corps did sustain it, and has covered itself with immortal honors by its constancy and courage. The total wreck of Cushing's battery; the lists of its killed and wounded; the losses of officers, men, and horses, Crowen sustained; and the marvellous outspread upon the board of death of dead soldiers and dead animals, of dead soldiers in blue, and dead soldiers in gray, more marvellous to me than any thing I have ever seen in war,— are a ghastly and shocking testimony to the terrible fight of the second corps, that none will gainsay. That corps will ever have the distinction of breaking the pride and power of the rebel invasion.

"The battle commenced at daylight on the side of the horse-shoe position, exactly opposite to that which Ewell had sworn to crush through. Musketry preceded the rising of the sun. A thick wood veiled this fight; but out of its leafy darkness arose the smoke; and the surging and swelling of the fire, from intermittent to continuous and crushing, told of the wise tactics of the rebels of attacking in force, and changing their troops. Seemingly, the attack of the day was to be made through the wood. The demonstration was protracted; it was absolutely preparative : but there was no artillery-fire accompanying the musketry; and shrewd officers in our western front mentioned, with the gravity due to the fact, that the rebels had felled trees at intervals upon the edge of the wood they occupied in face of our position. These were breastworks for the protection of artillery-men.

"Suddenly, and about ten in the forenoon, the firing on the east side and everywhere about our lines ceased. A silence as of deep sleep fell upon the field of battle. Our army cooked, ate, and slumbered. The rebel army moved one hundred and twenty guns to the west, and massed there Longstreet's corps and Hill's corps, to hurl them upon the really weakest point of our entire position.

"Eleven o'clock, twelve o'clock, one o'clock. In the shadows cast by the tiny farm-house, 16 by 20, which Gen. Meade had made his headquarters, lay wearied staff-officers and tired reporters. There was not wanting to the peacefulness of the scene the singing of a bird, which had a nest in a peach-tree within the tiny yard of the white-washed cottage.

"In the midst of its warbling, a shell screamed over the house, instantly followed by another and another; and in a moment the air was full of the most complete artillery prelude to an infantry battle that was ever exhibited. Every size and form of shell known to British and to American gunnery shrieked, whirled, moaned, whistled, and wrathfully fluttered over our ground. As many as six in a second, constantly two in a second, bursting and screaming over and around the headquarters, made a very hell of fire that amazed the oldest officers.

"They burst in the yard; burst next to the fence on both sides, garnished as usual with the hitched horses of aides and orderlies. The fastened animals reared and plunged with terror. Then one fell, then another: sixteen lay dead and mangled before the fire ceased, still fastened by their halters, which gave the impression of their being wickedly tied up to die painfully. These brute victims of a cruel war touched all hearts. Through the midst of the storm of screaming and exploding shells, an ambulance, driven by its frenzied conductor at full speed, presented to all of us the marvellous spectacle of a horse going rapidly on three legs. A hinder one had been shot off at the hock.

"A shell tore up the little step of the headquarters' cottage, cutting and ripping bags of oats as with a knife. Another soon carried off one of its pillars. Soon a spherical case burst opposite the open door; another ripped through the low garret. The remaining pillar went almost immediately to the howl of a fixed shot that Whitworth must have made. During this fire, the horses at twenty and thirty feet distant were receiving their death; and soldiers in Federal blue were torn to pieces in the road, and died with the peculiar yells that blend the extorted cry of pain with horror and despair. Not an orderly, not an ambulance, not a straggler, was to be seen upon the plain swept by this tempest of orchestral death thirty minutes after it commenced.

"Were not one hundred and twenty pieces of artillery trying to cut from the field every battery we had in position to resist their purposed infantry attack, and to sweep away the slight defences behind which our infantry were waiting?

Forty minutes, fifty minutes, counted on watches that ran, oh so languidly! Shells through the two lower rooms. A shell into the chimney, that fortunately did not explode. Shells in the yard. The air thicker and fuller, and more deafening with the howling and whirring of these infernal missiles. The chief of staff struck. Seth Williams, loved and respected through the army, separated from instant death by two inches of space vertically measured. An aide bored with a fragment of iron through the bone of the arm. Another cut with an exploded piece. And the time measured on the sluggish watches was one hour and forty minutes.

"Then there was a lull, and we knew that the rebel infantry was charging. And splendidly they did this work, — the highest and severest test of the stuff that soldiers are made of. Hill's division in the line of battle came first on the double-quick, their muskets at the ' right-shoulder-shift.' Longstreet's came as the support, at the usual distance, with war-cries and a savage insolence as yet untutored by defeat. They rushed in perfect order across the open field, up to the very muzzles of the guns, which tore lanes through them as they came.

"But they met men who were their equals in spirit, and their superiors in tenacity. There never was better fighting since Thermopylæ than was done yesterday by our infantry and artillery. The rebels were over our defences. They had cleaned cannoneers and horses from one of the guns, and were whirling it around to use upon us. The bayonet drove them back. But so hard pressed was this brave infantry, that at one time, from the exhaustion of their ammunition, every battery upon the principal crest of attack was silent, except Crowen's.

"His services of grape and canister were awful. It enabled our line, outnumbered two to one, first to beat back Longstreet, and then to charge upon him and take a great number of his men and himself prisoners. Strange sight! So terrible was our musketry and artillery fire, that when Armistead's brigade was checked in its charge, and stood reeling, all of its men dropped their muskets, and crawled on their hands and knees underneath the stream of shot, till close to our troops, where they made signs of surrendering. They passed through our ranks scarcely noticed, and slowly went down the slope to the road in the rear.

"Before they got there, the grand charge of Ewell, solemnly sworn to and carefully prepared, had failed. The rebels had retreated to their lines, and opened anew the storm of shell and shot from their one hundred and twenty guns. Those who remained at the riddled headquarters will never forget the crouching, dodging, and running of the butternut-colored captives when they got under this, their friends' fire. It was appalling to as good soldiers even as they were.

"What remains to say of the fight? It straggled surlily on the middle of the horse-shoe on the west; grew big and angry on the heel at the south-west; lasted there till three o'clock in the evening, when the fighting sixth corps went joyously by as a re-enforcement, through the wood bright with coffee-pots on the fire."

The following is from the invaluable pen of "Carleton," who was on the memorable spot:—

"At daybreak, I was in saddle for a ride over the battle-field. Reaching the top of the hill at the cemetery, I found the men of the first, eleventh, and twelfth corps, which took their positions on Wednesday, still in place. They had not moved. There was still a rattling fire along the picket-lines. Gen. Howard and staff were in the cemetery. How changed that spot! On Wednesday, its gravelled walks were smooth and clean, the flowers were in bloom, the shrubs and trees unscarred, the monuments undefaced, the marble slabs as pure and white as snow. There were broken wheels, splintered caissons, horses shot in the neck, in the head, with their bowels torn out, legs broken; here and there was a dead soldier wrapped in his blanket. The marble slabs were shivered, the iron railing around the enclosures of the dead broken, the ground ploughed up where solid shot had struck, holes excavated by exploding shells, — an indescribable scene of desolation.

"Fearful was the fire upon that point. Fifty shells a minute exploded around that spot; and yet it was held by the eleventh corps and by Osborne's batteries. Not for a moment was there a thought of abandoning that position.

"How these batteries flamed and smoked in that last terrible attack yesterday afternoon! It was as Sinai, fearful to behold. The earth quaked and trembled. How destructive the fire of those guns along that ridge from the cemetery down past the second and third corps, toward Round

Top! There, fifteen or twenty rods distant, was the left of the rebel columns of Hill and Longstreet, near the little white-washed cottage on the Emmettsburg Road. There you see the wind-rows of dead, lying just as Osborne's grape and canister raked them, in piles, as if a thunderbolt had fallen upon the one living mass.

. . . .

"There was determination on the part of the rebels to win, equal determination on the part of the Union men to hold the position. When the fight was hottest, a gunner in one of Osborne's batteries was severely wounded; and unable to stand, but seating himself behind the piece, he twice sighted it before he would allow himself to be carried to the rear.

"Men fired in each other's faces not five feet apart. There were bayonet-thrusts, cuttings with sabres, pistol-shots, cool, deliberate movements on the part of some; hot, passionate, desperate efforts with others; hand-to-hand contests. There were recklessness of life, tenacity of purpose, oaths, curses, yells, hurrahs, shoutings: men went down, some on their faces, some leaping into the air with exclamations wrung from their hearts. There were ghastly heaps of dead where the cannon tore open the ranks.

"The hours became eternities; the minutes, ages; and yet the line held out. Thin as it was, it was strong and tenacious, the best of mettle, not to be broken or twisted by the tremendous force beating and pounding at the centre.

. . . .

"Last night I rode along the ridge. It was past nine

o'clock. The pickets were at it, our own out by the Emmettsburg Road. Occasionally a shell screamed past them from the batteries opposite the third corps. The enemy were beaten. The troops were jubilant. The third corps was cheering: their shouts must have been very distinctly heard by the rebels across the fields.

"At headquarters, in the oak grove on the Taneytown Road, there was a collection of officers. Gen. Meade rode in, and sat down upon a stone, weary with the hard day's work. An officer reported that Pleasanton had taken several hundred prisoners.

"'Bully for him! — bully, bully, bully, all round!' was his good-natured, bluff, frank response.

"A band struck up, 'Hail to the Chief!' The music, never more pleasing to the ear than then, mingled with the cheers still ringing at the base of Round Top, and was borne on the evening air across the fields to the discomfited enemy. The men were in good heart to-day. They felt that at last the Army of the Potomac is a power in the world. It has worked hard, suffered much, has been abused, has been thought to be of no account; but it has written a page of history, — a bloody page, but one which will be forever honorable in the book of time."

In a previous narration of the day's events, Mr. Coffin says, —

"What deeds of valor were performed! There were many heroes that day. A rebel officer seized the colors of the Fourth Michigan. Col. Jefferds, seizing his revolver, shot him, and regained the flag. A rebel soldier with a bayonet-thrust run the colonel through the body, inflicting a mortal wound; but, as he fell, he held the flag he loved so well with a firmer grasp, clasping it in his arms, and pressing it to his heart. The rebel soldier, too, went down, his brain pierced by a bullet from Major Hall's revolver."

Among other thrilling scenes was the following: —

"When the fight was most terrific, Col. Hall, commanding the brigade, quietly ordered the color-bearer of the Fifteenth Massachusetts to advance upon the enemy alone. It was like an electric impulse. It thrilled the entire line. Men forgot that they were on the defensive; and, without an order from a commanding officer, the line, as if bent on one common purpose, surged ahead. Thousands of bayonets flashed in the beams of the setting sun. Then came a wild hurrah, and the mass of rebels melted away over the plain."

"Carleton" adds, in language that loyal hearts echo, —

"The invasion of the North was over; the power of the Southern Confederacy broken. There, at that sunset hour, I could discern the future, — no longer an overcast sky, but clear, unclouded starlight; a country redeemed, saved, baptized, consecrated anew to the coming ages.

"All honor to the heroic living! all glory to the gallant dead! They have not fought in vain: they have not died for nought. No man liveth to himself alone. Not for themselves, but for their children, for those who may never hear of them in their nameless graves, have they yielded life; for the future; for all that is good, pure, holy, true, just; for humanity, righteousness, peace; for paradise on earth; for Christ and for God, — they have given themselves a willing sacrifice. Blessed be their memory forevermore!"

One man who resided near the battle-ground has earned the title of "Hero of Gettysburg." His name is John Burns: he is of Scotch descent, but was born in New Jersey. He fought in the war of 1812.

"On the morning of the first day's fight at Gettysburg, he sent his wife away, telling her that he would take care of the house. The firing was near by, over Seminary Ridge. Soon a wounded soldier came into the town, and stopped at an old house on the opposite corner. Burns saw the poor fellow lay down his musket; and the inspiration to go into the battle seems then first to have seized him. He went over, and demanded the gun.

"'What are you going to do with it?' asked the soldier.

"'I'm going to shoot some of the damned rebels!' replied John.

"He is not a swearing man; and the strong adjective is to be taken in a strictly literal, not a profane sense.

"Having obtained the gun, he pushed out on the Chambersburg Pike, and was soon in the thick of the skirmish.

"'I wore a high-crowned hat and a long-tailed blue, and I was seventy years old,' said he.

"The sight of so old a man, in such costume, rushing fearlessly forward to get a shot in the very front of the battle, of course attracted attention. He fought with the Seventh Wisconsin Regiment, the colonel of which ordered him back, and questioned him; and finally, seeing the old man's patriotic determination, gave him a good rifle in place of the musket he had brought with him.

"'Are you a good shot?'

"'Tolerable good,' said John, who is an old fox-hunter.

"'Do you see that rebel riding yonder?'

"'I do.'

"'Can you fetch him?'

"'I can try.'

"The old man took deliberate aim, and fired. He does not say he killed the rebel, but simply that his shot was cheered by the Wisconsin boys, and that afterwards the horse the rebel rode was seen galloping with an empty saddle. 'That's all I know about it.'

"He fought until our forces were driven back in the afternoon. He had already received two slight wounds, and a third one through the arm, to which he paid little attention. 'Only the blood running down my hand bothered me a heap.' Then, as he was slowly falling back with the rest, he received a final shot through the leg. 'Down I went, and the whole rebel army ran over me.' Helpless, nearly bleeding to death from his wounds, he lay upon the field all night.

"'About sun-up, the next morning, I crawled to a neighbor's house, and found it full of wounded rebels.' The neighbor afterwards took him to his own house, which had also been turned into a rebel hospital."*

The writer of the above adds, —

"Of the magnitude of a battle fought so desperately dur-

* Atlantic Monthly, November, 1865.

ing three days, by armies numbering not far from two hundred thousand men, no adequate conception can be formed. One or two facts may help to give a faint idea of it. Mr. Culp's meadow, below Cemetery Hill, a lot of near twenty acres, was so thickly strewn with rebel dead, that Mr. Culp declared he 'could have walked across it without putting foot upon the ground!' Upwards of three hundred Confederates were buried in that fair field in one hole. On Mr. Gwynn's farm, below Round Top, near five hundred sons of the South lie promiscuously heaped in one huge sepulture. Of the quantities of iron, of the wagon-loads of arms, knapsacks, haversacks, and clothing, which strewed the country, no estimate can be made. Government set a guard over these; and, for weeks, officials were busy in gathering together all the more valuable spoils. The harvest of bullets was left for the citizens to glean. Many of the poorest people did a thriving business, picking up these missiles of death, and selling them to dealers, two of whom alone sent to Baltimore fifty tons of lead collected in this way from this battle-field!"

The Army of the Potomac were engaged in other battles, — those which resulted in the capture of many important towns and cities, and which gave a place to plant the flag of our country in most of the rebel States, long before the four battle-years were ended. Besides the famous battles already specially mentioned, the army wrought wonders under Gens. Grant, Sherman, and Sheridan, and fought other battles equally terrible and more decisive. But space cannot here be afforded to speak of the campaigns of those able generals in detail. We must be content with brief sketches. The following depicts Sheridan's splendid achievements at Five Forks: it is from the "New-York World:"—

"A colonel with a shattered regiment came down upon us in a charge. The bayonets were fixed: the men came on with a yell. Their gray uniforms seemed black amid the smoke. Their preserved colors, torn by grape and ball, waved defiantly. Twice they halted, and poured in volleys, but came on again like the surge from the fog, depleted, but determined: yet in the hot faces of the carabineers they read a purpose as resolute, but more calm; and while they pressed along, swept all the while by scathing volleys, a group of horsemen took them in flank.

"It was an awful instant. The horses recoiled; the charging column trembled like a single thing: but at once the rebels, with rare organization, fell into a hollow square, and with solid sheets of steel defied our centaurs. The horsemen rode around them in vain: no charge could break the shining squares, until our dismounted carabineers poured in their volleys afresh, making gaps in the spent ranks; and then in their wavering time the cavalry thundered down. The rebels could stand no more: they reeled and swayed, and fell back broken and beaten; and on the ground their colonel lay, sealing his devotion with his life.

"Through wood and brake and swamp, across field and trench, we pushed the fighting defenders steadily. For a part of the time, Sheridan himself was there, short and broad and active, waving his hat, giving orders, seldom out of fire, but never stationary; and close by fell the long yellow locks of Custar, sabre extended, fighting like a Viking, though he was worn and haggard with much work. At four o'clock, the rebels were behind their wooden walls at Five Forks; and still the cavalry pressed them hard, in faint rather than solemn effort; while a battalion, dismounted, charged squarely upon the face of their breastworks which lay in the main on the north side of the White-oak Road. Then, while the cavalry worked round toward the rear, the infantry of Warren, though commanded by Sheridan, prepared to take part in the battle.

"We were already on the rebel right in force, and thinly in their rear. Our carabineers were making feint to charge in direct front; and our infantry, four deep, hemmed in their entire left. All this they did not for an instant note, so thorough was their confusion; but, seeing it directly, they, so far from giving up, concentrated all energy, and fought like fiends. They had a battery in position, which belched incessantly; and over the breastworks their musketry made one unbroken roll, while against Sheridan's prowlers on their left, by skirmish and sortie, they stuck to their sinking fortunes, so as to win unwilling applause from mouths of wisest censure.

"It was just at the coming-up of the infantry that Sheridan's little band was pushed the hardest. At one time, indeed, they seemed about to undergo extermination; not that they wavered, but that they were so vastly overpowered. It will remain to the latest time a matter of marvel, that so paltry a cavalry force could press back sixteen thousand infantry; but, when the infantry blew like a great barn-door (the simile best applicable) upon the enemy's left, the victory that was to come had passed the region of strategy, and resolved to an affair of personal courage. We had met the enemy: were they to be ours?

"To expedite this consummation, every officer fought as if he were the forlorn hope. Mounted on his black pony, the same which he rode at Winchester, Sheridan galloped everywhere, his face flushed all the redder, and his plethoric but nervous figure all the more ubiquitous. He galloped once down to the rebel front with but a handful of his staff. A dozen bullets whistled for him together: one grazed his arm, at which a faithful orderly rode. The black pony leaped high in fright, and Sheridan was untouched; but the orderly lay dead in the field, and the saddle dashed afar empty.

"At seven o'clock, the rebels came to the conclusion that they were outflanked and whipped. They had been so busily engaged, that they were a long time finding out how desperate were their circumstances; but now, wearied with persistent assaults in front, they fell back to the left, only to see four close lines of battle waiting to drive them across the field decimated. At the right, the horsemen charged them in their vain attempt to fight 'out;' and, in the rear, straggling foot and cavalry began also to assemble. Slant fire, cross fire, and direct fire, by file and volley, rolled in perpetually, cutting down their bravest officers, and strewing the fields with bleeding men. Groans resounded in the intervals of exploding powder; and, to add to their terror and despair, their own artillery, captured from them, threw into their own ranks, from its old position, ungrateful grape and canister, enfilading their breastworks, whizzing and plunging by air line and ricochet; and, at last, bodies of cavalry fairly mounted their intrenchments, and charged down the parapet, slashing and trampling them, and producing inextricable confusion. They had no commanders, at least no orders; and looked in vain for some guiding hand to lead them out of a toil into which they had fallen so bravely and so blindly. A few more volleys, a new and irresistible charge, a shrill and warning command to die or surrender, and, with a sullen and fearful impulse, five thousand muskets are flung upon the ground, and five thousand hot, exhausted, and impotent men are Sheridan's prisoners of war.

"Acting with his usual decision, Sheridan placed his captives in the care of a provost-guard, and sent them at once to the rear. Those who escaped he ordered the fiery Custar to pursue with brand and vengeance: and they were pressed far into the desolate forest, spent and hungry; many falling, by the way, of wounds or exhaustion; many pressed down by hoof or sabre-stroke; and many picked up in mercy, and sent back to rejoin their brethren in bonds. We captured in all fully six thousand prisoners."

The allusion to Sheridan's black horse is explained by the following lyric, written by T. B. Read:—

SHERIDAN'S RIDE.

Up from the South at break of day,
Bringing to Winchester fresh dismay,
The affrighted air with a shudder bore,
Like a herald in haste to the chieftain's door,

The terrible grumble and rumble and roar,
Telling the battle was on once more,
And Sheridan twenty miles away.

And wider still those billows of war
Thundered along the horizon's bar,
And louder yet into Winchester rolled
The roar of that red sea uncontrolled,
Making the blood of the listener cold
As he thought of the stake in that fiery fray,
And Sheridan twenty miles away.

But there is a road from Winchester Town, —
A good broad highway leading down;
And there, through the flush of the morning light,
A steed, as black as the steed of night,
Was seen to pass as with eagle flight.
As if he knew the terrible need,
He stretched away with his utmost speed:
Hill rose and fell; but his heart was gay,
With Sheridan fifteen miles away.

Still sprung from those swift hoofs, thundering South,
The dust, like the smoke from the cannon's mouth,
Or the trail of a comet, sweeping faster and faster,
Foreboding to traitors the doom of disaster.
The heart of the steed and the heart of the master
Were beating like prisoners assaulting their walls,
Impatient to be where the battle-field calls:
Every nerve of the charger was strained to full play,
With Sheridan only ten miles away.

Under his spurning feet the road
Like an arrowy alpine river flowed;
And the landscape sped away behind
Like an ocean flying before the wind;
And the steed, like a bark fed with furnace ire,
Swept on, with his wild eyes full of fire.
But, lo! he is nearing his heart's desire;
He is snuffing the smoke of the roaring fray,
With Sheridan only five miles away.

The first that the general saw were the groups
Of stragglers, and then the retreating troops.
What was done? what to do? A glance told him both:
Then, striking his spurs, with a terrible oath
He dashed down the line 'mid a storm of huzzas;
And the wave of retreat checked its course there, because
The sight of the master compelled it to pause.
With foam and with dust the black charger was gray:
By the flash of his eye, and his red nostrils' play,
He seemed to the whole great army to say,
" I have brought you Sheridan all the way
From Winchester down to save the day!"

Hurrah, hurrah, for Sheridan!
Hurrah, hurrah, for horse and man!
And when their statues are placed on high,
Under the dome of the Union sky,—
The American soldier's Temple of Fame,—
There, with the glorious general's name,
Be it said in letters both bold and bright,
" Here is the steed that saved the day
By carrying Sheridan into the fight,
From Winchester, twenty miles away!"

The spring of 1865 brought the great battles which resulted in the fall of Richmond, the surrender of Gen. Lee, the final overthrow of the Rebellion, and the restoration of peace. A writer in the "Boston Journal" says (March 29) of the fight at Fort Steadman,—

"The rebels first made a dash on the Fifty-seventh; and, after the first fire, the brave soldiers of that regiment had no chance to load: but every man was a hero, and used his musket like a club, knocking them right and left. But it was of no use: they were overpowered by the enemy, and a number of brave men fell. Lieut. Murdoch fell with the color in his hand; Capt. Dougherty received his death-wound; and Capt. Ward is missing.

"Poor Dougherty! He was in his glory when fighting. He was taken to the hospital, and like a soldier he died. About twenty minutes before he expired, he sent his regards to Gen. Wilcox, and said, '*Tell him I hate to leave his command.*'

"The Twenty-ninth fought with equal bravery. Many were captured, and many that were captured escaped.

"The enemy was upon the Fifty-ninth in full force; but they showed the mettle of Massachusetts troops. They fought until they were almost surrounded, and only escaped by rushing over our works toward the enemy's, and round into Fort Haskell.

"I would mention Gen. Wilcox, who commands the division to which these regiments belong. His men think the world of him. When he found that the rebels had the fort, he sent one of his staff to order out part of the third division, which was in reserve near his headquarters, and sent another to the troops on the right and left of Steadman, ordering them to hold their ground at all hazards; and, when asked by one of his staff what he was going to do, replied, '*Charge, Steadman!*' He did so, assisted by Hartranft; and the fort was retaken.

"The colors of the One Hundreth Pennsylvania, of Wilcox's division, were the first planted on the fort; and his division 'captured seven rebel flags, together with one of our own, and fully one thousand prisoners,' as announced in general order."

"Carleton," in describing the final battles, thus writes:—

"It was my privilege to witness the second attack upon the ninth corps on Wednesday night. I was the guest of Surgeon White, of the first division hospital, which is located in rear of the battery. Precisely at ten o'clock, there was a signal-gun on the rebel lines; then a cheer,— the indescribable yell, the war-whoop, of the rebels; then a rattling fire of musketry, which deepened to a volley; then there came the roar of the cannonade.

"The ninth corps was prepared. All through the afternoon, they had seen suspicious movements along the rebel lines,—squads of men marching and countermarching. Deserters gave information that an attack was to be made. Besides, it was supposed that Lee might attempt to compel Grant to recall the fifth and second corps; and, having had one surprise, officers and men were determined not to be caught napping a second time. The picket-line was strengthened, and all the reserve batteries were brought up for use in case of emergency. The men were ordered to be on the alert; and they were.

"I was upon the west of the hill in three minutes after the signal-gun was fired; and there were at that moment not less than two hundred guns and mortars, Union and Rebel, in play. The night was dark: the clouds were hanging low. The wind was from the south, and rain-drops were beginning to fall; but the incessant flashing illumined the landscape. It surpassed all other firing I ever witnessed at night in beauty and grandeur. I counted thirty shells in the air at once, rising hundreds of feet high, remaining motionless a moment, then descending as rapidly as they rose, exploding, and leaving handfuls of white cloud where they disappeared. The air was filled with fiery arches crossing each other at all angles, — some from the north, east, south, and west, — passing and repassing, meeting midway, and cut across by lines of fire streaming from the rifled cannon, sending swiftly revolving bolts point blank into the rebel works.

"The arches began with a flash, and ended with a flash. Beneath these arches of fire, there were thousands of muskets flashing over the intrenchments. I watched it for two hours, till the rain drove me to dryer quarters. City Point was greatly alarmed. There was riding to and fro of orderlies. Timid civilians packed up their baggage, and made inquiries about how to get away if the rebels made their appearance. The gunboats in the stream swung their broadsides to bear upon the plain west of the Point. It certainly was one of the heaviest cannonades from field artillery I ever beheld, surpassed only by that of Gettysburg, Antietam, and Fredericksburg. An officer of Gen. Grant's staff says that it surpasses any thing he heard at Vicksburg; and yet, strange to say, there were but four or five killed and about thirty wounded on the Union side. Artillery firing is calculated to try the nerves of timid men; but old soldiers care but little about it. Sometimes it stirs their blood. While the cannonade was at its height, I heard a soldier who was wounded in the hand say, 'I wish I was down there with the boys!' There are many thousands in the ranks just like him; and they intend to win."

Petersburg and Richmond were at last in the hands of Union soldiers. The rebels evacuated them; at least, the rebel army departed from them; and the arch-rebel fled in haste and fear from his capitol. We must again receive "Carleton's" testimony concerning the occupation of those two long-besieged cities by the Federal troops. No better descriptions of war-scenes have ever been afforded than those from his graphic pen, and no volume relating to the Rebellion would be complete without them. Mr. Coffin wrote as follows:—

SPOTTISWOOD HOUSE, RICHMOND, VA.,
April 3, 1865.

To the Editor of the "Boston Journal," —

The stars and stripes wave over Petersburg and Richmond to-night. There is no longer a Confederacy. Jeff. Davis, Toombs, Breckinridge, and Gen. Lee, are fugitives, without a country or a home. The rebel army is broken and demoralized. The whole Rebellion in a night has disappeared. I am in a whirl of great events which will be forever prominent in history. I can give merely a summary of what has taken place since the sun went down last night. In a letter already forwarded, I have given an outline of the great movement of Gen. Grant, which, under the blessing of God, has given us not only a victory, but has blown up the whole Rebellion, routing the rebel army, and sending Jeff. Davis and the whole rebel government out of Richmond at a moment's notice.

On Saturday night, the "Five Forks" were carried by Sheridan and the fifth corps. It was an unexpected blow to Lee. He ordered down in hot haste nearly all the rebel troops north of the James; but they were too late to regain what had been lost. Before they arrived in Petersburg, the ninth corps, at four o'clock, had four forts. Then the second corps took the fort south of Hatcher's Run, on the Boydtown Road. Then the twenty-fourth corps made splendid assault, and swept over the embankments of two other fortifications; and the sixth corps, with irresistible impetuosity, broke through the rebel lines, and gained the rear of Petersburg. Through the day, I watched the rolling-on of the tide, the frantic efforts of the rebels to resist it, the commotion in Petersburg, the black columns of smoke ascending from burning buildings, and knew that Richmond must be ours to-day; for Petersburg is the key to the rebel capital, and the "Five Forks," in this instance, proved to be the key of Petersburg.

At three o'clock this morning, there was an explosion which shook Richmond to its foundations, and which made even the beds at City Point heave as if an earthquake had shaken the globe. It was the blowing-up of the iron-clads. Those who saw it describe it as a sight surpassingly grand. It roused the army from slumber: the hosts surrounding Petersburg needed no other *réveille*. The soldiers were on their feet in an instant; and Gen. Wilcox, commanding the first division of the ninth corps, accepted it as a signal to advance. He was lying east of the city, his right resting on the Appomattox. His men sprang forward, but found only deserted works. The last body of rebels — the lingerers, who were remaining to plunder the people of Petersburg — took to their heels; and the division entered the city without opposition.

The entire army were instantly put in motion. Engineers hurried up with pontoons, laid them across the Appomattox; and the army began its pursuit of Lee. I entered the town soon after sunrise. It was a scene of indescribable commotion; troops hurrying in from all quarters, cheering, swinging their caps, helping themselves to tobacco, rushing on upon the double-quick, eager to overtake Lee.

The colored population thronged the streets, swinging their dilapidated hats, bowing low, and shouting "Glory!" "Bless de Lord!" "I'se been a-praying for dis yare to happen; but I didn't spect it quite so soon." "It is jes like a clap of thunder," said an old negro.

"I'se glad to see you. I'm been trying and wishing and praying dat de Lord would help me get to de Yankees; and now dey has come into dis yere city," said another. The citizens of the place also were in the streets, amazed, confounded, and bewildered at what had happened. Gen. Macy, of Massachusetts, had a provost-guard established to prevent depredations, and to save the army from demoralization. The rebels set all the tobacco-warehouses on fire, and destroyed their commissary-stores. I took a hurried survey of the rebel works in front of Fort Steadman, and found them very strong. Our mortar-firing had been very destructive, sometimes blowing up their bomb-proofs. The ground is completely honeycombed by the shells which have been thrown from our mortars. The town is not very badly shattered. A great many houses were struck yesterday, and many of the people fled to the excavations which had been made in the hillsides.

Gen. Grant was early in the town with his staff, with the same cool, calm demeanor which he always wears. He was evidently well pleased with the aspect of affairs.

My stay in Petersburg was brief. Knowing that Richmond must be ours, although the intelligence that it had been evacuated had not reached Petersburg, I made haste to the cars in season to see President Lincoln.

He went up in a special car. The soldiers at Meade Station caught a sight of him, and cheered most heartily. He came upon the platform, and bowed. On Friday, he looked careworn. The failure of Grant's plans on Thursday troubled him; but the great victory had smoothed the deep wrinkles. He is much worn by constant work, care, and anxiety; but now he can take time to grow young again, for the nation's new lease of life is arrived. He acknowledged the enthusiasm and devotion of the soldiers by bowing, and by thanking them for the great victory they had won.

Reaching City Point at noon, I was soon in the saddle, galloping "on to Richmond," crossing the Appomattox at Broadway, riding to Varina on the James, crossing on the pontoons, and approaching the city by the New-Market Road, overtaking the twenty-fifth corps on the outskirts of the city, reaching the rebel capital at five o'clock in the afternoon.

At four o'clock in the morning, Major A. H. Stevens of the Fourth Massachusetts Cavalry, and provost-marshal of the twenty-fifth army corps, with detachments from Companies E and H, with Capts. Pray and Percy, started upon a reconnoissance of the enemy's lines. They found them evacuated, and the guns spiked. Major Stevens found a rebel deserter, who piloted the detachment safely over the torpedoes which had been planted in front of the enemy's works. A mile and a half out from the city, Major Stevens met a barouche, and five men, mounted, bearing a white flag. The party consisted of the mayor, Judge Meredith of the Confederate-States Court, and other gentlemen, who tendered the surrender of the city. Major Stearns entered the place amid the wildest demonstrations of joy on the part of the colored people and the poor whites. They danced and shouted and prayed, and blessed the Lord, and thanked him that the Yankees had come. Major Stevens informed me that some of the colored people threw themselves upon the ground, and prayed and laughed and shouted and cried for joy. He saw several Union flags thrown out from houses. He proceeded at once to the Capitol, ascended the roof, pulled down the State flag which was flying, and raised the guidons of the two companies upon the building. So Massachusetts was first in Richmond and in possession of the rebel Capitol. Gen. Weitzel and staff entered the city at eight o'clock, with the whole of his command following, bands playing, flags waving in the bright morning sun, the soldiers cheering, and singing the John Brown song. A delegation of the Christian Commission accompanied them, and had the blue flag of the Commission waving from a house before noon, ready to minister to the wants of the soldiers.

Going back now in the order of time to Sunday forenoon, I will endeavor to give a picture of what transpired in this city, as I have the information from the citizens.

On Saturday night, a despatch was received from Gen. Lee for Gen. Ewell to send all his available troops to Petersburg, as his lines were threatened. All Saturday night they were passing through the city, taking the Petersburg Railroad. The city patrols and government battalion were at the same time ordered to the trenches.

There was a jubilant feeling; for it was stated that Johnston had given Sherman the slip; that he was at Bellville, above Weldon, with thirty thousand men; and Hardee was on the Danville Road with twelve thousand, making a force of forty-two thousand, which would fall upon Grant's left at Hatcher's Run, and smash him to pieces. It was going to be Manassas over again. It was an execution of a plan which I discovered as a possible movement of Johnston in a letter written last week. It was the best thing that Johnston could do; but he was too late. The divine Providence which let Johnston reach

Manassas on Sunday, July 21, 1861, did not let him reach Hatcher's Run on Sunday, April 2, 1865.

Perhaps Jeff. Davis has had some misgivings as to the ability of Lee to hold Grant in check. There is no doubt he disposed of his plate two weeks ago. Mrs. Davis and the children left Richmond on Thursday last; but Jeff. remained. He was at church on Sunday morning. The minister was preaching, when an orderly entered, and handed a note to the President of the Confederacy. It was a despatch from Lee that his lines were broken in three places, and that Richmond must be evacuated. It was as if a hand had written once more, "Mene, mene, tekel. . . . Thou art weighed and found wanting: thy kingdom is defeated."

He turned pale; but, taking his hat, he hurriedly left the church. The hour of twelve came. The people, as they passed the Capitol on their way home from church, saw men hurriedly bringing out the State papers, piling them upon the ground, and setting them on fire. It was the first intimation they had that the city was to be evacuated.

There was commotion everywhere, among the officials, among the soldiers, among the citizens, and among the women: trunks were packed in hot haste; carpet-bags were stuffed in a moment. There was a stampede for the Danville Depot. Jeff. Davis went in the first train, leaving his housekeeper in charge of his house, important papers in his private room upon the table. Such hurry and confusion never were seen in Richmond before. Carriages were driven furiously to the depot. Citizens fled toward Lynchburg on horseback, in wagons, in coaches, and on foot.

So passed the afternoon and the night. People who could not get away did not dare to go to bed; for the order was issued to withdraw all the troops at daybreak, spike the guns, and blow up the gunboats. They were afraid that the city would be fired by Gen. Ewell, who swore that the Yankees should find only a heap of smouldering ruins. They were afraid also that the rearguard would give themselves up to pillage. It was a horrible night, — a night which tires nerves, which makes young men grow old. I speak now not only of those who are hostile in feeling, but of those who longed to see the stars and stripes once more in Richmond. They feared the transition period, — the hour of no government.

At four o'clock, the iron-clads one after another were blown up, shaking the city, rattling the glass from the windows, jarring down chimneys, and almost taking away the breath of men in the streets. At the same moment, the torch was applied to several unfinished rams and boats on the shore, also to several tobacco-warehouses.

Gen. Breckinridge, the Secretary of War, protested to Gen. Ewell that it would be an act of inhumanity to fire the city; but Ewell, who is a brutal man, who is brutal to his soldiers, coarse and rude in all his acts, swore that the tobacco should be destroyed, and the arsenal. He sent a man to fire the Tredegar Iron-works: but the man in charge said, "These are private works, sir; and, if you undertake to fire them, I'll shoot you." The officer charged with the execution of the burning withdrew; but the tobacco-houses, and the arsenal, and a large flouring-mill on the bank of the river, were fired at five o'clock. It was at that hour that Ewell with his rabble, and Breckinridge, mounted their horses, and rode out of the city towards the west, turning their backs upon what had been the rebel capital. Like assassins, burglars, and villains of the deepest dye, after the robberies and murders, they applied the torch to the place where they had revelled in crime, and disappeared from the place, carrying with them the execrations of all, — of foes, and of those, who, till this morning, were their friends. History will hold Breckinridge responsible for the act of burning the city. He was Ewell's superior; was in the city till the last moment: he could have prevented the act, but did not. How fallen! In 1856 he was Vice-President of the United States, and no man had a fairer prospect than he of honor. Four years ago he turned his back upon his country, fled from the city of Louisville on a dark and stormy night, and became a traitor, a rebel. This morning he became an incendiary, and to-night he is fleeing on horseback to escape falling into the hands of Sheridan's troopers. His game is played. He threw honor, reputation, family, name, every thing, into the Rebellion, and against his country, and has lost all. But to resume the narrative: —

When Major Stevens entered the city, the flames were leaping from house to house, and devouring block after block in the centre of the town. Capt. Percy went to see about the arsenal, but found it on fire. It contained several thousand shells, which began to explode, scattering firebrands in every direction, filling the air with iron fragments, driving the people from that section of the city.

The poor people helped themselves to the commissary supplies, broke open stores, and made free with whatever they saw. Some of the citizens rushed to the liquor-stores, and, with commendable forethought, dashed in the heads of several hundred barrels of whiskey.

The prisoners in the Libby Prison were removed on Saturday evening, being sent off by the Danville Road. The flames spread from the tobacco-warehouses to the Libby, and that prison-house is now nothing but ruins. The flames spread towards the Penitentiary, and the convicts were set at liberty. The building was burned, and the city has now this class of depraved men at large.

On, on, from building to building, from warehouse to warehouse, from store to hotel, from hotel to bank, to the newspaper-offices, to the churches, all along Main Street, from near the Spottiswood House to the eastern end of the town, back to the river, to the bridges across the James, up to the large stone fire-proof building erected by the United States for a post-office, now full of Confederate promises to pay, all around this building, on both sides of it, up to the Capitol Square, the flames leaped, licking up all the business part of the city. Strange to say, the Spottiswood Hotel is saved. I look out from my window upon a mass of ruin, of tall chimneys, of tottering walls; upon streets impassable from piles of brick and stones and rubbish; upon smoking ruins. Richmond is a sea of fire to-night. It is the most complete scene of devastation I ever beheld, excepting Charleston: there the streets echoed only to my own footsteps. and to the cry of buzzards; but here I look down

16

from my window to-night upon a woe-begone crowd of human beings, gazing at the ruins, moving here and there, gathering up broken furniture. Elaborate cornices, marble mantles, broken looking-glasses, piles of bedding, chairs, tables, barrels, and boxes, are piled in Capitol Square. The ground is thick with feathers, with broken crockery, with scattered books and papers, *débris* of all kinds. Millions of dollars will not cover the loss. All the banks, all the newspaper-offices, except the "Whig" and the "Examiner," the bridges across the Appomattox, Dr. Reed's Presbyterian church, hundreds of houses and acres of ground,—the heart of the city is eaten out.

Four years ago, on the second Sunday in April, there was great rejoicing in Richmond when the flame of war was lighted around Sumter; but what a contrast is the scene to-day! Men who swung their hats and hurrahed on that occasion, who celebrated it by drunken orgies, who looked forward to dominion and empire, walk these streets to-night penniless, poverty-stricken, broken-hearted, beholding a future illumined by no ray of hope. The flame of war has consumed them at last. Loud and long and terrible are their execrations of Jeff. Davis and Ewell; but they forget the part they have taken, that they urged on secession, hurrahed for it, shouted for it, prayed for it, gave thanks for the victory of Manassas. They forget that God's throne is built on justice,—justice on earth as well as in heaven.

When Major Stevens entered the city, the people were beholding the fire, and making little effort to stay its progress. He issued an order calling upon the police and fire department to set about extinguishing the flames. Citizens were pressed into the service; and thus the flames are stopped at last.

My note-book is full of other events; but the mail-messenger is waiting, and I come to an abrupt close for to-day.

CARLETON.*

Many and important incidents of the war are necessarily left out. Sherman's grand march, so ably and fully described by Major Nichols,† deserves to be remembered through all time; and the valor of his men at Atlanta will will never be forgotten. But of all this, and of Lee's surrender to Gen. Grant, and many another episode connected with the closing of the war and the dawn of peace, which, like the sun-rays on the ancient statue, evoked the music of the joy-bells throughout the land, these pages may not speak.

We have reason to thank God for the glorious achievements of the Potomac Army, and impartial history will assign to it a high and noble place.

---

* The author of this volume feels under great obligation to C. C. Coffin, Esq., for kind permission to use freely in its preparation whatever he may have written. The whole country is under obligation to him for the finely written and reliable letters which have made the name of "Carleton" a household word; and his books, "My Days and Nights on the Battle-field," "Following the Flag," &c., are acceptable everywhere.

† Story of the Great March, by Major Nichols: Harper & Bros.

CHAPTER V.

BATTLE-SCENES. — WEST AND SOUTH-WEST.

"By the flag of my country, through weal or through woe,
On the tempest-tossed ocean while battling the foe,
In the morning of hope when with victory 'tis crowned,
Through the night of despair when with mourning 'tis bound,
Through Maine's dreary winter, on Texas' hot sand,
By the flag of my country undaunted I'll stand."*

WHILE the patriot soldiers of the Potomac Army were bravely defending the flag, the soldiers of the Western armies were no less valiant. Fort Donelson, Pittsburg Landing, Shiloh, Vicksburg, and other now historic names, telling of bloodshed and of glory, bring up the memory of patriotism and of valor such as might make any people proud. The attempt will be made in this chapter to present a few pictures of battle and other scenes in connection with Western and South-western campaigns.

One of the important battles fought by our Western army was that of Fort Donelson, in February, 1862. A writer

---

* The first stanza of a song by J. M. F., dedicated to that gallant standard-bearer of the Second Massachusetts, who, when five ensigns had been shot down, seized the tattered flag, and bore it on to victory.

in the "Chicago Post" gives the following description of the final struggle and the victory: —

"FIELD OF BATTLE, FORT DONELSON,
"Sunday Night, Feb. 16.

"The day is ours. All honor and glory to our brave volunteers of the West! They have wiped out the disgrace of Bull Run. They have taken a position stronger than Manassas, and gained a position more important in its results and its moral effect than any that has yet been won. But they have bled terribly to gain it; and the blackening corpses that strew the heights around this fortification furnish terrible evidence of the unflinching courage and awful determination with which they fought.

"How shall I describe that fight, — that series of terrible engagements constituting one grand battle, beginning on Thursday morning, and terminating in glorious triumph on the Sabbath morn? No one person could behold it all, nor in any possible way qualify himself to testify as an original witness to the many events that were transpiring at one and the same time on different parts of the extensive and mountainous field. Those who have seen both, say that the ground, in its unevenness and wooded character, much resembles that of Manassas, but that the inequalities are greater, the hills higher, the ravines deeper, and roads (where there were any) muddier. It was a region extending for some five or six miles around the extensive fortifications.

"In order to gain a correct idea of the battle, it will be necessary to have a correct idea of the character and extent of the rebel fortifications. The fort (so called, though properly an intrenched camp) crowns the summit of a hill one hundred feet high, on the left bank of the stream, just where its general course turns toward the north. It encloses an area of about a hundred and sixty acres. The hill slopes gradually down to the river; and on its face, some thirty or forty feet above the water, is a range of water-batteries, mounting twelve guns, — eight thirty-two pounders, one ten-inch shell-gun (manufactured at the Tredegar Works, Richmond), one immense rifled gun (from the same works), and two sixty-four-pound howitzers.

"These constitute the defences of the place against assault by water. On all other sides of the fort, the ground sinks immediately into a deep ravine, where, and on the opposite side-hills, the ground is covered with felled trees. Across this ravine, intrenchments and ranges of rifle-pits are thrown up on the surrounding hills, in such a way, that each hill is made an independent redan, yet supported by and supporting each of its fellows. I am told that the engineer, Capt. Dixon, who constructed the works, selected as his plan that of the famous Russian engineer, Totleben, for the works in the Crimea. It is said by skilful engineers in our army, that, if the rebels had had a force sufficient to man all parts of the fortifications, an army of three hundred thousand could not have dislodged them.

"But their strength was their weakness. Instead of having an army of fifty thousand, the least number that would be required, they had less than twenty-four thousand. Many of their officers say they had only twelve thousand; but the figures show fully fifteen thousand. This force was insufficient to defend all parts of the extensive works against a force of more than double their number.

"But the Southerners fought bravely and desperately, if not at all times quite honestly. When, on the first day of the battle, our infantry on the right attempted to storm their position on one of their fortified hills, they repulsed them, because they were able to shoot in safety from rifle-pits; while our soldiers were in the open field, or sheltered only by thin woods.

"But, when they came out of their pits after us, we stood on equal terms; and our boys, after some hard fighting, drove them back. If our soldiers did not stand their bullets where they had no chance to play back, theirs did not stand our bullets in a fair stand-up fight. And the next day showed that the rascals were not willing to take their chances of being shot, even in their rifle-pits; for they had placed a parapet of logs on their breastworks, with a crack wide enough to shoot through, thus protecting their heads from the never-failing aim of Birge's sharpshooters. These fellows, with their heavy Western rifles, would clip the whiskers of a squirrel at eight hundred yards.

"The results of the fighting on Thursday were, that our troops were repulsed on the right flank, and the enemy gained possession of the ground which Gen. McClernand had occupied for three days. The gunboat 'Carondelet' had wasted about a hundred shot and shell at long range, without doing them any damage. The enemy were highly elated and confident.

"On Friday, ten thousand fresh troops arrived, and entered the field; but fighting between the infantry was not resumed till towards evening. The gunboats opened their batteries at three, P.M., and poured a terrific storm of shot and shell until half-past four, when two of them were temporarily disabled, and the cannonading ceased. The rebels fired three shots afterward, and then set up a yell of exultation which shook the hills around.

. . . .

"About three o'clock, P.M., the turning-point of the struggle arrived. Gen. Smith, who commanded our left wing, ordered a charge upon the enemy's breastworks in front of him. The Second Iowa and Seventh Illinois and another regiment dashed up the declivity in face of the enemy's musketry, drove the rascals out of their pits, and dashed over the breastworks. Other regiments followed; and speedily the hill was in our possession. The enemy was completely outflanked. The position commanded his line in such a manner as to render it impossible for him to hold the neighboring heights. He must abandon his rifle-pits, and fight honestly in the open field, or retreat into his fort.

"Nobody expected, however, that he was going to give up quite so soon. Our soldiers went to their cold rest, confident in their ability to whip the rebels the next day; but they expected to fight for it. Not a man in the army but expected with the coming daylight to snatch his musket, and re-enter the combat. There had been during the bloody day one circumstance, which, to many of the thinking ones, cast a shade of gloom upon their spirits. The gunboats had not renewed the bombardment. Why was it? Were they disabled? or were the rebel batteries too much for them? In either case, land forces must fight and conquer alone. They laid down to sleep feeling that they could do it.

"At daylight Sunday morning, Commodore Foote opened a gun upon the fort. Three or four shots were fired; but no response was heard. Then it was reported a white flag was flying, and then that the enemy had got away during the night. A tug started with a flag of truce, and ran up to the fort; and the news came back, that the rebels had surrendered. Such was the fact. The rebel commanders, Pillow, Floyd, Buckner, and Bushrod Johnson, had held a council of war during the night, at which it had been decided to surrender; and no sooner had this decision been arrived at, than Floyd, true to his instincts, took his brigade, and ran away.

"Pillow also 'skedaddled,' as did a portion of Forest's Kentucky cavalry brigade. Such was Pillow's haste to depart, that (a rebel officer tells me) he knocked two men off the boat with his sword who were trying to go with him. Buckner and Bushrod Johnson remained, and are among our prisoners.

"The spectacle presented as our troops entered the place was one to which no description can do justice. As our fleet of transports, preceded by the gunboats, moved slowly up toward the fort, the rebel soldiers collected in groups and squads, and gazed upon them in apparent wonder."

A writer in the "New-York Tribune" thus depicts

the horrors of war as displayed at the Fort-Donelson battle : —

"The distance between the two armies during the three days, in many cases, was so slight, that we could not bring off our dead; and the wounded who could neither walk nor crawl remained where they fell until Sunday morning, some even till late that day. A prisoner told me that some Germans lay wounded before their earthworks on Friday night, calling for help and water, and that they went out to bring them in; but, it being moonlight, our men fired on them, and they were obliged to go back. It was early Sunday morning when they ventured out again, and brought them in. They were still alive, but blue with cold, and covered with frost and snow. They did what they could for them; but it was not much, and for this reason: For a week, they had been guarding their earthworks, three miles in length; and, from Thursday, they had been out in force night and day. Many of them in the rifle-pits froze their feet and hands. On the boats, I saw young officers whose slaves pulled off their stockings; and, as they did so, the skin from various parts of their feet came along with them. In passing from their works to their quarters, they frequently had to wade sluices waist-deep, and then lie down to sleep in their wet clothes. The least result was violent cold. In addition, our gunboats kept them in constant alarm, and their artillerists were worn out with constant watching,

"The Eleventh Illinois, suddenly coming upon the enemy, was forced to retreat beneath an awful shower of balls. The major then called for volunteers to bring off the wounded.

Twenty or thirty started, crawling; and they brought off a few, but some of them were wounded in the attempt. Again volunteers were called for; and they approached amid an awful fire, when one of our wounded beckoned them away. The attempt was madness. Just then, the leaves took fire; and, covered by the smoke, our men rushed in and saved a few more: but their clothes had taken fire, and some perished miserably. Those who were left, of course, perished.

"The severity of the cold is well illustrated by the statement made by our field-officers, who rode from post to post during the night, that, in the morning, their clothes were so stiff, that, could they have been taken off, they would have stood alone. It is doubtful whether suffering was greater, though it was longer, in the retreat of the French from Moscow.

"Most of the horses of many of our batteries were shot down. They had been well trained, and stood fire well. The horse is the most intelligent of all animals. He has a thinking eye: it sparkles with inquiry as you approach him. He loves music; and, in the horrors of battle, he is not afraid. Herodotus calls the horse a stranger; perhaps because he was so little understood.

"Saturday morning, when the enemy came out in heavy columns, and three times were driven back with tremendous slaughter, some batteries were ordered to positions which the enemy had a little while before occupied. The horses hesitated not to tread on the wounded, dying, and dead; and the ponderous artillery-wheels crushed limbs and skulls,

It was an awful sight to behold weak, wounded men lifting their feeble hands beneath the horses' hoofs. Sighs, at least, are due to the noble horses which fell. Going over this part of the field on Sunday, where the dead lay thickly, and where the track of the artillery could be traced, some words of the old poet came to mind: —

> 'So the fierce coursers, as the chariot rolls,
> Tread down whole ranks, and crush our heroes' souls;
> Dashed from their hoofs, while o'er the dead they fly,
> Black, bloody drops the smoking chariot dye;
> The spiky wheels through heaps of carnage tore,
> And thick the groaning axles dropped with gore.'

"The town of Dover, containing perhaps one hundred houses, must be considered a part of the battle-field, as it was within the rebel lines. Every room contained sick, wounded, or dead men. The inhabitants had fled. Some of our soldiers were sacking it, contrary to express orders. I saw plates, knives and forks, and articles of fine female wearing apparel, on the floor; bloody rags were everywhere, and often pieces of raw human flesh cut away by the surgeons; and you could not open a door without hearing groans. No matter how grand or how low, how retired or how public, the house might be, it was all the same. Thunder and lightning, cholera or other pestilence, or the most awful earthquake, could not have caused such a scene of horror."

These are horrible pictures; but, alas! they are true. Yet while our gallant defenders were full of pluck, and true to their country, on the battle-field, they were not inhuman;

nor were there instances wanting of humane action on the part of both Federals and Rebels. Both were, doubtless, sometimes humane and hospitable, except in the stern hour of conflict. B. F. Taylor, in the "Chicago Journal," says, —

"Now and then a little human smile brightens war's grim visage, like a flash of sunshine in an angry day. I remember one that I wish I could daguerrotype. The amenities of battle are so few, how precious they become! Let me give you that little 'touch of nature that makes the whole world kin.' A few months ago, the Third Ohio, belonging to Streight's command, entered a town *en route* for Richmond, prisoners of war. Worn down, famished, hearts heavy, and knapsacks light, they were herded, like dumb, driven cattle, to wear out the night. A rebel regiment, the Fifty-fourth Virginia, being camped near by, many of its men came strolling about to see the sorry show of poor supperless Yankees. They did not stare long, but hastened away to camp, and came streaming back with coffee-kettles, corn-bread, and bacon, the best they had, and all they had; and straightway little fires began to twinkle, bacon was suffering the martyrdom of the saint of the gridiron, and the aroma of coffee rose like the fragrant cloud of a thank-offering. Loyal guests and rebel hosts were mingled. Our hungry boys ate, and were satisfied; and for that one night our common humanity stood acquitted of the heavy charge of total depravity with which it is blackened. Night and our boys departed together. The prisoners in due time were exchanged, and are now encamped within rifle-shot of

Kelly's Ferry, on the bank of the Tennessee. But often, around the camp-fires, I have heard them talk of the Fifty-fourth Virginia, that proved themselves so immeasurably better ' than a brother afar off; ' heard them wonder where they were, and discuss the chance that they might ever meet. When they denounced the 'damnable Johnny Rebs,' the name of one regiment, you may be sure, was tucked away in a snug place, quite out of the range of hard words.

" And now comes the sequel, that makes a beautiful poem of the whole of it. On the day of the storming of Mission Ridge, among the prisoners was the Fifty-fourth Virginia; and on Friday it trailed away across the pontoon-bridge and along the mountain-road, nine miles, to Kelly's Ferry. Arrived there, it settled upon the bank, like wasps, awaiting the boat. A week elapsed, and your correspondent followed suit. The major of the Third Ohio welcomed me to the warm hospitalities of his quarters; and almost the first thing he said was, ' You should have been here last Friday: you missed the *dénoûment* of the beautiful little drama of ours, whose first act I have told you. Will you believe? — the Fifty-fourth has been here. Some of our boys were on duty at the landing when it arrived. "What regiment is this?" they asked; and, when the reply was given, they started for camp like quarter horses, and shouted, as they rushed in and out among the smoky cones of the Sibleys, "The Fifty-fourth Virginia is at the ferry!" The camp swarmed in three minutes. Treasures of coffee, bacon, sugar, beef, preserved peaches, every thing, were turned out in force; and you may believe they went laden with plenty, at the double-quick, to the ferry.' The same old scene, and yet how strangely changed!—the twinkling fires, the grateful incense, the hungry captives: but guests and hosts had changed places; the starlit folds floated aloft for the bonny blue flag; a debt of honor was paid to the uttermost farthing. If they had a triumph of arms at Chattanooga, hearts were trumps at Kelly's Ferry. And there it was that horrid war smiled a human smile; and a grateful, gentle light flickered for a moment on the point of the bayonet. And yet, should the Fifty-fourth Virginia return to-morrow, with arms in their hands, to the Tennessee, the Third Ohio would meet them on the bank, fight them foot to foot, and beat them back with rain so pitiless, the river would run red."

The following extract from a letter by "Carleton," giving credit to some Western regiments which fought at Mill Springs, Ky., may be of interest to many readers:—

"Exaggerated statements have been made relative to Zollicoffer's force. I think, from all information received, that he had about seven thousand men in the fight. The forces of Gen. Thomas engaged were the Tenth Indiana (which sustained the fight nearly an hour before re-enforced), Fourth Minnesota, Ninth Ohio, and Walford's Cavalry. Other regiments came up just as the rebels fled; but these regiments achieved the victory. Each one of these regiments arrived upon the ground in the nick of time. They were not encamped in a body, but were separated each about a mile from the others. The Tenth Indiana was obliged to fall back at first to save itself from being surrounded. There was no running, but a deliberate retreat, and a return-fire for every volley from the enemy. They fell back till joined by the Fourth Kentucky, which closed upon their left flank just in season to prevent Zollicoffer's right wing from closing in their rear. Then the stand was made and held. The enemy, being baffled there, attempted to outflank Thomas's right wing; and there the Second Minnesota came up just at the right moment. It was, throughout, a series of fortuitous circumstances and well-timed movements on our part.

"There was very close fighting. A portion of the rebels were behind a brush fence when our line advanced, and they fought hand to hand across the fence. The Fourth Kentucky, at the moment of Zollicoffer's death, was about fifteen paces from the right of the 'Mississippi Butcher.'

"The battle was fought by Gen. Thomas's forces, and not by Gen. Schoepff's, or a portion of the last-named troops, as has been stated by some persons who were ignorant of the facts. Col. Monson, of the Indiana Tenth, was in command of the second brigade, which did the fighting; and to him belongs the credit of the victory. Gen. Thomas did not arrive upon the ground till the battle had raged a long while; but he did not interfere with Col. Monson's plans, which were made with admirable judgment and precision. He is represented to have been very cool, watching every movement with great complacency. He was at Rich Mountain, in Western Virginia, and was highly praised for his admirable bearing. The Tenth Indiana thus far stands probably first on the roll of fame. They fought bravely at Rich Mountain; and here, at Mill Springs, they were in at the beginning, the middle, and the end.

"When the rebels gave way, Col. Monson proposed that they be followed to their intrenchments. Gen. Thomas hesitated. 'What shall we do for provisions?' he asked. 'Oh, never mind provisions! now is the time to pitch in,' said Monson. Thomas acquiesced; and the troops passed on, only to find the rebels swifter-footed than they, and the road strewed with blankets, guns, knapsacks, caps and coats, with cannons and caissons, wagons and provisions. They came close upon the intrenchments at night, but were too much exhausted to attempt an attack; and rested on their arms.

"I need not recapitulate what followed, — how they found the camp deserted, how the batteries set the steamboat on fire; for it is an old and familiar story. The prisoners taken tell hard stories of their officers. They report, that, when the officers were escaping across the river in some flatboats, a soldier sprang into the water, and grasped the sides; and that the officers drew their swords, and cut off the fingers of the man! I give it as it was told me by one who had it from the lips of the prisoners. He reports that a large number were drowned.

"It is not pleasant to hear such a story, or accept it as truth; but panic-stricken men will do almost any thing. It is related by the historian of Old Newbury, that, when the news of the battle of Lexington reached that town, there was great excitement. Men ran through the streets, crying that the red-coats were at Ipswich, cutting and slashing all before them; that the inhabitants immediately packed up their valuables, and prepared to get across the river; that one man had his family in a boat, and one of his children, an infant, cried, and he exclaimed, 'Throw the brat overboard, or we shall all be found out and killed!' A lady seized what she supposed to be her infant, which was lying on the bed, and ran in great terror till exhausted; when, stopping to rest a moment, she discovered that she had a big black cat in her arms! It is possible, therefore, that the statements of this prisoner may be correct."

Among the duties of our soldiers, sometimes, were those of raiders,—men who would fearlessly scour the country, crippling the enemy, and, while failing to engage in battle with the foe, would yet do much to aid the cause of liberty. A few details of the great raid in Mississippi, by Col. Grierson's cavalry, may be of interest:—

"In obedience to orders of Col. B. H. Grierson, commanding the first cavalry brigade, Col. Edward Prince moved with his regiment, the Seventh Illinois Cavalry Volunteers, five hundred and forty-two officers and men, from Lagrange, Tenn., at ten o'clock, A.M., on the 17th of April, on the Ripley Road, and camped on the plantation of Dr. Ellis, four miles north-west of Ripley, Miss., distance about thirty miles.

"The order of march for this day was to be as follows: Sixth Illinois in advance, Lieut.-Col. Reuben Loomis commanding, followed by the Seventh Illinois and Second Iowa; but the Sixth Illinois, taking the wrong road near Lagrange, was thrown to the west, and did not rejoin the command till near camp. As the Seventh Illinois was just going into camp, Col. Prince discovered a party of five or six rebels crossing a field; and immediately sent a party in pursuit, who captured three of the number.

. . . .

"The march of the 22d was terrible, because the swamps of the Okanoxubee River were overflowed. After moving four miles south of Louisville, they marched a distance of eight miles through a swamp. On each side of the road were enormous trees; and the water was everywhere from three to four feet deep, with, every few hundred yards, a mire-hole, in which frequently, for a few moments, man and horse were lost to view. The Seventh Illinois, being in the rear, found these holes almost impassable, from the action of the large body of cavalry which had preceded them; and they were compelled to leave drowned some twenty noble animals, whose strength was not equal to such an emergency. The men so dismounted removed their saddles, placed them on some other led beasts, and pushed onward cheerfully.

. . . .

"At ten o'clock, P.M., Col. Blackburn, of the Seventh Illinois, was sent forward with two hundred men to Decatur; which place he passed through at four, A.M., of the 24th, and captured two trains of cars and two locomotives at Newton Station at seven o'clock. The rest of the command arrived at nine o'clock. The bridges and trestles were found burned six miles each side of the station, seventy-five prisoners captured and paroled, two warehouses full of commissary-stores utterly destroyed by fire, and also four car-loads of ammunition, mostly for heavy artillery. The bridges, &c., on the east side of the station, were destroyed by the second battalion of the Sixth Illinois, under Major M. H. Starr. The whole command left Newton at eleven, A.M., of the 24th, and marched through Garlandville to the plantation of Mr. Bender, about twelve miles from Newton, where they encamped. The distance traversed on the 23d and 24th was eighty miles, and all this without scarcely stopping.

. . . .

"Although Col. Prince had marched his regiment forty-one miles, — during a large portion of the time through drenching rain, — he believed, that as the citizens were arming themselves, and the news about them was flying in all directions, Pearl River should be crossed, and the New-Orleans and Jackson Road reached without any delay whatever. He therefore obtained permission from Col. Grierson to move directly forward, with two hundred picked men of his regiment, to secure the ferry across Pearl River before the enemy should be able to destroy it. The distance to the river was thirteen miles, and from there to Hazlehurst's Station was twelve miles. The remainder of the two regiments were to come forward as soon as they were sufficiently rested.

"Col. Prince started with the two hundred at one, A.M., and reached the bank of the river before daylight; when, contrary to his information, the flatboat was upon the opposite side of the river. Not daring to call out, he spoke to a volunteer, who, with a powerful horse, undertook to swim the river; but the rapidity of the swollen stream carried him below the landing, where there was a quicksand, and he barely returned to shore with his life.

"A few moments later, a man came down from the house, toward the river, and, in true North-Carolina accent, asked, in a careless way, if we wanted to cross; to which he got a reply,— in a very capital imitation of his twang,— that a few of them did want to go across, and that it seemed harder to wake up his nigger ferryman than to catch the conscripts. The proprietor took the bait, apologized for the detention, and woke up his ferryman, who immediately brought over the boat, which thenceforward became the property of Uncle Sam; the proprietor all the while believing he was lavishing his attention on the First Regiment of Alabama Cavalry, fresh from Mobile! The breakfast given to the Alabama colonel that morning was highly relished and appreciated; but too much time was not spent over it, and the importance of speed was clearly proved only half an hour afterwards, when they caught a courier flying to the ferry with the news that the Yankees were coming, and that all the ferries were to be immediately destroyed.

"At Hazlehurst Station, Col Prince succeeded in capturing a large number of cars; four or five being loaded with shell and ammunition, and others with army-stores. The whole of this property was utterly destroyed.

"And here comes one of the most amusing episodes of the whole affair. Capt. Forbes, who, it will be remembered, had been sent to Macon from near Starkville, rejoined the command just as they had all crossed Pearl River. Having been unable to take Macon, he followed their trail to Newton, where he was informed that they had gone to Enterprise, on the Mobile and Ohio Railroad. He followed on to that place, and marched with his little squad into town, where he found about three thousand rebel troops just getting off the cars. He promptly raised a flag of truce, and boldly rode forward, demanding the surrender of the place in the name of Col. Grierson.

"The commanding rebel officer, Col. Goodwin, asked one hour to consider the proposition, and wished to know where Capt. Forbes would be at that time. The captain answered that he would go back with the reply to the reserve, which he did pretty rapidly, after having shrewdly ascertained the strength of the enemy. It is not known whether Enterprise ever surrendered or not, or whether the rebel colonel is still trying to find the 'reserve' to make his penitent bow; but one thing is certain, that Capt. Forbes, with his little squad of thirty-five men, did not intend to take those three thousand rebel prisoners that time at least, and was laughing in his sleeve many miles off while those Enterpris-ing people were trembling in their boots.

"This noble band of heroes arrived at Baton Rouge about noon of May 2, where their triumphal entry created a furor of joyful excitement that will not cease till it has thrilled every loyal heart upon this continent; ay, every heart that loves liberty and human bravery throughout the civilized world.

"Some idea of the endurance of these men can be gleaned from the fact, that during the last thirty hours, in which they had ridden eighty miles, fought two or three skirmishes, destroyed bridges, camps, equipage, &c., swam a river, and captured forty-two prisoners, and quantities of horses, they had scarcely halted at all, and went through these terrible exertions without food for man or beast! During the last night, it was observed that nearly the entire column, worn out almost beyond human endurance, were fast asleep upon horseback, except when a sharp report of a carabine told of the nearness of the enemy; and all this was rendered without one word of murmur or complaint from any lip, either of officers or privates.

"The only casualties and losses among them which we have to deplore are one killed, and fourteen wounded, — all of the Seventh Illinois.

"While several of our scouts were feeding their horses at the stables of a wealthy planter of secession proclivities, the proprietor, looking on, apparently deeply interested in the proceeding, suddenly burst out with —

"'Well, boys, I can't say I have any thing against you. I don't know but, on the whole, I rather like you. You have not taken any thing of mine except a little corn for your horses, and that you are welcome to. I have heard of you all over the country. You are doing the boldest thing ever done: but you'll be trapped, though; you'll be trapped; mark me!'

"At another place, where our men thought it advisable to represent themselves as Jackson's Cavalry, a whole company was very graciously entertained by a strong secession lady, who insisted on whipping a negro because he did not bring the hoecakes fast enough.

"On one occasion, seven of Col. Grierson's scouts stopped at the house of a wealthy planter to feed their jaded horses.

Upon ascertaining that he had been doing a little guerilla business on his own account, our men encouraged him to the belief, that, as they were the invincible Van Dorn Cavalry, they would soon catch the Yankees. The secession gentleman heartily approved of what he supposed to be their intentions, and enjoined upon them the necessity of making as rapid marches as possible. As our men had discovered two splendid carriage-horses in the planter's stables, they thought, under the circumstances, they would be justified in making an exchange; which they accordingly proceeded to do.

"As they were taking the saddles from their own tired steeds, and placing them on the backs of the wealthy guerilla's horses, the proprietor discovered them, and at once objected. He was met with the reply, that, as he was anxious that the Yankees should be speedily overtaken, those after them should have good horses.

"'All right, gentlemen,' said the planter: 'I will keep your animals until you return. I suppose you'll be back in two or three days at the farthest. When you return, you'll find they have been well cared for.'

"Our soldiers were sometimes asked where they got their blue coats. They always replied, if they were travelling under the name of Van Dorn's Cavalry, that they took them at Holly Springs, of the Yankees. This always excited great laughter among the secessionists. Our scouts, however, usually wore the regular secesh uniform."

The Army of the West cannot be mentioned without a thought of Gen. Frémont, who was such a favorite with our Western soldiers, and who so reluctantly obeyed the summons to leave them. This is not the place to discuss his merits as a man or a leader; but at least it may be said that in him the slave had a friend, and that his proclamation of freedom has to-day all the grandeur of a mighty and a fulfilled prophecy.

The following extract from a letter in the "Boston Journal" may interest many by its personal allusions: —

"On returning from a visit to the arsenal this morning, I had the pleasure of witnessing the presentation of a flag to the body-guard by Mrs. Frémont. It was a piece of good fortune wholly unexpected; but, looking up Chateau Avenue as we passed along, we noticed an unusual crowd before the 'palatial mansion of Mrs. Brant,' and, of course, wished to see what was going on.

"The body-guard were drawn up in two long lines in front of the house, with drawn swords, all looking straightforward, very fierce and solemn, — the celebrated, dashing, daring Major Zagonyi at their head, on a magnificent horse, which he caused to jump about in a most extraordinary manner.

"There were so many about the house, it would have been impossible for me to have seen any thing, if the awe-inspiring sentries on either side of the gate had not been so much modified by the eloquence of a friend as to allow me the privilege of entering the yard, where I had a fine view of every thing.

"Mrs. Frémont did not appear for some time. The guard sat patiently on their horses, solemn and immovable. I sat, impatient, conversing with one of the guard, who, being delayed at Warsaw on account of illness, was not one of those who made the brilliant but reckless dash into Springfield. He was very communicative, and pointed out those who had fought most bravely. I stared in mute astonishment at an orderly-sergeant, who, he assured me, had killed *nine men!* His imperfect English was extremely amusing. He said that 'the first horse the sergeant rode was badly wounded. He *yumped* off that, and yumped on to a second: that was immediately killed. He yumped off that, and yumped on to a third, which was soon killed also. Then he yumped back on to the wounded horse, and soon got a bad wound himself.'

"The two sons of Gen. Frémont, fine black-eyed little fellows of ten and twelve, also attracted my notice. They were in military dress, and stood on the steps talking with the officers, apparently great favorites. The oldest accompanied his father to Warsaw and Springfield.

"At last, there was a general whisper of 'She's coming!' and I started up to see the ceremony. The staff formed a double semicircle around the door; Gen. Frémont, his wife, and Major Zagonyi, in front. 'Madame,' as they call her, then presented a handsome flag, draped with crape, to the major, who replied briefly, and then received a few congratulatory words from the general himself. Then, committing the colors to the care of the orderly-sergeant who had fought so gallantly, he mounted his fiery steed once more, and made a pleasant, touching address to the body-guard. Three hearty cheers were then given for Frémont, three more for 'Madame' (who responded by a most gracious bow, taking off the slightly jaunty black hat she wore), and the scene closed.

"Every one — every lady at least — will like to know how 'Jessie' looked, and how Major Zagonyi impressed your correspondent. She is tall and stout, with a striking face, — not handsome at all; but meet her anywhere, and you would feel sure that she was no common person. There is an entire forgetfulness of self, an entire absence of affectation and embarrassment, that is charming. She presented the flag with the same careless ease that you would feel in giving a bouquet to a friend. Her features are large, and slightly coarse; but her dark, handsome eyes, full of life and intelligence, and a very pleasant smile, fully atone for that. The soldiers are devoted to her. She has taken great interest in them; visiting their barracks, and going to the hospitals, where she shakes hands with as many as possible, adding for each a kind, cheerful word.

"But I am running away from Major Zagonyi, who certainly deserves a description. He is rather short and slender, with a sharp, wide-awake face, brown hair, cut close, dark eyes, full of fire, and such a mustache!"

Horace Greeley, in his "History of the American Conflict," thus refers to the gallant major, who was at Springfield with only three hundred companions, and was to meet there twelve hundred infantry and four hundred cavalry: —

"Zagonyi did not quail. To his officers he said, 'Follow me, and do like me!' To his soldiers, —

"'Comrades, the hour of danger has come: your first

battle is before you. The enemy is two thousand strong, and you are three hundred. If any of you would turn back, you can do so now.'

"Not a man stepped from the ranks. He then added, 'I will lead you. Let the watchword be, *The Union and Frémont!* Draw sabres! By the right flank; quick trot; march!'

"With a ringing shout, the third battalion dashed eagerly forward.

"A miry brook, a stout rail-fence, a narrow lane, with sharpshooters judiciously posted behind fences and trees,— such were the obstacles to be overcome before getting at the enemy. A fence must be taken down, the lane traversed, the sharpshooters defied, before a blow could be struck. All was the work of a moment; but, when that moment had passed, seventy of their number were stretched dead, or writhing on the ground. Major Dorsheimer, an aide to Frémont, who came up soon after, thus describes the close of the fight:—

"'The remnant of the Guard are now in the field under the hill; and, from the shape of the ground, the rebel fire sweeps with the roar of a whirlwind over their heads. A line of fire upon the summit marks the position of the rebel infantry; while nearer, and on the top of a lower eminence, to the right, stand their horse. Up to this time, no Guardsman has struck a blow; but blue-coats and bay horses lie thick along the bloody lane. Their time has come. Lieut. Maytheuzi, with thirty men, is ordered to attack the cavalry. With sabres flashing over their heads, the little band of heroes spring toward their tremendous foe. Right upon the centre they charge. The dense mass opens, the blue-coats force their way in, and the whole rebel squadron scatter in disgraceful flight through the corn-fields in the rear. The boys follow them, sabring the fugitives. Days afterward, the enemy's horse lay thick among the uncut corn.

"'Zagonyi holds his main body until Maytheuzi disappears in the cloud of rebel cavalry; then his voice rises through the air, "In open order, charge!" The line opens out to give play to their sword-arm. Steeds respond to the ardor of their riders; and quick as thought, with thrilling cheers, the noble hearts rush into the leaden torrent which pours down the incline. With unabated fire, the gallant fellows press through. The fierce onset is not even checked. The foe do not wait for them: they waver, break, and fly. The Guardsmen spur into the midst of the rout, and their fast-falling swords work a terrible revenge. Some of the boldest of the Southrons retreat into the woods, and continue a murderous fire from behind trees and thickets. Seven Guard horses fall upon a space not more than twenty feet square. As his steed sinks under him, one of the officers is caught around the shoulders by a grape-vine, and hangs dangling in the air till he is cut down by his friends. The rebel foot are flying in furious haste from the field. Some take refuge in the fair-ground, some hurry into the corn-fields; but the greater part run along the edge of the wood, swarm over the fence into the road, and hasten to the village. The Guardsmen follow: Zagonyi leads them. Over the loudest roar of battle rings his clarion voice, "Come on, Old Kentuck!* I'm with you!" and the flash of his sword-blade tells his men where to go. As he approaches a barn, a man steps from behind the door, and lowers his rifle; but, before it has reached a level, Zagonyi's sabre-point descends upon his head, and his life-blood leaps to the very top of the huge barn-door.

"'The conflict now rages through the village, in the public square, and along the streets. Up and down the Guards ride in squads of three and four, and, wherever they see a group of the enemy, charge upon and scatter them. It is hand-to-hand. No one but has had a share in the fray.'

"Zagonyi wisely evacuated the town at nightfall, knowing that, by night, he was at the mercy of the rebels if they should muster courage to return and attack him. Of his three hundred men, eighty-four were dead or wounded."

Passing from Zagonyi's brilliant charge at Springfield to the great battle at Pittsburg Landing, "Carleton's" description of the scene on the night of Buell's advance to the re-enforcement of Gen. Grant and his weary soldiers, who had fought well, but were exhausted, is here given. It is taken from the first of his series of battle-histories for the American youth, whose value will only increase as years go on. He says, "Through the night, the shells from the gunboats crashed along the rebel lines. So destructive was the fire, that Beauregard was obliged to fall back from the position he had won by such sacrifice of life. There was activity at the Landing. The steamers went to Savannah, took on board McCook's and Crittenden's divisions of Buell's army,

* Of the Guard, one hundred were Kentuckians.

and transported them to Pittsburg. Few words were spoken as they marched up the hill in the darkness, with the thousands of wounded on either hand; but there were many silent thanksgivings that they had come. The wearied soldiers lay down in battle-line to broken sleep, with their loaded guns beside them. The sentinels stood, like statues, in silence on the borders of that valley of death, watching and waiting for the morning.

"The battle-cloud hung like a pall above the forest; the gloom and darkness deepened; the stars, which had looked calmly down from the depths of heaven, withdrew from the scene, — a horrible scene! for the exploding shells had set the forest on fire. The flames consumed the withered leaves and twigs of the thickets, and crept up to the helpless wounded, to friend and foe alike. There was no hand but God's to save them. He heard their cries and groans. The rain came, extinguishing the flames: it drenched the men in arms, waiting for daybreak to come to renew the strife; but there were hundreds of wounded, parched with fever, restless with pain, who thanked God for the rain."

Again Mr. Coffin writes: —

"On the Sabbath after the battle, the chaplains of the regiments had religious exercises. How different was the scene! Instead of the cannonade, there were prayers to God; instead of the musketry, there were songs of praise. There were tears shed for those who had fallen; but there were devout thanksgivings that they had given their lives so freely for their country, and for the victory they had achieved by their sacrifice.

"One of the chaplains, in conducting the service, read a hymn, commencing, —

> 'Look down, O Lord! O Lord, forgive;
> Let a repenting rebel live!'

But he was suddenly interrupted by a patriotic soldier, who cried, 'No, sir; not unless they lay down their arms, every one of them.'

. . . .

"After the battle, a great many men and women visited the ground, searching for the bodies of friends who had fallen. Lieut. Pfieff, an officer of an Illinois regiment, was killed, and his wife came to obtain his body. No one knew where he was buried. The poor woman wandered through the forest, examining all the graves. Suddenly a dog, poor and emaciated, bounded towards her, his eyes sparkling with pleasure, and barking his joy to see his mistress. When her husband went to the army, the dog followed him, and was with him through the battle, watched over his dead body through the terrible contest, and, after he was buried, remained day and night, a mourner! He led his mistress to the spot: the body was disinterred. The two sorrowful ones, the devoted wife and the faithful brute, watched beside the precious dust till it was laid in its final resting-place beneath the prairie-flowers." *

---

* Two Kentucky regiments met face to face, and fought each other with terrible resolution; and it happened that one of the Federal soldiers wounded and captured his brother, and, after handing him back, began

Among the battles fought by the Army of the South-west was that of Prairie Ridge, Benton County, Ark., in 1862. A correspondent of the "New-York Herald" thus describes the final day of the three-days' struggle: —

"Daybreak and sunrise at last; not the bright clear sun that rose over Austerlitz, and cheered Napoleon to his great victory, but a dull, copper-tinted globe, slowly pushing itself up through the murky cloud of cannon-smoke, that even the long hours of a winter night had not dispelled. The heavens soon became overcast, as if the elements themselves foreshadowed an impending calamity.

"The fortune of the day was depending upon Gen. Sigel; and that officer calmly but carefully prepared his command for the conflict. Our whole force was concentrated to the north of our camp; and what till then had been our rear became our front. Col. Carr's division was placed in the centre, occupying the road a short distance on either side. The enemy during the night had planted some of his batteries on an eminence about two hundred feet high, sloping away to the north, but precipitous on the side in our front. Batteries and large bodies of infantry were posted at his right base of this hill, and at the edge of some timber to its left. Infantry and cavalry, with a few guns, were posted

---

firing at a man near a tree; when the captured brother called to him, and said, "Don't shoot there any more! — that's father!"

A Federal volunteer and a Rebel soldier were found dead, with hands clasped. It is supposed that they fell side by side, mortally wounded, and, making friends, died in peace. What a contrast to the spectacle around!

on his extreme left beyond the road; and, to oppose these, Col. Davis was sent to our extreme left.

"It was apparent, that, if we could dislodge the rebels from this hill, the victory would be with our banners. With the skill of an expert in military science, Gen. Sigel arranged his columns for the coming action. His foremost line was drawn up in battle-array, with infantry, cavalry, and artillery, all in their proper positions. At a suitable distance in the rear his reserves were placed, ready to be brought forward at any needed moment. A level, open field, of great extent, gave splendid opportunity for an imposing display. It had last been a corn-field; and the white and withered stalks were still on the ground, forming a fine background for the dark-blue uniforms worn by our men. Throughout the morning, skirmishing and light encounters had transpired with the portion of the enemy opposed to our centre and right; but, on the left, not a gun was fired until the whole of Gen. Sigel's command was in readiness.

"At a little past eight o'clock, the decisive portion of the engagement commenced. Along the entire line, the cannoneers stood to their guns; and, at the word of command, fire was opened. A brisk cannonade was kept up for upwards of two hours, with occasional intervals of from five to fifteen minutes' duration. The sharp booming of six, twelve, and eighteen pounders followed each other in rapid succession.

"The shot from the rebel batteries were well directed, but failed of execution equal to those from ours. Several guns were disabled and taken to the rear, and their places speedily supplied by others. During the cannonade, Col. Carr's and Col. Davis's divisions advanced slowly upon the enemy until they held the edge of the timber, where the rebels had position in the morning. A battery of three guns, in front of a wooded space on the left of the road, at length became troublesome ; and orders were issued for a bayonet charge to capture it. Just at this moment, a gust of wind blew away the smoke from the front of the rebels, revealing their exact position. The Twelfth Missouri was designated for the honor of taking the battery, and nobly acquitted themselves, advancing at the *pas de charge* under a terrible musketry-fire, possessing themselves of the guns, and holding them until their supports came up. Twelve of their men were killed in this charge, and a large number wounded. Another gun was shortly after taken in the timber near by, and still another spiked piece on the extreme right of Davis's division.

"After sustaining a heavy cannonade for two hours and a half, the rebels showed signs of a desire to leave the ground. Their batteries were withdrawn from the hill, and their infantry was fast melting away; large numbers of them, as we since learn, fleeing in terror at the fearful fire under which they had stood. The Eighteenth and Twenty-second Indiana Regiments were ordered to charge, and did so in gallant style ; but the rebels were too quick for the movement to succeed in taking the guns. Their infantry fled in disorder ; and their artillerymen had barely opportunity to attach their horses to the guns, and move them from the field. It was useless to pursue with cavalry, the country being too densely wooded to admit of using this arm of the service. The entire line moved forward to the support of the Indiana regiments; and, up and down its entire length, the air resounded with cheer upon cheer from our exultant troops. The enemy had been driven from his stronghold, and victory was upon our banners.

"Gen. Sigel went in pursuit of the fleeing rebels, following their main body for twelve miles, and capturing a considerable quantity of wagons, supplies, &c., several ammunition-wagons, a load of powder, and nearly a thousand stand of arms. They fled too rapidly to permit of a capture of the entire force; and, on the morning of the 9th, Gen. Sigel's division returned to camp. A portion of the rebels fled to the eastward, felling timber across the road to prevent pursuit. Another portion turned to the westward, fleeing by the way of Bentonville towards the sunny South. When last heard from, they were in camp eight miles to the southward. A flag of truce came in to-day to arrange for burying the dead, and making exchange of prisoners.

. . . .

"The appearance of the hill and woods shelled by Gen. Sigel's division attests the terrific shower of missiles that fell upon them. Walking over the ground immediately after the flight of the enemy and the pursuit of our forces, I found it thickly strewn with dead and wounded, most of them having fallen by the deadly artillery projectiles. On the hill, where the cannonade had been severe, trees, rocks, and earth bore witness to its fierceness. Fifteen wounded rebels lay in one group, and were piteously imploring each passerby for water, and relief for their wounds. A few rods from them was another, whose arm had been torn off by a cannon-shot, leaving the severed member on the ground a few feet distant: near him was the dead body of a rebel, whose legs and one arm had been shattered by a single shot. Behind a tree, a few yards distant, was stretched a corpse, with two-thirds of its head blown away by the explosion of a shell, and near it a musket broken into three pieces. Still farther along was the body of a rebel soldier, who had been killed by a grape-shot through the breast. A letter had fallen from his pocket, which, on examination, proved to be a long and well-written love-epistle from his betrothed in East Tennessee. It was addressed to Pleasant J. Williams, Churchill's regiment, Fayetteville, Ark. Around him in all directions were his dead and dying comrades, some stretched at full length on the turf, and others contorted as if in extreme agony.

"The bursting of shells had set fire to the dry leaves on the ground, and the woods were burning in every direction. Efforts were made to remove the wounded before the flames should reach them, and nearly all were taken to places of safety. Several were afterwards found in secluded spots, some of them still alive, but horribly burned and blackened by the conflagration.

"The rebels, in nearly every instance, removed the shoes from the dead and mortally wounded both of their own army and ours. Of all the corpses I saw, I do not think one-twentieth had been left with their shoes untouched. In some cases, pantaloons were taken, and occasionally an overcoat or a blouse was missing. A large number of the killed among the rebels were shot through the head, while the majority of the dead were shot through the breast.

"Col. Hendricks of the Twenty-second Indiana was killed while gallantly leading his men in the action of the 7th, under Col. Davis. Two of the German regiments illustrated the Teutonic love of music by singing one of the songs of Faderland while they stood under fire of the rebel batteries on the morning of the 8th. The Illinois regiments were not prominent in the action, with the exception of the Thirty-fifth, Col. William Smith (wounded), and he Thirty-sixth, Col. Greusel; but they were all prompt to execute every order which they received. The Forty-fourth Illinois was in the pursuit of the rebels, and returned, bringing nearly a hundred prisoners and as many horses.

"There are no data, as yet, by which we can estimate the loss of the enemy. Their dead and wounded on the ground were much more numerous than ours; at least one-half or two-thirds more. For ten miles on the road by which they retreated, the houses were full of wounded. The whole line of buildings on the route hence to Keetsville is one grand hospital. Our entire loss is estimated at a little more than a thousand, of whom about one-fourth are killed."

Gen. Grant and the Army of the West conquered Vicksburg. An account of the siege of that city is given in the following spirited poem : * —

* By Mrs. Caroline A. Hayden.

"Day broke; and on the crested hill where heavy earthworks frowned,
In narrow gorge and valley fair where stillness reigned profound,
Along the edge of dark ravines, and up the craggy steeps
Of summits where the crispy grass and blackened rock-moss creeps,
'Neath gloomy battlements that fling their shadows miles away,
Are gathered countless numbers in battle's grim array,
Watching now the curling, wreathing smoke from many a hamlet green;
And now the spires of Vicksburg, for the first time dimly seen.

There was silence, oh, so deep and still! as if the very air
Were loath to stir the silken banners trailing idly there,—
The dear old stars and stripes below; and up on many a height
The blood-red bars of treason, flaunting proudly in their sight.
Oh! long before the sun shall gild yon city in its pride,
Full many a messenger of death along our ranks shall glide;
Yet firm the solid columns stand, and breast the battle's shock,
As if each separate form was cut from out the quarried rock.

While yet the glancing sunbeams kiss each lofty spire and tree,
The clarion's blast is thrilling forth, wild, glorious, and free;
And, ere its sound had died away, another, wilder still,
Comes hissing with a shower of lead from valley, glade, and hill.
The air is rent with fearful yells while charge on charge is made;
The firm earth trembles at each shock of heavy cannonade;
And, when the curling vapor lifts, it shows our dauntless men
With trailing muskets sweeping onward to the front again.

On, on, through rifts which Death has made, through sheets of flaming fire,
Through rifle-pit and deep morass, through blood and slime and mire,
Adown the steeps of dark ravine, and up the ragged sides
Of beetling cliffs, where scarcely even the hardiest plant abides,
To gain yon towering battlement, down its traitorous ensign tear,
And plant the glorious stars and stripes with shouts of victory there!

'Tis *noon*, and still our army ranges seven miles in length;
'Tis *night*, and still our army proves its undiminished strength:
For, though the battle-field is strewn with heaps on heaps of slain,
A countless host, with nerves of steel, for vengeance yet remain;
And tireless feet, and watchful eye, and dauntless hearts, now wait
Round that beleaguered city, struggling wildly with its fate.

The hush precedes the tempest: they will rally yet once more,
With the strength of desperation, more reckless than before;
Will pour their murderous volleys out, until the air is rife
With sulphurous smoke, and hideous sounds of wailing, death, and strife.
But God has given us a Grant; and when again we rest,
'Twill be to plant the stars and stripes on yonder green hill's crest;
And, though a legion more should fill yon proud beleaguered towers,
They must yield; for Right is on our side, and Vicksburg must be ours."

The victory was not gained at Vicksburg without severe fighting, and the loss of many noble men. One of the most touching incidents in connection with it is that told of a dying drummer-boy, who did not fail to do an errand to Gen. Sherman with all needful accuracy. George H. Boker has put the incident into most vivid pictorial-poetical form, as follows:—

BEFORE VICKSBURG, MAY 19, 1863.

BY GEORGE H. BOKER.

While Sherman stood beneath the hottest fire
  That from the lines of Vicksburg gleamed,
And bomb-shells tumbled in their smoky gyre,
  And grape-shot hissed, and case-shot screamed,
    Back from the front there came,
    Weeping and sorely lame,

    The merest child, the youngest face,
   Man ever saw in such a fearful place.

  Stifling his tears, he limped his chief to meet;
   But when he paused, and tottering stood,
 Around the circle of his little feet
   There spread a pool of bright, young blood.
     Shocked at his doleful case,
      Sherman cried, "Halt! front face!
    Who are you? Speak, my gallant boy!"
    "A drummer, sir, — Fifty-fifth Illinois."

"Are you not hit?" — "That's nothing! Only send
  Some cartridges: our men are out,
And the foe press us." — "But, my little friend" —
  "Don't mind me! Did you hear that shout?
    What if our men be driven?
    Oh for the love of Heaven,
  Send to my colonel, general dear!"
   "But you?" — "Oh! I shall easily find the rear."

"I'll see to that," cried Sherman; and a drop
  Angels might envy dimmed his eye,
As the boy, toiling toward the hill's hard top,
  Turned round, and, with his shrill child's cry,
    Shouted, "Oh, don't forget!
    We'll win the battle yet!
   But let our soldiers have some more,
   More cartridges, sir, — caliber fifty-four!"

One brilliant episode of the operations of the Army of the West was the "Battle of the Clouds," as the assault of Lookout Mountain has been called.

Gen. Grant gave Gen. Hooker permission to assault the rebels on the mountain with all his force. "This order was received about noon on the 25th of November; but, before nightfall, he had planned and had executed an attack which was as brilliant as daring. Two months' observation of the mountain, from his camp in the valley, had given him full knowledge of all its outlines, its roads, &c.; and it is easy to believe that the plan which Hooker decided upon had had for some time a place in his mind. It was as unique in conception as it proved successful in execution. A small force, under Osterhaus, was ordered to make a feint upon the enemy's rifle-pits at the point (or 'nose,' as Rosecrans calls it) of the mountain, while, with Geary and Ireland and Crafts and Whitaker, he moved up the valley until in rear of the enemy's position, ascended the side of the range until the head of his column reached the palisades, marched forward, taking the rebel works in flank and rear, and secured about thirteen hundred prisoners. The enemy fled around the nose of the mountain, closely pursued to a position on the opposite side, where Hooker again attacked. After one or two desperate efforts, the rebel works were carried; but it was at such a late hour (midnight), that it was impossible to dislodge them from a position controlling a mountain-road, by which they evacuated during the night. The mountain thus assaulted is fourteen hundred feet above the Tennessee River, and was held by a force of at least six thousand strongly fortified. He must be a regular mountaineer, who can, unopposed, make the ascent of the mountain without halting several times to rest; and the story of the assault seems incredible to one standing on the summit, where the rebels were posted, and looking at the rough ascent over which Hooker charged."*

This wonderful passage in the history of the Chattanooga campaign has been made the subject of a song written by our consul at Venice, W. D. Howell, Esq., which is as follows: —

"Where the dews and the rains of heaven have their fountain,
   Like its thunder and its lightning our braves burst on the foe,
Up above the clouds, on Freedom's Lookout Mountain,
   Raining life-blood like water on the valleys down below.
        Oh! green be thy laurels that grow,
        Oh! sweet be the wild-buds that blow,
In the dells of the mountain where the braves are lying low.

Light of our hope, and crown of our story,
   Bright as sunlight, pure as starlight, shall their deeds of daring glow,
While the day and the night out of heaven shed their glory
   On Freedom's Lookout Mountain whence they routed Freedom's foe.
        Oh! soft be the gales when they go
        Through the pines on the summit where they blow,
Chanting solemn music for the souls that passed below."

And thus may close this chapter, in which the writer has desired to twine a chaplet of unfading laurels for the brows of our Western and South-western heroes. More might have been said of Corinth, Iuka, Shiloh, Atlanta, and other places which have so lately won historic fame, but limited space forbade. Enough, however, has been recorded here to show that our pioneer-boys fought bravely, and did not fight in vain.

* Harper's Monthly, October, 1865.

CHAPTER VI.

HOSPITAL-SCENES.

'Into a ward of the whitewashed walls,
   Where the dead and the dying lay,
Wounded by bayonets, shells, and balls,
   Somebody's darling was borne one day;
Somebody's darling so young and so brave,
   Wearing yet on his pale, sweet face,
Soon to be hid by the dust of the grave,
   The lingering light of his boyhood grace.

Matted and damp are the curls of gold
   Kissing the sun of that fair young brow;
Pale are the lips of delicate mould:
   Somebody's darling is dying now.
Back from the beautiful blue-veined brow
   Brush all the wandering waves of gold;
Cross his hands on his bosom now:
   Somebody's darling is still and cold.

Kiss him once for 'somebody's' sake;
   Murmur a prayer soft and low;
One bright curl from its fair mates take,—
   They were somebody's pride, you know.
'Somebody's' hand hath rested there:
   Was it a mother's, soft and white?
And have the lips of a sister fair
   Been baptized in those waves of light?

God knows best! He was 'somebody's' love;
 'Somebody's' heart enshrined him there;
'Somebody' wafted his name above,
 Night and morn, on the wings of prayer;
'Somebody' wept when he marched away,
 Looking so handsome, brave, and grand;
'Somebody's' kiss on his forehead lay;
 'Somebody' clung to his parting hand.

'Somebody's' watching and waiting for him,
 Yearning to hold him again to their heart;
And there he lies with his blue eyes dim,
 And the smiling childlike lips apart.
Tenderly bury the fair young dead,
 Pausing to drop on his grave a tear;
Carve at the wooden slab at his head,
 'Somebody's darling slumbers here.'"

ANONYMOUS.

MANY of these "darlings" filled our hospitals during the war; and often they were tenderly nursed: for the work which Margaret Fuller Ossoli inaugurated in Rome, when Italian patriots struck an unsuccessful blow for liberty, and which Florence Nightingale continued in the Crimea, was nobly taken up by Dorothea L. Dix, and her band of assistants, whose name was Legion, but who were a band of angels instead of demons; till, at this hour, to have been a nurse in a hospital is a title-deed to respect and honor. All the nurses were not perfect; but many, perhaps most, were worthy of a place beside Miss Nightingale, whose very shadow the sick and wounded soldiers of the Crimea would fain kiss. One of those good nurses has given, in a volume whose only fault is its brevity, entitled "Hospital Sketches," a graphic picture of scenes constantly occurring amid hospital-life. Both witty and pathetic, its irresistible humor sometimes moves the risibles, and anon its pathos calls forth a tear. With the wish that the whole could be enjoyed by the reader, the following extracts are given. After telling of the arrival of some eighty wounded men, she goes on to say, —

"I pitied them so much, I dared not speak to them; though, remembering all they had been through since the rout at Fredericks, I felt ready to be handmaid to the dreariest and dirtiest of them all. Presently Miss Blank tore me from my refuge behind piles of one-sleeved shirts, odd socks, bandages, and lint; put basin, sponge, towels, and a block of brown soap, into my hands, with these appalling directions : —

"'Come, my dear, begin to wash as fast as you can. Tell them to take off socks, coats, and shirts; scrub them well; then put on clean shirts; and the attendants will finish them off, and lay them in bed.'

"If she had requested me to shave them all, or dance a hornpipe on the stove-funnel, I should have been less staggered; but to scrub some dozen lords of creation at a moment's notice was really — really ——. However, there was no time for nonsense; and having resolved, when I came, to do every thing I was bid, I drowned my scruples in my wash-bowl, clutched my soap manfully, and, assuming a business-like air, made a dab at the first dirty specimen I saw, bent on performing my task *vi et armis* if necessary. I chanced to light on a withered old Irishman, wounded in the head, which caused that portion of his frame to be tastefully laid out like a garden, the bandages being the walks, his hair the shrubbery. He was so overpowered by the honor of having a lady wash him, as he expressed it, that he did nothing but roll up his eyes, and bless me in an irresistible style, which was too much for my sense of the ludicrous: so we laughed together. And, when I knelt down to take off his shoes, he 'flopped' also, and wouldn't hear of my touching 'them dirty craters. May your bed above be aisy, darlin', for the day's worrk ye are doon! Whoosh! there ye are; and, bedad, its hard tellin' which is the dirtiest, the fut or the shoe.' It was; and, if he hadn't been to the fore, I should have gone on pulling, under the impression that the 'fut' was a boot; for trousers, socks, shoes, and legs were a mass of mud. This comical tableau produced a general grin; at which propitious beginning I took heart, and scrubbed away like any tidy parent on a Saturday night. Some of them took the performance like sleepy children, leaning their tired heads against me as I worked; others looked grimly scandalized; and several of the roughest colored like bashful girls. One wore a soiled little bag about his neck; and, as I moved it to bathe his wounded breast, I said,—

"'Your talisman didn't save you, did it?'

"'Well, I reckon it did, marm; for that shot would a' gone a couple a' inches deeper but for my old mammy's camphor-bag,' answered the cheerful philosopher.

"Another, with a gunshot wound through the cheek, asked for a looking-glass, and, when I brought one, regarded his swollen face with a dolorous expression, as he muttered, —

"' I vow to gosh, that's too bad! I warn't a bad-looking chap before; and now I'm done for. Won't there be a thunderin' scar! and what on earth will Josephine Skinner say?'

"He looked up at me with his one eye so appealingly, that I controlled my risibles, and assured him, that, if Josephine was a girl of sense, she would admire the honorable scar as a lasting proof that he had faced the enemy; for all women thought a wound the best decoration a brave soldier could wear. I hope Miss Skinner verified the good opinion I so rashly expressed of her; but I shall never know.

. . . .

"Having done up our human wash, and laid it out to dry, the second syllable of our version of the word ' war-fare' was enacted with much success. Great trays of bread, meat, soup, and coffee, appeared; and both nurses and attendants turned waiters, serving out bountiful rations to all who could eat. I can call my pinafore to testify to my good will in the work; for in ten minutes it was reduced to a perambulating bill of fare, presenting samples of all the refreshments going or gone. It was a lively scene,—the long room lined with rows of beds, each filled by an occupant whom water, shears, and clean raiment, had transformed from a dismal ragamuffin into a recumbent hero with a cropped head. To and fro rushed matrons, maids, and convalescent 'boys,' skirmishing with knives and forks, retreating with empty plates, marching and countermarching with unvaried success; while the clash of busy spoons made most inspiring music for the charge of our Light Brigade.

'Beds to the front of them,
Beds to the right of them,
Beds to the left of them:
  Nobody blundered.
Beamed at by hungry souls,
Screamed at with brimming bowls,
Steamed at by army rolls
  Buttered and sundered.
With coffee, not cannon, plied,
Each must be satisfied,
Whether they lived or died:
All the men wondered.'

" Very welcome seemed the generous meal after a week of suffering, exposure, and short commons. Soon the brown faces began to smile, as food, warmth, and rest did their pleasant work; and the grateful 'thankees' were followed by more graphic accounts of the battle and retreat than any paid reporter could have given us.

. . . .

" At five o'clock, a great bell rang; and the attendants flew, not to arms, but to their trays, to bring up supper, when a second uproar announced that it was ready. The new-comers woke at the sound; and I presently discovered that it took a very bad wound to incapacitate the defenders of the faith for the consumption of their rations. The amount that some of them sequestered was amazing; but, when I suggested to the matron the probability of a famine hereafter, that motherly lady cried out, 'Bless their hearts! why shouldn't they eat? its their only amusement: so fill every one; and, if there's not enough to-night, I'll lend my share to the Lord by giving it to the boys.' And, whipping up her coffee-pot and plate of toast, she gladdened the eyes and stomachs of two or three dissatisfied heroes by serving them with a liberal hand; and I haven't the slightest doubt, that, having cast her bread upon the waters, it came back buttered, as another large-hearted old lady was wont to say.

"Then came the doctor's evening visit, the administration of medicines, washing feverish faces, smoothing tumbled beds, wetting wounds, singing lullabies, and preparations for the night. By eleven, the last labor of love was done, the last 'good-night' spoken; and, if any needed a reward for that day's work, they surely received it in the silent eloquence of those long lines of faces, showing pale and peaceful in the shaded rooms as we quitted them, followed by grateful glances that lighted us to bed, where rest the sweetest made our pillows soft, while Night and Nature took our places, filling that great house of pain with the healing miracles of Sleep, and his diviner brother Death."

Miss Alcott bears the following testimony to the patience of those who were under her care:—

"It is all very well to talk of the patience of woman, and far be it from me to pluck that feather from her cap; for, Heaven knows, she isn't allowed to wear many: but the patient endurance of these men, under trials of the flesh, was truly wonderful. Their fortitude seemed contagious; and scarcely a cry escaped them, though I often longed to groan for them, when pride kept their white lips shut, while great drops stood upon their foreheads, and the bed shook with the irrepressible tremor of their tortured bodies."

Hospitals and hospital-scenes can never in future be mentioned in our land without the mind's reverting to the noblest charity the world ever knew, — the Sanitary Commission. Armed and equipped for its country's service by the loyal women at home, through their various general and auxiliary societies, this Commission gave comfort and material aid to hundreds of thousands among our brave defenders, and doubtless saved many thousands of valuable lives. No language can express what the Federal forces owe to the Sanitary Commission; and in this obligation many a rebel shared. The following touching incident is but one among many similar scenes witnessed by the employés of the Sanitary Commission: —

"A rebel prisoner asked a clean shirt for his young comrade, whose fresh but bloodstained bandages told of a recent amputation just above the knee. One of the Sanitary Commission gave the shirt, but said the boy must first be washed. 'Who will do that?'—'Oh! any of those women yonder.' A kind-looking woman from Philadelphia was asked if she was willing to wash a rebel prisoner. 'Certainly,' was the prompt reply: 'I have a son in the Union army; and I would like to have somebody wash him.' With towel and water in a tin basin, she cheerfully walked through the mud to the tent. Careful not to disturb the amputated leg, she gently removed the old shirt, and began to wash him; but the tenderness of a mother's heart was at work, and she began to cry over him, saying that she imagined she was washing her own son. This was more than he could bear. He, too, began to weep, and to ask God to bless her for her kindness to him. The scene was too much for the bystanders; and they left the Northern mother and the Southern son to their sacred grief, wishing that tears could blot out the sin of this Rebellion, and the blood of this unnatural war."

The noble self-sacrifice of our loyal women, who left the comforts of home for the dreary hospital and its often unpleasant duties, cannot be too highly commended; and the value of their presence to many a sick, wounded, and dying soldier, can never be computed. They were truly ministering spirits; and in the land of angels alone can they ever be fully appreciated. The following incident, given by Prof. Hackett in his excellent "Memorials of the War," illustrates the value of their presence in one case: —

"Among the many brave, uncomplaining fellows who were brought up to the hospital from the battle of Fredericksburg, was a light-eyed, intelligent youth, sixteen years old, who belonged to a Northern regiment. He appeared more affectionate and tender, more refined and thoughtful, than many of his comrades, and attracted a good deal of attention from the attendants and visitors. Manifestly the pet of some household, which he had left, perhaps, in spite of entreaty and tears, he expressed an anxious longing for the arrival of his mother, who was expected, having been informed that he was mortally wounded, and failing fast. Ere she arrived, however, he died.

"But, before the end, almost his last act of consciousness was the thought that she had really come; for as a lady sat by his pillow, and wiped the death-sweat from his brow, just as his sight was failing, he rallied a little, like an expiring taper in its socket, looked up longingly and joyfully, and, in tones that drew tears from every eye, whispered audibly, 'Is that mother?' Then, drawing her toward him with all his feeble power, he nestled his head in her arms like a sleeping infant, and thus died, with the sweet word 'mother' on his quivering lips."

Those "little gifts," how they have cheered our soldiers! Prof. Hackett felicitously calls these gifts, and their inscriptions, "The Current between Home and Camp;" and goes on to say, —

"Some of the marks fastened on the blankets, shirts, and other gifts sent to the Sanitary Commission for the soldiers, showed the thought and feeling at home. Thus on a homespun blanket, worn, but washed as clean as snow, was pinned a bit of paper, which said, 'This blanket was carried by Miles Aldrich (who is ninety-three years old), down hill and up hill, a mile and a half, to be given to some soldier.'

"On a bed-quilt was pinned a card, saying, 'My son is in the army. Whoever is made warm by this quilt, which I have worked on for six days and the greater part of six nights, let him remember his own mother's love.'

"On another blanket was this: 'This blanket was used by a soldier in the war of 1812. May it keep some soldier warm in this war against traitors!'

"On a pillow was written, 'This pillow belonged to my little boy, who died resting on it. It is a precious treasure to me; but I give it for the soldiers.'

"On a pair of woollen socks was written, 'These stockings were knit by a little girl five years old; and she is going to knit some more, for mother says it will help some poor soldier.'

"On a box of beautiful lint was this mark: 'Made in a sick-room, where the sunlight has not entered for nine years, but where God has entered, and where two sons have bid their mother good-by as they have gone out to the war.'

"On a bundle containing bandages was written, 'This is a poor gift; but it is all I had. I have given my husband and my boy, and only wish I had more to give; but I have not.'

On some eye-shades was marked, 'Made by one who is blind. Oh, how I long to see the dear old flag you are all fighting under!'"

Kindred to all these was this impromptu, by a lady of Salem, Mass.,* now first published. It was placed on a pair of stockings for the army.

"Go forth on thy mission, this work of my hand;
Make warm the cold feet that now shivering stand;
For they wander from home and loved ones to-day:
But tell the brave hearts that for them we pray;
That our work with our prayers shall follow them now,
Till the wreath of the victor is placed on their brow;
That our Father will guide their feet from all harm,
And shield by his love from danger and storm;
That he'll give the strong arm the strength of his might,
And peace to the cause that is right in his sight."

---

* Mrs. M. G. Farmer ("Mabelle").

The lady who thus helped to form the above links between home and camp or hospital, was then, and is still, an invalid; having been much of the time, for several years, confined to her room and bed. Yet she did enough for our sick and wounded soldiers to shame those in health who did nothing. She planned, and, by the efficient aid of her husband and many friends, conducted, a Fair in the city of Salem, in 1864, which brought her eight hundred dollars for the use of the soldiers. This sum was faithfully expended: a part of it was used to provide a library for Jefferson Barracks, Missouri, in response to a call from Mr. C. H. Talmadge; and three hundred dollars of it, at least, went to our soldiers through an agent of the Christian Commission, — Rev. J. W. Dadmun. Such devotion to country cannot go unappreciated. Our soldiers were cheered by it, and her own heart was blessed.

"Carleton" wrote concerning the Fair, to the "Boston Journal," as follows: —

"One of the many affecting incidents in connection with this enterprise is that of a little blind girl, who heard of what this lady had undertaken, and her sympathy was at once aroused. What could she do for the soldiers? The active brain and tender heart soon found work for the willing hands. Various kind of bead and needle work were soon fashioned into forms of beauty by her delicate sense of touch. Her heart was in the work, and she did what she could. When the articles were finished, she gathered them up in her arms, and was led by two little girls to a house where the contributions were being collected; and there she presented her gifts to the soldiers' Fair."

The "New-Bedford Mercury" sends the following:—

"Yesterday forenoon, a poor woman, earning but twenty-five cents a day by sewing, entered a grocery-store in the west part of the city, and paid for ten packages of cornstarch, to be sent to the City Hall, and thence to the sick and wounded soldiers of the army. 'Verily I say unto you, that this poor widow hath cast more in than all they which have cast into the treasury.'"

That these self-denying ones did not give in vain, no candid mind can doubt. Through those noble charities, the Sanitary and Christian Commissions, those benefactions were honestly and liberally dispensed. Yet there were some opposed to the elder Commission, and undoubtedly without sufficient cause.

It has been thought by some that the Christian Commission was needed to care for the souls of the soldiers, because the Sanitary Commission "cared for none of these things." This is a mistake. Many of the agents and nurses belonging to the Sanitary Commission were earnest and active Christians; and the sick and wounded did not lack for friends in them, who would point them to "the Lamb of God, who taketh away the sins of the world."

The following remarkable narration, having reference to a hospital visit, is from the "New-Bedford Mercury," and believed to be reliable in every particular:—

"Elizabeth Comstock, a lady of English birth, and a resident of Michigan, is an eloquent preacher of the Society of Friends. For some years, she has devoted herself particularly to visiting prisons and hospitals, and, with the self-denying spirit of a Fry or a Howard, has ministered to the miserable inmates. She was in attendance at the recent Yearly Meeting of Friends at Newport, and, at the close of it, was urged to visit Salem, and spend last First Day with Friends there. This invitation she declined, saying there were no hospitals or prisons there; and to these was her mission. Soon after, however, yielding to a strong impression upon her own mind that it was her duty, she announced that she would go to Salem. She attended Friends' meeting, and preached; her subject being 'the Value of Early Religious Training.' Illustrative of this, she narrated the following touching incident:—

"Soon after the terrible battle of Fredericksburg, some year and a half since, she visited one of the hospitals in the vicinity of Washington, going from ward to ward, and from cot to cot, comforting and consoling the wounded sufferers. Upon one bed lay a young man, with eyes closed, and apparently insensible. The attendant remarked, that it would be useless to speak to him, as he had been constantly delirious since his arrival, and had now relapsed into a death-like stupor. But the good lady, full of motherly, Christian sympathy, stopped by the bedside, and repeated Dr. Watts's hymn, in her sweet tones,—

'Jesus can make a dying bed
Feel soft as downy pillows are,' &c.

"As she closed, the young man looked up with an intelligent smile, and, seeing a female form, said, 'I knew you would come, mother, and speak to me of Jesus.' By his side the good woman remained, we believe, till the spirit left him, catching his last accents on earth, 'Mother, I am going to Jesus.'

"But the most remarkable part of our story is to come. As the meeting broke up, and the Friends were leaving, the preacher's attention was arrested by a female face in the throng; and she remarked to a friend, 'That must be the mother of the young soldier of whom I spoke.' They met, the preacher and the mother; and, upon comparing notes, the fact was established that it was the son of that mother to whom Elizabeth Comstock had ministered in his dying hour, and had thus brought to her the first knowledge of his death. Our readers can imagine the consolation thus given by the assurance, that, in his dying hour, the young soldier thought of his mother, and coupled her name with that of Jesus, whom she had taught him to revere. Who shall say that the Good Spirit did not lead Elizabeth Comstock out of her chosen path of labor to carry comfort to the heart of that Salem mother?"

Volumes might be filled with incidents of thrilling interest which have occurred at our hospitals, both among the rebel as well as among the loyal soldiers.

The loyal hearts at home deserve great credit for their efficient aid to the agents in the field. The great Sanitary Fairs of our large cities furnished thousands of dollars to carry on the work; and, as we have seen, even children and invalids lent their little aid, made "mighty through God," to save their Country in her hour of peril. The benefactions of loyalists are worthy of mention and remembrance, and make one proud of a country whose inhabitants are so liberal and benevolent. One of our religious papers thus sums up the money in various ways laid upon the altar of patriotism and humanity : —

"The total contributions from states, counties, and towns, for the aid and relief of soldiers, amounted, during the war, to $187,209,608.62. The contributions of associations and individuals for the care and comfort of soldiers were $24,044,863.96 ; for sufferers abroad, $380,040.74 ; for sufferers by the riots of July, for freedmen and white refugees, $639,633.13 ; making a grand total, exclusive of expenditures of the Government, of $212,274,248.45."

THE SOLDIER'S FRIEND. — To no single individual in our land, so far as private contributions and personal efforts are concerned, can the title of "The Soldier's Friend" be more appropriately given than to Count L. B. Schwabe, at the present time a resident of Boston, Mass. We have endeavored to obtain from him some facts with regard to his munificent charities during the past four years ; but he persistently refuses to parade his generous deeds before the public gaze. We are consequently obliged to give but a meagre account of one, who, though a native of a far-distant country (Germany), and independent of any claims, which we, as a people, could make upon his generosity, has been one of the truest and most liberal friends which the officers and soldiers in our army have had during the late Rebellion. In a thousand ways, frequently untold and unknown, his generous bounty has found its way to some soldier or officer, some company or regiment, some camp or hospital, in some part of the land. We know that he now has in his possession thousands of letters of thanks and recommendations, which he has received from our most distinguished generals and the governors of States, but which he is not willing to make public.

Count Schwabe is now creating a most magnificent memorial of our heroic dead, — THE NATIONAL GALLERY OF FALLEN HEROES; in which work he is engaged with all the enthusiasm of his ardent nature and the resources of his generous purse. This gallery he designs shall be an enduring monument to the memory of the gallant men who have laid down their lives for their country. Several of the portraits already completed were on exhibition at the Mechanics' Fair in Boston, and attracted universal attention for their excellence, and truthfulness to nature. These portraits are in oil, life-size, and from the hands of the best artists. They represent officers and men of all ranks in the army and navy, and from every loyal State. Secretary Stanton, who was present at the opening of the fair, spoke of them in the warmest manner, congratulated Count Schwabe on the success which has thus far attended his efforts to form such a gallery, and expressed his desire to be present at its inauguration.

The interesting theme is left with the pleasant thought, that, in the book of heavenly remembrance, no act of mercy, or deed of divine charity or loyal devotion, will be unrecorded.

CHAPTER VII.

PRISON-HORRORS.

> "In the prison cell I sit,
>   Thinking, mother dear, of you,
> And our bright and happy home so far away;
>   And the tears they fill my eyes,
>   Spite of all that I can do,
> Though I try to cheer my comrades, and be gay.
>
> *Chorus.*—Tramp, tramp, tramp, the boys are marching:
>   Cheer up, comrades; they will come;
>   And beneath the starry flag
>   We shall breathe the air again
>   Of the free land in our own beloved home.
>
>
>   In the battle front we stood
>   When their fiercest charge they made,
> And they swept us off, a hundred men or more;
>   But before we reached their lines
>   They were driven back dismayed,
> And we heard the cry of victory o'er and o'er.
>   *Chorus.*—Tramp, tramp, tramp, &c.
>
>
>   So, within the prison-cell,
>   We are waiting for the day
> That shall open wide the iron door;

> And the hollow eye grows bright,
> And the poor heart almost gay,
> As we think of seeing home and friends once more.
>
> *Chorus.*— Tramp, tramp, tramp," &c.— ANONYMOUS.

THIS popular song, which was first sung at the Centennial celebration at Ashfield, June 21, 1865, has been sung in cot and hall, by road and fireside, with tearful eyes and aching hearts, because it pictured (alas! too truly) the sufferings of Union soldiers in rebel prisons, starving to death, but longing for liberty.

It is a matter of profoundest mystery to all, except those who understand, in a measure, the baleful influence of slavery even upon the whites, how our "Southern brethren" could ever be so cruel to their prisoners of war. But the testimony is too strong to be denied; and from nameless graves at the South, and graves at the North untimely filled, goes up to heaven the cry against the pitiless cruelty of Southern captors. The record of rebel atrocities is dark and damning. There is no language but that of Scripture to express the character of those who tortured their prisoners unto death, following them with merciless hatred even unto the grave: they were truly "earthly, sensual, *devilish.*".

The following extracts from the "Report of the Committee appointed by the United-States Sanitary Commission to investigate the Treatment of Union Prisoners by the Rebel Authorities" will unfold a horrible tale of barbarities, fit for the dark ages, with their blind superstitions, rather than for the nineteenth century, with its light and freedom:—

"In entering upon their duties, the commissioners had no other wish than to ascertain the truth, and to report the facts as they were. For this they endeavored to collect all the evidence within their reach, and to hear and record all that could be said on every side of the subject. They were accompanied by a United-States commissioner; and in every case the testimony was taken on oath or affirmation before him, or, in his absence, before other officers equally empowered.

. . . .

"The commissioners, at the very outset, were brought face to face with the returned captives. They first visited the two extensive hospitals in Annapolis, occupying the spacious buildings and grounds of the Naval Academy and St. John's College, where over three thousand of them had been brought, in every conceivable form of suffering, direct from the Libby Prison, Belle Isle, and two or three other Southern military stations. They also visited the West's Buildings Hospital, and the Jarvis General Hospital in Baltimore, where several hundreds had been brought in an equally dreadful condition.

"The photographs of these diseased and emaciated men, since so widely circulated, painful as they are, do not, in many respects, adequately represent the sufferers as they then appeared.

. . . .

"The first fact developed by the testimony of both officers and privates is, that prisoners were almost invariably robbed of every thing valuable in their possession; sometimes on the field, at the instant of capture; sometimes by the prison authorities, in a 'quasi official way,' with the promise of return when exchanged or paroled, but which promise was never fulfilled. This robbery amounted often to a stripping of the person of even necessary clothing. Blankets and overcoats were almost always taken, and sometimes other articles; in which case, damaged ones were returned in their stead. This preliminary over, the captives were taken to prison.

"The Libby, which is best known, though also used as a place of confinement for private soldiers, is generally understood to be the officers' prison. It is a row of brick buildings, three stories high, situated on the canal, and overlooking the James River; and was formerly a tobacco warehouse. The partitions between the buildings have been pierced with doorways on each story. The rooms are one hundred feet long by forty feet broad. In six of these rooms, twelve hundred United-States officers of all grades, from the brigadier-general to the second lieutenant, were confined for many months; and this was all the space that was allowed them in which to cook, eat, wash, sleep, and take exercise! It seems incredible. Ten feet by two were all that could be claimed by each man, — hardly enough to measure his length upon; and even this was further abridged by the room necessarily taken for cooking, washing, and clothes-drying.

"At one time, they were not allowed the use of benches, chairs, or stools; nor even to fold their blankets, and sit upon them: but those who would rest were obliged to huddle on their haunches, as one of them expresses it, 'like so many slaves on the middle passage.' After a while, this severe restriction was removed, and they were allowed to make chairs and stools for themselves out of the barrels and boxes which they had received from the North.

"They were overrun with vermin, in spite of every precaution and constant ablutions. Their blankets, which averaged one to a man, and sometimes less, had not been issued by the rebels, but had been procured in different ways,—sometimes by purchase, sometimes through the Sanitary Commission. The prisoners had to help themselves from the refuse accumulation of these articles, which, having seen similar service before, were often ragged, and full of vermin. In these they wrapped themselves at night, and lay down on the hard plank-floor in close and stifling contact,—'wormed and dovetailed together,' as one of them testifies, 'like fish in a basket.' The floors were recklessly washed late in the afternoon, and were therefore damp, and dangerous to sleep upon. Almost every one had a cough in consequence.

"There were seventy-five windows in these rooms, all more or less broken; and in winter the cold was intense. Two stoves in a room, with two or three armfuls of wood to each, did not prove sufficient, under this exposure, to keep them warm.

"The regulations varied, at different periods, in stringency and severity; and it is difficult to describe the precise condition of things at any one time; but the above comes from two officers, Lieut.-Col. Farnsworth and Capt. Calhoun.

As it happens, they are representatives of the two opposite classes of officers confined in the Libby. The former, coming from Connecticut, and influentially connected at the North, was one of a mess to which a great profusion of supplies, and even luxuries, were sent. The latter, coming from Kentucky, and being differently situated, was entirely dependent upon the prison-fare. These officers were there during the same season, but never became acquainted. The accounts of each, found in the evidence side by side, are here combined, and run together.

"From their statements, it appears that the hideous discomfort was never lessened by any variation in the rules, but often increased. The prison did not seem to be under any general and uniform army regulations; but the captives were subject to the caprices of Major Turner, the officer in charge, and Richard Turner, inspector of the prison.

"It was among the rules, that no one should go within three feet of the windows, — a rule which seems to be general in all Southern prisons of this character, and which their frequently crowded state rendered peculiarly severe, and difficult to observe. The manner in which the regulation was enforced was unjustifiably and wantonly cruel. Often by accident, or unconsciously, an officer would go near a window, and be instantly shot at without warning. The reports of the sentry's musket were heard almost every day; and frequently a prisoner fell, either killed or wounded. It was even worse with a large prison near by, called the 'Pemberton Buildings,' which was crowded with enlisted men. The firing into its windows was a still more common occurrence. The officers have heard as many as fourteen shots fired in a single day. They could see the guards watching an opportunity to fire; and often, after one of them had discharged his musket, the sergeant of the guard would appear at the door, bringing out a dead or wounded soldier.

"So careless as this were the authorities as to the effect of placing their prisoners in the power of the rude and brutal soldiery on guard. It became a matter of sport among the latter 'to shoot a Yankee.' They were seen in attitudes of expectation, with guns cocked, watching the windows for a shot. Sometimes they did not even wait for an infraction of the rule. Lieut. Hammond was shot at while in a small boarded enclosure, where there was no window, only an aperture between the boards. The guard caught sight of his hat through this opening, and aiming lower, so as to reach his heart, fired. A nail turned the bullet upward, and it passed through his ear and hat-brim. The officers reported the outrage to Major Turner, who merely replied, 'The boys are in want of practice.' The sentry said 'he had made a bet that he would kill a damned Yankee before he came off guard.' No notice was taken of the occurrence by the authorities. The brutal fellow, encouraged by this impunity, tried to murder another officer in the same way. Lieut. Huggins was standing eight feet from the window, in the second story. The top of his hat was visible to the guard, who left his beat, went into the street, took deliberate aim, and fired. Providentially he was seen: a warning cry was uttered. Huggins stooped, and the bullet buried itself in the beams above.

"Very much the same thing is mentioned as happening to the prison-buildings at Danville. A man was standing by the window, conversing with Private Wilcox: at his feet was the place where he slept at night, close under the window, and where his blanket lay rolled up. He had his hand on the casement. The guard must have seen his shadow, for he was invisible from the regular beat, and went out twenty feet to get a shot at him. Before the poor fellow could be warned, the bullet entered his forehead, and he fell dead at the feet of his companion. Almost every prisoner had such an incident to tell. Some had been shot at themselves a number of times, and had seen others repeatedly fired upon. One testifies that he had seen five hundred men shot at.

"The same brutal style of 'sporting,' while on guard, seems to have prevailed wherever the license was given by this cruel and unnecessary rule. Capt. Calhoun mentions, that while he and his companions were on their way to Richmond from North-eastern Georgia, where they were captured, they stopped at Atlanta; and, just before they started, a sick soldier, who was near the line beyond which the prisoners were not allowed to go, put his hand over to pluck a bunch of leaves that were not a foot from the boundary. The instant he did so, the guard caught sight of him, fired, and killed him.

"Another instance of equal skill in 'shooting on the wing' will be noticed in the case of the soldier who only exposed his arm an instant in throwing out some water, and was wounded, fortunately not killed, by the rebel bullet. Something of the same kind was related in the course of conversation, but is not in the evidence, as happening at the Libby, when an officer was shot while waving his hand in farewell to a departing comrade.

"But there were cruelties worse than these, because less the result of impulse and recklessness, and because deliberately done. There opens now a part of the narrative which is as amazing as it is unaccountable. The reader will turn to the heart-rending scenes of famine which the testimony before the Commission has exposed.

"The daily ration in the officers' quarter of Libby Prison was a small loaf of bread, about the size of a man's fist, made of Indian-meal. Sometimes it was made from wheat-flour, but of variable quality. It weighed a little over half a pound: with it was given a piece of beef weighing two ounces. But it is not easy to describe this ration, it was so irregular in kind, quality, and amount. Its general character is vividly indicated by a remark made in conversation by one of the officers. 'I would gladly,' said he with emphatic sincerity, — '*gladly* have preferred the horse-feed in my father's stable.'

"During the summer and early part of the fall, the ration seems to have been less insufficient, and less repulsive, than it afterwards became. At no period was it enough to support life, at least in health, for a length of time; but, however inadequate, it was not so to such a remarkable degree as to produce the evils which afterward ensued.

"It was about the middle of last autumn that this process of slow starvation became intolerable, injurious, and cruel to the extent referred to. The corn-bread began to be of the roughest and coarsest description. Portions of the cob and husk were often found ground in with the meal. The crust was so thick and hard, that the prisoners called it 'iron-clad.' To render the bread eatable, they grated it, and made mush out of it; but the crust they could not grate. Now and then, after long intervals, often of many weeks, a little meat was given them, perhaps two or three mouthfuls. At a later period, they received a pint of black peas, with some vinegar, every week: the peas were often full of worms, or maggots, in a chrysalis state, which, when they made soup, floated on the surface.

"Those who were entirely dependent on the prison-fare, and had no friends at the North to send them boxes of food, began to suffer the horrible agony of craving food, and feeling themselves day by day losing strength. Dreams and delusions began to distract their minds. Although many were relieved through the generosity of their more favored fellow-prisoners, yet the supply from this source was, of course, inadequate. Capt. Calhoun speaks of suffering 'a burning sensation on the inside, with a general failure in strength. I grew so foolish in my mind, that I used to blame myself for not eating more when at home. The subject of food engrossed my entire thoughts.'

"Capt. Stevens, having received a box from home, sat down and ate to excess, and died a few hours afterward.

'A man had a piece of ham, which I looked at for hours, and would have stolen if I had had a chance.'

"One day, by pulling up a plank in the floor, they gained access to the cellar, and found there an abundance of provisions, — barrels of the finest wheat-flour, potatoes, and turnips. Of these they ate ravenously, until the theft was discovered.

"But the most unaccountable and shameful act of all was yet to come. Shortly after this general diminution of rations, in the month of January last, the boxes, which before had been regularly delivered and in good order, were withheld. No reason was given. Three hundred arrived every week, and were received by Col. Ould, commissioner of exchange; but, instead of being distributed, they were retained, and piled up in warehouses near by, and in full sight of the tantalized and hungry captives. Three thousand were there when Lieut.-Col. Farnsworth came away. There was some show of delivery, however, but in a manner especially heartless. Five or six of the boxes were given during the week. The eager prisoner, expectant perhaps of a wife's or mother's thoughtful provision for him, was called to the door, and ordered to spread his blanket, when the open cans, whether containing preserved fruits, condensed milk, tobacco, vegetables, or meats, were thrown promiscuously together, and often ruined by the mingling.

"It is stated that for offences, whether trivial or serious, the prisoners were consigned to cells beneath the prison, the walls of which were damp, green, and slimy. These apartments were never warmed, and often so crowded, that some were obliged to stand up all night. It was in these dungeons that the hostages were placed."

Well might the poet's lyre give forth most sad and plaintive notes at the knowledge of such barbarity. Our brave boys died by scores and hundreds; but, alas! —

> "Not on the battle-field
> Did they their brave lives yield,
> In gallant onslaught 'gainst a treacherous foe;
> But slowly, day by day,
> Their warm blood oozed away
> In lingering agonies but God may know!"*

The horrors of Libby Prison were duplicated at Andersonville. The following is the evidence of Dr. John C. Bates, a contract-surgeon employed by the rebels in the Andersonville Hospital, given on the trial of Wirz, the rebel prison-keeper:—

"I was ordered to report to J. H. White, the surgeon in charge; but, hearing he was injured by a railroad accident, I reported to R. A. Stevenson. On going into ward fifteen of the hospital, I saw a number of men, and was rather shocked. Many of them were lying partially naked, dirty, and lousy in the sand; others were crowded together in small tents, the latter unserviceable at the best. I examined all who were placed in my charge. On further investigation of matters, to make myself acquainted with the mode of doing business, the disagreeable feeling at first made on me wore off more or less, as I was becoming more

---

* Miss L. L. A. Very.

familiar with the effect of misery. I inquired into the rations, and talked about them. I felt disposed to do my duty, and aid all the sufferers I could. They frequently asked me for a teaspoonful of salt, or for orders for a little sifting that came out of meal, as they wanted to make some bread. If I found something better than siftings, I ordered it. I spent considerable of my time in writing orders. The meat ration was cooked in a different part of the hospital. The men would gather round me, and ask for a bone. Of clothing we had none: the living were supplied with the clothing of those who died. There was a prolific crop of vermin and lice. I understand the term 'lousy' from prison-experience. On retiring from the hospital, I examined myself. It was impossible for a surgeon to leave there without bringing some with him. As to medical attendance, I found the men destitute; and of clothing, bedding, and fuel, there was only a partial supply. As the officer of the day, shortly after I arrived there, I was in supreme command; and it was my business to rectify any thing wrong. I found the men, as a general thing, destitute, partly naked, sick, and diseased. Their disposition only was to get something to eat. They asked me for orders for potatoes, biscuit, siftings of meal, and other things. The following morning, I sat down, and made a report on the condition of things I found at the hospital. The report was sent up. Being a novice, for some of the things I said, I received a written reprimand, signed by Dr. Dillard for Dr. R. A. Stevenson. Medicines being scarce, I gathered up a large quantity of what were the best attainable,—antiscorbutic, as well as to soothe the alimentary canal, and to cure complaints of gangrene. I think the reports were not heeded. My attention was called to a patient in my ward who was only fifteen or sixteen years of age. I took much interest in him, owing to his youth. He would ask me to bring him a potato, bread, or biscuit, which I did. I put them in my pocket. He had the scurvy and gangrene. I advised him not to cook the potato, but to eat it raw. He became more and more emaciated, his sores gangrened; and for want of food, and from lice, he died. I understood that it was against orders to take anything in to the prisoners; and hence I was shy in slipping food into my pockets. Others in the ward came to their deaths from the same causes. When I went there, there were two thousand or two thousand five hundred sick. I judge twenty or twenty-five thousand persons were crowded together. Some had made holes and burrows in the earth: those under the sheds were doing comparatively well. I saw but little shelter, excepting what ingenuity had devised. I found them suffering with scurvy, dropsy, diarrhœa, gangrene, pneumonia, and other diseases. When prisoners died, they were laid in wagons, head-foremost, to be carried off. I don't know how they were buried. The effluvia from the hospital was very offensive. If by accident my hand were abraded, I would not go into the hospital without putting a plaster over the affected part. If persons whose systems were reduced by inanition should perchance stump a toe, or scratch the hand, the next report to me was gangrene, so potent was the regular hospital gangrene. The prisoners were more thickly confined in the stockade, like ants and bees. The dogs referred to were to hunt the prisoners who escaped. Fifty per cent of those who died might have been saved. I feel safe in saying seventy-five might have been saved, had the patients been properly cared for. The effect of the treatment of the prisoners was morally as well as physically injurious. There was much stealing among them. All lived each for himself. I suppose this was superinduced by their starving condition. Seeing the dying condition of some of them, I remarked to my student, 'I can't resuscitate them; the weather is chilling: it is a matter of impossibility.' I found persons lying dead sometimes among the living: thinking they merely slept, I went to wake them up, and found they had taken their everlasting sleep. This was in the hospital. I judge it was about the same in the stockade. There being no dead-house, I erected a tent for that purpose: but I soon found that a blanket or quilt had been clipped off of the canvas; and, as the material could not be readily supplied for repairs, the dead-house had to be abandoned. I don't think any more dead-houses were erected. The daily ration was less in September, October, November, and December, than it was from the 1st of January to the 20th of March. The men had not over twenty ounces of food for twenty-four hours."

Of course, there were sometimes gleams of sunlight in those dreary prison-cells; but the hours of brightness were "few, and far between," while the night of horror generally settled down upon the occupants, — a night of dense, starless, rayless obscurity, — a darkness which, like that of Egypt, could be felt.

A member of an Illinois veteran battalion * was captured, with three hundred and seventy others, by the rebels, and taken to Andersonville, but, after some months of imprisonment, escaped. From his own account, published in the "Woodstock Sentinel," the following is taken: —

"We were then turned over to the Alabama State troops, and marched across the country to Columbus, some thirty miles, and treated more like brutes than human beings. If a man became tired, and began to straggle, or stop for a drink of water, they would take out their revolvers, and threaten to shoot us; and at night they camped us where we could get neither water nor wood. We arrived at Columbus, Oct. 10, and, the next morning, took the cars for Andersonville. While at Columbus, we found a paper, in which notice was given that there would be eight thousand Union soldiers in that day; and, when we (three hundred and seventy men) marched into town, they asked where the eight thousand were. We told them that they had gone the other way; and that Sherman had taken them, instead of Hood.

"There we bought a pail of water, for which we paid fifty cents: and while some eight or ten were standing about it, drinking, the officers rode up, and ordered us away; but, as we did not move quite quick enough to suit them, one fired his pistol among us. Fortunately no one was hurt. Oct. 11, we arrived at Andersonville. After taking our names, searching us closely, and taking our knapsacks from

---

* Frank E. Hanaford, of Woodstock.

us (fortunately we had but little money for them, as we had not been paid for a long time), we were counted into squads of a hundred, and turned into the bull-pen, where we remained just one month; and good Lord deliver me from ever getting in such a place again! I have heard and read of the horrors of a prison-life; but I never could believe from another one-half of what I have seen. I saw many there who seemed lost to all reason; and I have seen men lay there in the sand, and die, and others begging to be shot to end their misery, with no one to help them in the least. Oh! I saw far more suffering there than I ever saw on the battle-field. From the last of March, 1864, to September, there were fifteen thousand men died at Andersonville, as I had it from those who were there, and kept account of the dead that were carried out each day.

"There was a gang there called the Raiders, who, when they saw a prisoner come in with any thing they wanted, would kill and rob him. Finally the rebel officers refused to serve any more rations until there was a stop put to it. Then the prisoners took a lot of them, organized a court-martial, tried them, and sentenced five to be hung. A gallows was erected in the centre of the prison, and they were launched into eternity. This put a stop to it in a measure."

The narrative of Lieut. Hanaford's escape is of such interest, that the closing portion of it is here given. He, with four others, started from a place in Georgia, about twelve miles from Thomasville, where the cars which contained prisoners were detained in the woods, because the locomotive gave out. He says, —

"We threw our blankets over our shoulders, and walked boldly out through the guard-lines, though trembling with fear. We ate our supper just before we started, and took with us one quart of meal, one quart of beans, an old tin pail, and a gourd, for five of us. This was on the night of the 11th of December. We found no place where we dare make a fire to cook any thing, until the third night after we started; consequently we fasted until then. We happened to have one prairie-match with us, with which we struck a fire. There is seldom a match to be found there. On the fourth night, we were compelled to go in search of fire and food. As good luck would have it, we came to a house where they had had a fire outside during the day; and there we found an iron kettle without a bail. We hunted around, and found a rope, and put through the ears; then scraped up some coals from their fire, and put them in the kettle, which two of us took on a pole; and in that we did our cooking by day, and carried our fire by night, never losing it but twice on our journey. Then the way we got it once, we went to a man's house in the night, and told them we had a team broke down, and wanted to get a light to see to mend it up: so the good woman gave us a torch-light; and then, when we had searched the potato-hole and chicken-roost, we were all right. Twice we were hunted by blood-hounds; but a kind Providence delivered us from them. While in prison, we procured a map from which we drew a sketch of the southern part of Georgia; and this, with the stars, was our only guide. We used all the caution possible; never spoke to a person on our way, except when we called for the light;

never allowed ourselves to speak above a whisper, or step on the ties, when walking on the railroad.

"After travelling about two hundred miles by land, we came to St. Mary's River, where we found two small boats, which we confiscated; broke open a blacksmith-shop near by, and found the oars, and some other things of use, which we confiscated also: but on the river, as well as the land, we were obliged to travel by night, and hide in the woods and swamps by day, and rob potato-holes, hen-roosts, bee-hives, &c., for our subsistence, and drag our boats into the woods and swamps with us every morning. After we took to the river, we were rather short of provisions; and what we got we had to go back some four or six miles in the country for (in the night at that), as most of the plantations on the river were deserted as far up as our gunboats went.

"While on the river, we suffered a great deal from cold, as we were poorly clothed; and some nights we were obliged to lay by on that account. On the night of Jan. 31, we went ashore, on account of cold, in what proved to be the town of St. Mary, twelve miles from Fort Clinch; found an unoccupied house, procured fuel, went in, closed the doors, and made a fire in the fireplace. After getting well warmed, went out to get something to eat; but there was nothing to be found. The whole town was unoccupied; we were the only inhabitants: so we went back to our fires, and staid there until morning, and concluded we would lay by that day, and go back far enough to get something to eat, as we had been living on half-rations some two or three days. We started out, and had not gone far, when I chanced to find a spy-glass. Oh, what a treasure it proved to us! It was truly a God-send to me. We knew we had travelled a long distance, and were footsore and weary, our shoes nearly worn out, but supposed we had still many miles to travel. I raised the glass to my eye, looked southward, and saw a flag waving. The glass was not very clear, and I could not tell whether it was our flag at first, or not. I looked again: truly it was our flag. Words cannot describe the joy I felt when I beheld once more that glorious old banner floating in the breeze from Fort Clinch. We then took our boats, and started; and I doubt if ever men worked with a better will than we, or if ever a boat cut through the water faster than ours by a single pair of oars. In less than two hours, we were within our lines, at Fernandina, Fla., having travelled about two hundred and eighty miles in twenty-three days."

A Detroit paper thus speaks of one who was starved to death by the rebels: —

"There died in this city on Tuesday, of starvation, a man named Edgar B. Trumbull. We relate his story as told just before his death. He belonged to the first cavalry, was taken prisoner at the same time as the lamented Brodhead, and was sent, along with five thousand others, to Belle Isle, N.C., where they were confined in a space about as large as two ordinary city-lots. All the food allowed them was five ounces each of musty bread per day, to be washed down with an equal proportion of miserable water. Under this kind of treatment, his one hundred and eighty pounds of flesh wasted away to seventy-five pounds of skin and bones, when he was exchanged. By taking large potions of whiskey and quinine, he succeeded in keeping body and soul together until he reached this city, where he died in a few hours."

Since the close of the war, successful efforts have been made to bury properly the victims of the rebels in Andersonville. The following, from the "Springfield Republican," concerning prison-horrors, is appropriate in this chapter. We cannot wonder that our brave men died there.

"The sad duty of recovering and interring the remains of the poor fellows who died or were killed at the Andersonville prison-pen by rebel starvation and barbarity has been completed. Capt. James M. Moore, to whom the work was intrusted, has returned to Washington, and reports that he has buried, and designated the graves by head-boards, — on which were painted the name, company, and regiment of the deceased, — about thirteen thousand Union soldiers. The dead were usually buried in trenches, each trench containing about one hundred. The cemetery, which comprises in all about fifty acres, is situated about three hundred yards from the prison stockade. A neat white fence has been erected around it, and an abundance of trees have been planted to shade the graves of those who would have been more than thankful for a bit of shade when confined in the prison-pen. By means of a stake at the head of each grave, as made by the rebels, which bore a number corresponding with a similar numbered name upon the Andersonville hospital-records, the bodies of all but about five hundred of our prisoners were recognized, and proper headstones placed above their remains in the new cemetery.

"Capt. Moore found the prison-pen in a perfect state of preservation, just as it was left by the rebels; and even the dead-line could be plainly seen. Near the enclosure also were the dog-kennels, where the blood-hounds were kept that were used to hunt up those prisoners who had made their escape. The inhabitants in the vicinity call the place the most unhealthy in all Georgia; and indeed there is but one house in Andersonville proper. One of Capt. Moore's party died of the fever before they could complete their work and get away. Andersonville at present is guarded by a small force of Federal soldiers; and a superintendent is left in care of the buildings and grounds, who will see that every thing that pertains to the place is carefully preserved. Miss Clara Barton returns with Capt. Moore; and the whole party deserve great credit for the way in which they have performed their delicate and arduous duties."

Miss Barton, the annalist of our Union martyrs, said at that time, —

"Two hundred and seventy-six bodies were recovered yesterday from the ground known as outside of the 'dead-line,' or, as it was generally known to the public, outside of a prohibited line, beyond which they had accidentally strayed for the purpose of procuring a little fresh water, or the roots of shrubs or trees, to allay the pangs of thirst and hunger, and for so doing were barbarously murdered."

Much more might be adduced to show that the treatment

of prisoners and of Union men by the rebels was such as to call down upon the authors and perpetrators of such cruel wrongs the obloquy of the world, and that vengeance of Heaven which aways follows the violated laws of justice and humanity.

The Sanitary Commission's report concerning the sufferings and privations of United-States officers and soldiers, and a volume entitled "Atrocities of the Rebellion," by a Southern Unionist, who barely escaped with his life, contain proof enough to blacken the pages of Southern history, so that no partial historian can ever bleach or whitewash it. To use the language of the author of the latter volume, in his preface, "It may be said that the atrocities recorded in this book are isolated and extreme cases, and do not present a fair view of the matter. Would that this were true! But so far is this from being true, that the picture is altogether too faint. The atrocities related are only specimens; mere selections from an immense mass of hideous deeds of barbarism. Were the whole to be recorded, the mind would tire of and recoil from the recital; were the whole to be recorded, volumes would be required. Barbarism has characterized the Rebellion from the beginning to the present hour in every state and county and town and village and hamlet. It originated in barbarism; has been prosecuted with barbarism; and may its overthrow be the overthrow of barbarism, and give place to a higher civilization and a purer Christianity!"

The loyal heart beats sadly over the record of these infamous deeds, and remembers with pain the horrors of guerilla warfare, the atrocious attack on sleeping and defenceless men in Kansas, and all the many acts of diabolical barbarity; and mourns, as well it may,

> "Man's inhumanity to man."

Alas! the chariot-wheels of moral progress seem to have been greatly retarded in this age of unparalleled intellectual advancement; the inhabitants of a nominally Christian land thus "crucifying the Son of God afresh," and putting him to an open shame. Can the broken-hearted ones, who sigh for the absent whom angels released from the prison-horrors of the South, lift toward heaven, with tearful eyes, but forgiving hearts, a petition in the spirit of Him who prayed on cross-crowned Calvary, "Father, forgive them: they know not what they do"? It may be so, but only when they hear rumbling along the heavens, and then bursting in thunder-tones upon their ears, the assurance, "Vengeance is mine, I will repay, saith the Lord;" or when, in the stillness of that hour of spirit-communion with God, when the soul has truly "fellowship with the Father and with his Son Jesus Christ," they hear the whisper of Immanuel, "Forgive, and ye shall be forgiven."

As we peruse these records of battle and prison horrors, how blessed the thought that the promised day *shall* come, when "the sword shall be beaten into the plough-share, and the spear into the pruning-hook, and the nations shall learn war no more"!

> "Fly swiftly round, ye wheels of time,
> And bring the welcome day!"

CHAPTER VIII.

CHRISTIAN LIFE IN THE ARMY AND NAVY.

"Am I a soldier of the cross,
A follower of the Lamb?
And shall I fear to own his cause,
Or blush to speak his name?"

THE profession of arms is not necessarily one antagonistic to the possession of a Christ-like spirit, or the practice of Christian virtues. England had her "Havelock and his saints" to prove this; and America has had her scores and hundreds who have been valiant soldiers in the Union army and navy, and, at the same time, faithful servants of Christ Jesus. Above the radiant banner of their beloved land, they have seen the sacred splendors of the cross of Christ. No temptation of the camp, no privation or suffering in the hospital, no scene of reckless carnage on the battle-field or loathsome horror in the prison-cell, has been sufficient to cause their trust in God to waver, or the light of their faith in Christ and immortality to flicker in the gloom of doubt, or die out in the darkness of despair. The promise, "My grace is sufficient," has been graciously fulfilled to the soldiers of Christ and Liberty; and the weary, feeble, wounded, suffering, dying soldier has been able to say, "I can do all things through Christ which strengtheneth me."

In the present chapter, it is designed to present some examples of faith and Christian effort as evinced by men in the Union army and navy. The first is from the interesting pages of Prof. Hackett's memorial volume:—

"Among the men at the New-England Rooms, in New York (says a visitor to that place), is one from Michigan. He was shot in the head at Malvern Hill, and the optic nerve was carried away; so that he has become stone-blind. He is now well, in his general health; but will never see again. He is one of the happiest men in the land. He is a person of cheerful, but open and decided piety. 'Happy as the day is long' has its literal and expressive meaning as applied to him. It is delightful to listen to him as he speaks of what he did for the old flag while he could see, and still more to observe how he strives to be useful still, since his injury, in such ways as he can. He feels his way from couch to couch; drops, as he moves along, fitting words of sympathy and counsel; cheers up the despondent; and makes the heart glad. Those connected with the rooms assure me (says this visitor) that the tone of his happy speech and pious resignation impress all who have an opportunity to see and hear him."

The lamented Admiral Foote was a man of the Havelock stamp. Prof. Hackett says of him, "Hardly any one has appeared on the stage of action during the war more distinguished for the highest qualities of the patriot, hero, and Christian, than Admiral Foote."

Another anecdote in point, from the "Memorials," is entitled "Last Interview of the Heroes," and is as follows:—

"While at Gettysburg (says a visitor to that place), I learned the following incident from the lips of Prof. Stoever: 'At the close of the bloody battles of the 2d and 3d of July, while thousands of the soldiers were lying wounded side by side, and before even the officers could seek out and speak to their bleeding and dying friends, the command came to pursue the flying Confederates. Major-Gen. Howard, at the head of the eleventh army corps (who has been called the Havelock of the American army), hastened to the bedside of Capt. Griffeth of his staff, between whom and the general a strong personal attachment existed, to take his last farewell. He closed the door; and, after a brief interchange of sympathies, the general took his New Testament, and read to him the fourteenth chapter of John. The consolatory words have been often heard at the bed of the dying, giving strength to the soul for the last conflict. "Let not your heart be troubled: ye believe in God; believe also in me. In my Father's house are many mansions: if it were not so, I would have told you. I go to prepare a place for you: and, if I go and prepare a place for you, I will come again, and receive you unto myself; that where I am, there ye may be also."

"'The general then knelt in prayer, and commended his wounded friend to the compassionate God and Father of all those who trust in him, and, rising from his knees, clasped him in one long, fond, weeping embrace. Thus parted the heroes. One went to pursue the rebels against his Government: the other died in a few days in perfect peace, cordially acquiescing in God's will, and firmly relying on the merits of his Saviour.'"

The following anecdote is from the same volume, all whose pages demonstrate the value of the lives and services of those who have been soldiers of Liberty in our land:—

"When Col. Herman Canfield was wounded at the battle of Pittsburg Landing, knowing that his wound would be fatal, he expressed a wish to his young brother-in-law that he might be taken to his home and family. But, as the battle raged, the enemy pressed upon them; so that they were in momentary fear of being made prisoners. The surgeon, chaplain, and others who were looking after the wounded, were taken and borne away. Strange as it may appear, the two relatives were left unmolested. Alone, and in such a condition, the moment was one of anxiety and of trial to them both. His brother-in-law was not able, without aid, to convey him to a place of safety; and he expressed a fear that he should not be able to comply with his request. To this apprehension the colonel calmly replied, 'Never mind, Charley: Jesus will take me home.'

"Oh! what child-like trust, what Christian faith, is there expressed! Having lived near to God, and long trusted in his sure promises, he had no doubts now. He knew that the Lord of hosts was present on the battle-field as well as in the peaceful home. As he lay there, with his life-blood ebbing from a ghastly wound in his lungs, he testified of the goodness of God, and showed with what fearlessness a Christian may yield his soul to Him who gave it.

"At last assistance arrived, and the wounded man was borne on a stretcher through low, marshy defiles, and over rough, pathless woodland, toward the Tennessee. At night, they encamped upon its bank. It was the last night he passed upon earth: a dark and fearful one it was to his companions. A storm raged about them: the very elements seemed pouring forth their sad requiems for the dying and the dead. During the vivid flashes of lightning, they had glimpses of the agonized features of their loved commander. And many were their anxious inquiries; but he assured them, that, though his physical sufferings were great, his soul was at peace with God, and he knew he soon would be at rest. Doubtless he caught glimpses of that brighter world, where darkness and death cannot enter, because God is the light and life thereof. What that brave soldier and Christian suffered during that night of agony, none but God can know. He did not murmur at his fate, and thought not his life too great a sacrifice for the cause in which he fell.

"The following day he was removed to a hospital-ship, where his wounds were carefully dressed; but he gradually grew weaker, until evening, when, leaving tender messages for his loved wife and children, he calmly committed his soul to God, and Jesus took him home."

The following digest of letters contributed by H. C. Gannett to the "United-Service Magazine" for October, 1863, shows the state of religious feeling and effort in the navy:—

United-States Steamer "South-Carolina."

We hold service on board Sundays; and I am happy to state that many of our ship's company appear inclined to serve God. I have also set apart for the service of God a portion of Tuesday and Friday evenings, and hope we shall be rewarded with the grace and love of God. Remember this ship's company in your prayers. Trusting in the Almighty Father, who alone rules the universe, and spreads out the seas, I remain yours,

J. W. Magune.

United-States Steamer "Sonoma."

Some of our men seem neither to fear God nor man; and do not like us much, because we read the Testament and Psalms on deck. Our profession, and rebuke of swearing, cause talk about the ship; but I care not. I feel more determined than ever to serve my God and King. There are several religious men on the vessel besides myself.

William T. Walcott.

United-States Steamer "Genesee."

In trying to follow in the footsteps of our blessed Redeemer, we get along with the crew nicely. The books and tracts which you gave us have been distributed freely among the crew, all of whom seem to read with interest the printed truths they contain. Our prayer to God is that those who read may be benefited thereby. We go on deck with our Bibles; and, to all who would like to listen to the reading of it, we give an earnest invitation to join us. Some are pleased to listen, while others laugh and scoff. We are not cast down, neither are we discouraged: for the Lord he is our God; in him do we trust.

G. W. MARSTON.

Simple and unpretending as these records are, they show an amount of religious feeling which it is pleasant to know existed among our brave sailor-boys. Nor, as we have seen, were their officers deficient in genuine piety. Another anecdote of one already mentioned may illustrate this: —

"It has been mentioned, as characteristic of Commodore Foote, that he prayed as if every thing depended on God, and fought as if every thing depended on man. On a certain occasion, says the correspondent of a St. Louis paper, the commodore was present at a meeting on the Sabbath, shortly after one of his signal victories, when the minister of the church failed to appear, and the audience was kept waiting for the opening of the service. It seemed as if the opportunity for instruction and worship would be lost. The elder of the church was unwilling to officiate. Under these circumstances, Commodore Foote, on the impulse of the moment, went up to the pulpit, read a chapter in the Bible, prayed, and delivered a short discourse from the text, 'Let not your heart be troubled: ye believe in God; believe also in me.' It was unexpected to the people; nor was their wonder less when they saw his self-possession, his readiness, and the pertinence of his remarks. He seemed to be as much at home in the pulpit as he was on the deck of the 'Cincinnati' during the bombardment of Fort Henry. The audience were much affected at hearing the voice from which so lately rang out the word of command

> 'In worst extreme, and on the perilous edge
> Of battle when it raged,'

lifted up in humble acknowledgment to Heaven for the recent victory, and in earnest supplication for protection and success in days to come. Some of his own soldiers were among the hearers. They were expecting to be called to go into battle again at any moment. They could have heard nothing from any one better fitted to tranquillize their minds, and nerve them for the conflict.

"On coming down from the pulpit, the minister, who had arrived just after the prayer, approached, and tendered his thanks; but the commodore rebuked him for his tardiness, and also for his neglect to take the pulpit immediately on his arrival."

Prof. Hackett also says, "Commodore Foote, the praying commodore, as he has been truthfully called, acted often as his own chaplain. The following sketch of the services on his flatboat, on a certain Sunday, was given in a letter from the Mississippi fleet. It affords another proof of the anxiety of this noble man for the spiritual welfare of those who served under him, and of his conviction that he would have better soldiers in them, if he could lead them to honor God, and trust in him.

"'The sailors, clad in their clean, plain blue uniforms, congregated on the forward port-side. We look around us, and a scene presents itself very different from the ordinary employment of warlike men. Here, in line on the starboard, we see the marines drawn up in line, as at ease, with their muskets and fixed bayonets resting on their left shoulder. In the foreground is the capstan, covered with the "Union Jack," its blue field and white stars adorning the patriotic pulpit. Around it stand Flag-officer Foote, Lieut. Phelps, Col. Buford, and other officers. As the flag-officer approaches, he is saluted by all hands, who stand with uncovered heads. The gay, glittering, showy uniforms of the officers are in striking contrast with the plain garb of the seamen and marines. The flag-officer, in a few brief and eloquent remarks, reminds us that this is the Sabbath,— the day set apart for rest, and the worship of the Most High. It is the first religious service, we are told, held on this flagship, because, on the last Sabbath, we could not perform it, owing to an engagement with the enemy, which could not be avoided.

"'In the course of his address, he urged us to bear in mind our duty, to be prepared to meet our Maker; and hoped that all, officers and men, would refrain from intemperance, profanity, every immoral practice, and be ready to give their account to God, let the summons come when and as it might. He also offered up a prayer from the Episcopal service. The services were impressive and interesting. While Flag-officer Foote was praying, "Our Father who art in heaven," the report, and zip, zip, zip, of shot or shell from the enemy's guns, could be distinctly heard by all present. The flag-officer was calm and unmoved, however: he went forward eloquently and feelingly with the service, until all was concluded in due form.'"

In answer to the question, "Can the soldier be a Christian?" read the following from the "Soldier's Friend:"—

"At a prayer-meeting of soldiers in the tent of the Christian Commission, in September last, a wounded soldier arose, and, commencing with the above proposition, said, 'I find that a great many of my comrades do not believe that a soldier can be a Christian; but I *know* that they are mistaken, for I have tried it, and have found that it has power to give peace to the soul, and lift it above the fear of death. I do not believe that God saves his children from the deadly bullet by any miracle; and yet I have stood calm and peaceful while bullets rattled thick as snow-flakes about my head. And in that hour of danger, when death was reaping a rich harvest, I have looked up, and my heart has said, "Father, not my will, but thine, be done. I stand here in defence of my country and the dear flag. I desire to do my duty to it and to thee; and, in the consciousness of thy friendship and thy presence, though I walk through the valley of the shadow of death, I will fear no evil." Yes, comrades, a man *can* be a Christian and a soldier; and the Christian soldier is the happiest and serenest in every time of trouble and every hour of danger.'"

One peculiar feature in connection with the war of the Rebellion deserves special notice; viz., the revival spirit which was manifested among the soldiers from time to time. Faithful men of God were among the chaplains, who did not fail to speak to men of duty and destiny; of God's great goodness, and man's obligations. Private soldiers as well as officers were among the praying souls of many churches;

and, when they went to camp, they carried their religion with them. Some of them labored in season and out of season for the moral and religious benefit of those around them. And the ever-waiting spirit came in answer to prayer,— prayer from the camp and hospital, and prayer from pious friends at home too; and many a heart which had long resisted the influences of divine grace amid old scenes and familiar haunts, there, away from home and the dear ones of the family circle,— the heart that longed for the communion of loved friends on earth so far away,— learned to confide in and hold sweet communion with its Father in heaven.

CHAPTER IX.

LAST HOURS OF SOME OF FREEDOM'S CHAMPIONS.

> "Rest, soldier, rest; thy task is done;
> The battle calls no more for thee:
> Thou hast a nobler victory won
> Than Spartan at Thermopylæ!
> Rest thou in peace: the flag still waves,—
> The dear flag of thy love and pride;
> Its stars watch o'er our myriad graves,
> And guard our heroes who have died."
>
> DR. ARTHUR E. JENKS.

THE closing hours of a human life are always full of interest. Though they can scarcely be regarded as a criterion of character, and hopes concerning the fitness of the soul for companionship with angels, based only upon the final acts or words of the parting spirit, may be to the last degree fallacious, yet, as every act and word of each immortal is the result of influence, and exerts influence, being a part of the divine chain which links all worlds and all time in one grand whole, all have a measure of interest for the thoughtful mind; while those which precede or follow momentous changes must have a peculiar charm. It may be pleasing, and perhaps also instructive, to pause over the death-hours of some of Freedom's noble champions, and learn how Christian heroes sometimes die, cheered by an ever-brightening hope, and sustained by a trust that never faltered.

To speak of all who passed on to eternal life thus cheered and supported would be a task of too great magnitude for these pages. The flowers must be gathered here and there for the bouquet thus to be placed on martyr-graves.

And first may be remembered the earliest victims of the Rebellion, — "our Massachusetts dead in Baltimore."

"It is said that one of them, Ladd, struck by the fatal ball, struggled, stood erect, with his face towards the blue sky above him, his dying eye having caught for the last time a glimpse of the flag, and, extending his hands in joyful greeting, cried out with unfaltering voice, 'All hail to the stars and stripes!' and expired. In his agony of glory, he spoke for a continent.

"From that moment, the pavement on which he fell, the city where he so gloriously died, the States with their homes and hearts, were consecrated to Liberty and Union. And now the acclaim sounds forth from millions of hearts, from coast to inland, from mountain-top to peaceful vales and outstretching prairies. Age and infancy, manhood and womanhood, the hopeful nations, the good and brave, chant that anthem, and catch up the inspiring strain, 'All hail to the stars and stripes'!" *

Among the earliest martyrs was Col. Ellsworth, who commanded a regiment of Zouaves. The following, from the "Bugle Blast," is an account of his last moments. The regiment of Zouaves formed a part of the thirteen thousand

* H. P. Shed, Esq.

troops sent across the Potomac to Alexandria on the 24th of May, 1861. They reached Alexandria; and "after detailing Company E, Capt. Leveridge, to destroy the railroad track leading to Richmond, Col. Ellsworth directed the adjutant to form the regiment, and then with his aide, Lieut. Winser, and a file of men, proceeded, in double-quick time, up the street for the telegraph-office, to cut the wires.

"Having proceeded about three blocks, Col. Ellsworth's attention was attracted by a large secession flag flying from the roof of the Marshall House, kept by J. W. Jackson. He entered the hotel, and inquired of a man there, 'Who put that flag up?' The man answered, 'I don't know: I'm a boarder here.'

"Col. Ellsworth, Lieut. Winser, the chaplain of the regiment, a volunteer aide, and the four privates, went up to the roof; and Col. Ellsworth cut down the obnoxious flag. As the party were returning down the stairs, Francis E. Brownell, a private of Company A, being foremost, they met the man in the hall who had said he was a boarder, but who proved to be the landlord, Jackson, having a double-barrel gun, which he levelled at Brownell. Brownell struck up the gun with his musket; and Jackson, at the same instant pulling both triggers of the gun, lodged the contents of both barrels in the body of Col. Ellsworth, who was descending next to Brownell.

"Col. Ellsworth, who was at that time rolling up the flag, received the fatal charge between the second and third ribs, and immediately fell forward upon the hall floor, and exclaiming, 'My God!' instantly expired.

"Brownell instantly levelled his musket at Jackson's head, and fired. The ball struck on the bridge of the nose, and, crashing through the skull, killed him on the spot. As he fell forward, Brownell followed the shot by a bayonet-thrust through the body, pinning him to the floor." Thus was Ellsworth's death speedily avenged. Thus fell an *officer*, in the peaceful discharge of his duty, by the hand of a ruthless murderer. How die the *privates?* Let the following thrilling incident, which occurred at City-Point Hospital, answer : —

"A chaplain of the Christian Commission, while moving through the long line of sufferers, administering the consolation of the gospel, approached the bedside of a gallant fellow who was severely wounded. His earthly march was nearly ended : but, when the chaplain asked him if he was prepared to die, he motioned for pencil and paper, and with a tremulous hand wrote, ' I am prepared to go to heaven ; my trust in Jesus Christ is perfect ; ' and, immediately under, these words of assured victory over the grave, ' Come, rally round the flag, boys ! ' The chaplain took the paper, and, standing up, read it with a loud voice. Just as he concluded, a soldier, who had recently lost a hand, sprang from his bed, and, waving the mutilated stump in the air, burst forth with the glorious song his dying comrade had suggested. The effect was electric. A thousand voices took up the chorus, and the place of suffering was made to fairly rock with thunder of melody. As that vast soldier-choir ceased singing, the chaplain turned to look upon the dying brave. He was just in time to catch the last faint smile that flickered across the sunburnt face, as the soul was wafted on the strains of that Union-music to the throne of Liberty."

The following incidents were published in a Christian-Commission pamphlet: —

"On the damp ground at Falmouth lay a poor sufferer, whose body gave him no rest. Said he to the Rev. A. S. Twombly, 'Please talk to me about those things (meaning God and heaven) some more.' — 'I continued,' says Mr. Twombly, 'the conversation I had begun; when, turning about, I found him indeed *tranquilly asleep.*'"

"A dying boy from Venango County, Penn., said to a delegate, as he took his hand and placed it on his breast, 'Stay with me, oh! stay with me, and talk of Jesus until I die.' He fell asleep in that same Jesus at sundown."

"A young man from Vermont, suffering excruciating pain from the loss of his leg, said to the same delegate, 'My sufferings are beyond language to describe; but the sweetness of the precious Jesus you have brought me exceeds them.' With these words he closed his eyes on his earthly trials, to look upon the face of his Saviour."

Among our fallen heroes was Col. Baker, who fell at Ball's Bluff. He was a senator from California, and laid aside the toga for a sword, under the sense of duty. Thus speaks the "Cincinnati Commercial" concerning him and his last hours: —

"The writer met Col. Baker, in June last, on a steamer going from Baltimore to Fortress Monroe. He said he did not expect to survive the war; that, in his judgment, he never should see the shores of the Pacific again. This was hardly so much a presentiment on his part as a calculation. He said the troops were green, and it would be necessary for the officers to expose themselves. He had seen service, and would feel it a duty to lead his regiment. The enemy had plenty of sharpshooters, and he presumed they would pick him off. He said he believed it would be his fate to die at the head of his regiment; and so he died.

"It may illustrate the temper and character of the man to mention, that after saying with as perfect calmness as he could have named the most trivial circumstance, that he believed it would be his fate to fall in battle, and that he should never see his home on the Pacific again, he retired from the guards, where he had been engaged in conversation, to the cabin, and, seating himself at the piano, played, with grace and skill remarkable for a gentleman amateur on that instrument, several touching airs, among them the favorite of the English soldiers before Sevastopol, — sweet and mournful 'Annie Laurie.'"

Thus "Carleton" narrates the manner of his death : —

"The force behind the hill suddenly came over it, yelling and whooping like savages. Col. Baker was in front of his men, urging them to resist the impending shock. He was calm and collected, standing with his face to the foe, his left hand in his bosom. A man sprang from the rebel ranks, ran up behind him, and, with a self-cocking revolver, fired six bullets into him. Two soldiers in front of him fired at the same time. One bullet tore open his side;

another passed through his skull. Without a murmur, a groan, or a sigh, he fell dead.

"But, as he fell, Capt. Beirel, of the California regiment, leaped from the ranks, and blew out the fellow's brains with his pistol.

"There was a fierce and terrible fight. The Californians rushed forward to save the body of their beloved commander. They fell upon the enemy with the fury of madmen. They thought not of life or death. They had no fear. Each man was a host in himself. There was a close hand-to-hand contest, bayonet-thrusts, desperate struggles, trials of strength. Men fell, but rose again, bleeding, yet still fighting, driving home the bayonet, pushing back the foe, clearing a space around the body of the fallen hero, and bearing it from the field." *

As one thinks of the noble souls that "counted not their lives dear unto them," and passed away gloriously to their reward, he wishes for the privilege of covering acres of paper with the record. Only a meagre report can, however, here be given. Many stars in our brilliant constellation of heroes must be barely named; and many more, stars, too, "of the first magnitude," cannot be named at all.

There was Gen. Lyon, who fell at the head of the First Iowa Regiment, which had lost its colonel, while making a gallant charge upon the enemy.

The soldier-astronomer, Gen. Mitchell, — a devotee of science, whose writings are both popular and useful, —

* Following the Flag.

"His mighty life was burned away
  By Carolina's fiery sun:
The pestilence that walks by day
  Smote him before his course seemed run.

The constellations of the sky —
  The Pleiades, the Southern Cross —
Looked sadly down to see him die,
  To see a nation weep his loss."

The martyr-chaplain, Arthur Buckminster Fuller (a brother of one of America's representative women, Margaret Fuller, Countess d'Ossoli), who fell at Fredericksburg, Dec. 11, 1862. The loyal heart will never forget his noble patriotic words as he rushed forward to cross the river under fire of the enemy: "*I must do something for my country.*"

The "Knightly Soldier," how brave and noble! His last words, except words of cheering to his men, were, "*I do trust Jesus fully, wholly;*" and so the name of Major Henry W. Camp is embalmed forever.

Young Sneider, son of a veteran missionary, who was shot near Petersburg. His farewell words will sound through the ages: "Tell my brother *to stand by the flag, and cling to the cross of Christ.*"

Young Trask, the late editor of the "Kansas State Journal," who fell in the rebel raid at Lawrence. His answer will not soon be forgotten. When asked, "What will you do if the guerillas invade your State?" his reply was brave and characteristic, "I'll die for Kansas!"

"O fateful prophecy ! O fresh young lips,
  That uttered it half smiling ! did no drear
  Forecast of evil, like a dark eclipse,
Blanch their bright bloom the while, as with a mortal fear ?

'I'll die for Kansas!' Ay ; and he *has* died, —
  Died in the freshness of his young renown :
  Oh ! reverently, my country, yet with pride,
Give him his well-earned due, — a martyr's name and crown." *

The following newspaper record is of unusual interest, because it describes the patriotism of John Goldsmith Hanson, a great grand-nephew of Oliver Goldsmith, the celebrated poet : —

"When his grandmother and aunt urged on him the dangers of a soldier's life, he repeatedly said, 'God can defend me on the battle-field as well as in any other place. I can be a Christian soldier.' His spirit was a cheerful, uncomplaining one. He bore the hardships of a soldier's life without a murmur, jesting over his discomforts. He survived a dreadful attack of typhoid-fever, which confined him four months to the hospital. In the midst of camp-life, he wrote, 'I read my Bible every day.' His first battle-field was at Culpepper, Aug. 9 ; and his last letters describe the part his regiment took in the engagement. The concluding words of the letter are, 'The Union forever!' He was not heard from again till his name appeared among the list of the killed. A letter from a friend describes his death as in-

* Mrs. Caroline A. Mason.

stantaneous. He was shot through the head; and the same volley killed his friend, J. R. Mitchell."

One brave fellow, named Broad, from Concord, Mass., a member of the Massachusetts Fifty-seventh, must be mentioned, though more briefly than his heroism deserves. Seeing an officer lying in front, who had nearly lost his leg by a solid shot, and being assured, that, if he was brought in and cared for, his life might be saved, this hero said, "I have neither wife nor child to suffer if I am killed; and, if I can save that man's life, I will do it." He went therefore, and brought him in safely, but was himself wounded, so that he died shortly after.*

Brave Ulric Dahlgren, whose beautiful portrait adorns this volume, should receive in these pages more than a passing notice; and from the columns of the "American Volunteer" the following article is taken, to vindicate the character of one unjustly aspersed, and to assist in preserving unimpaired the memory of one of the most gallant and honored of the young heroes of the late Rebellion. The article is from the pen of Major Sidney Herbert, aide-de-camp, who was associated with Col. Dahlgren in the army.

"I have yet to learn that the written programme of Col. Dahlgren, which designed the burning of Richmond, the ravaging of its women, and the murder of President Davis and all his cabinet, has ever been disavowed or denounced by the *Washington* (?) Government, or by the newspapers that support it." — GEORGE AUGUSTA SALA.

"The above paragraph forms a portion of this gentle-

---

* A letter in the "Boston Journal," from Capt. H. H. Buttrick, narrated the above heroic deed.

man's introduction to a scurrilous publication entitled 'Belle Boyd in Camp and Prison.' The character of the author of the book, — Belle Boyd herself, — and the vile calumnies which its pages contain, would deter us from any notice of this infamous slander of one of the noblest and bravest heroes of this or any age of civilized warfare, were it not for the high literary reputation of its English author. He has once visited our country, and, while here, enjoyed, as we believe, to its fullest extent, the hospitality of our leading literary characters. And yet, in the hour of our deepest distress and greatest peril, he lends his name and literary talents to as vile a slander (which he repeats in his extended introduction to the book) as ever was aimed at a chivalrous and humane, but defeated and slaughtered foe. But, thank God! the foul slander lives only as a lasting reproach upon those who welcomed its birth, nourished its infancy, and then gave it wings to fly. And we now call upon all true Americans, as they have regard for the honor and fair fame of their heroic and lamented dead, to *forever* set their faces against this vile slanderer of our country, her cause, and her fallen heroes. Let him write, henceforth, if he must write for American readers, for the men and women whose cause he so readily espoused and so earnestly defended.

"Of Col. Dahlgren's last gallant exploit, which proved so fatally unsuccessful, and in which he lost his own life, his father, Rear-Admiral J. A. Dahlgren, then in command of our naval force at Charleston, thus tenderly but severely and justly speaks, in a letter which bears date July 24, 1864. He says, 'I have patiently and sorrowfully awaited the hour when I should be able to vindicate fully the memory of my gallant son, Col. Ulric Dahlgren, and lay bare to the world the atrocious imposture of those, who, not content with abusing and defacing the remains of the noble boy, have knowingly and persistently endeavored to blemish his spotless name by a forged lie.

"'That hour has at last come. I have before me a photolitho copy of the document which the inhuman traitors at Richmond pretend was found upon the body of my son after he had been basely assassinated by their chivalry at midnight, and who, on the pretext that this paper disclosed an intent to take the lives of the arch-rebel and his counsellors, and to destroy Richmond, have not hesitated to commit and commend the most shocking barbarities on the remains of the young patriot, and to exult like dastards over his sad fate.

"'I can now affirm that the document is a forgery, — a barefaced, atrocious forgery, — so palpable, that the wickedness of the act is only equalled by the recklessness with which it has been perpetrated and adhered to; for the miserable caitiffs did not confine themselves to the general terms of a mere allegation, but published the paper in all the precision of a photographic *fac-simile*, as if not to leave a doubt or cavil. I felt from the first just as if I knew the fact that my son never wrote that paper, — that it was a forgery; but I refrained from giving utterance to that faith until I had seen a sample of the infamous counterfeit, and, having seen it, could say, as I say now, that a more fiendish lie never was invented.

. . . .

"'It is well known that the cruel usage practised on the Union soldiers who were imprisoned at Richmond had become a theme at the North, and that their release from slow and horrid death was the object of the expedition. My son had just returned from a visit to me off Charleston when he learned of the project. Every one was aware that he was in no condition to take the field just then: for he had lost a leg by a wound received in a charge through Hagerstown, pending the battle of Gettysburg; and the consequent illness nearly cost him his life. The vigor of his frame had carried him through the crisis; but the wound was not perfectly healed: he was still weak, and could only move on crutches.

"'No sooner was he apprised of what was contemplated than he sought to join the enterprise, in remembrance of comrades pining in loathsome dungeons, — of men with whom he had ridden side by side amid the deadly conflict; and, a strong conviction of their sufferings animating every pulse of his gallant heart, he felt that duty called him there, and the reluctant consent of the authorities was at last yielded to his earnest entreaties.

"'It is not my purpose here to narrate the whole course of this noble enterprise; that will be the duty of a future day: but no one had seen Col. Dahlgren in his full vigor sit his charger more gracefully, or better endure the incessant and multiplied hardships of that ride, by day and by night, in shine and storm.

"'The failure of his column to connect with that of Gen. Kilpatrick led to the failure of the expedition, and the death of as noble a soldier as ever gave life to a great cause.

. . . .

"'The gallant youth fell, pierced by many balls, at the head of his men; and, even while his brave spirit lingered about its scattered tenement, the chivalry began to strip him of his clothing. Whether the detestable purpose was accomplished before he was dead, I know not; nor whether the infamous wretches paused to make sure that life was extinct before they severed a ring given by a departed sister, and deeply prized by the heart that is now as still as her own.

"'It was not until daylight disclosed the utter helplessness of the survivors that the victors took heart of grace, and consummated their brave deed by marching the wearied and famished troopers along the road, regardless of the fact that this led them by the body of their young chief, just as it lay, stripped, and covered with mud, but yet honored by the sad tokens which it exhibited of love and loyalty to the cause of his country. The absent limb told of recent battle-fields; and the breathless body gave assurance that the last sacrifice had been made. The young life, rich in promise, had been laid down; and thus was redeemed the solemn oath of fealty to the Union.

"'No respect for the well-known gallantry of their victim, no feeling for his extreme youth, entered into the thoughts of these atrocious ruffians; and only when sated with the mournful sight were the relics of the noble dead permitted such sepulture as a hasty grave could afford.

"'Be it remembered, that, to this time, nothing was known of the forged document. But presently it came to the upper chivalry of Richmond that one of the leaders of the expedition had fallen. Frenzied with terror at the possible consequences of the success of the undertaking, — for they had every reason to dread that the vengeance of the released prisoners would respect no person, — they sought a pretext for the meditated villany on the body of Col. Dahlgren, in a forgery, which, they thought, would extenuate all disregard of every dictate of manhood and humanity.

"'So they forged the lie, and gave it currency in all the minuteness of a seeming *fac-simile;* while the original counterfeit was so recklessly executed, that the shameful deceit could not fail to be apparent to any one having the least knowledge of Col. Dahlgren's handwriting.

"'So the remains of the heroic dead were torn from the grave, conveyed to Richmond, and there exposed to the taunts and gaze of a mob; then hurried away, in the obscurity of the night, to some nameless spot, whence it was intended they should never be recovered. There was an ingenuity in the contrived villany, from which the mind recoils with horror.

. . . .

"'He had not completed the first year of his manhood when he was so basely assassinated; yet, by his bravery and devotion on many a battle-field, he had won the high but well-deserved rank of colonel of cavalry. He was tall, well-built, and graceful: his frame gave every promise of future strength, but, as yet, lacked the development of the matured man, and was divested of all spare flesh by a life of constant activity in the saddle.

"'To the casual observer, he appeared like a very young and a very diffident man, gentle and unobtrusive, a moderate talker, and always of pleasant mood. But beneath lay a character of the firmest mould, a constancy of purpose never to be diverted from its object, courage that was never disturbed by any danger, impulses of the purest nature habitually in exercise, producing a course of life unblemished by the least meanness, — a good son, a warm friend, dutiful alike to God and man. I can now look back over the whole of his young life, and declare, that in no instance did he ever fail in the most respectful obedience to my least wish. A more perfect and lovely character I cannot conceive.

. . . .

"'His courage was not of that rampant character so troublesome to friend as well as to foe, but came forth instantly at the first sign of danger. To these qualities he added a deep sense of religious obligation, having been carefully trained by a departed mother to the Church and the Sunday School. But in this, as in many other respects, he was not demonstrative. When apparently at the verge of death from a wound, and reminded of the danger, he smiled, and said that he had never gone into battle without asking forgiveness of his sins, and commending his soul to his Maker. And so passed away this bright young life, so radiant in promise. Nor is it only a father's love and affection that prompts such praise, as the many who knew him will confirm.

. . . .

"'The last letter that he ever wrote was to myself. It was from camp, just before putting foot in stirrup, and about to set out on the last of a brilliant and eventful career. He directed that it should only be given to me in the event of his not returning. He speaks of the enterprise as "glorious, and that he would be ashamed to show his face again if he had failed to go in it." He expressed himself as fully sensible of the danger, and concludes thus: "If we do not return, there is no better place to give up the ghost."'

"Such was the brave and generous spirit whose light has been so early quenched forever. That of itself might have sufficed to sate the vengeance even of traitors. The shocking cruelty that has been exhibited to his inanimate body, and the perpetration of a forgery to justify it, will, in the end, recoil on the infamous ruffians.

"To the gallant young soldier it has been as nothing. He had passed away to his final account, leaving behind him a name far beyond the reach of the chivalry. There are those left, however,—his distinguished father, two lovely and bereaved sisters, and a patriotic and heroic brother, who, with the father, has done good service for the country,—whose pride and pleasure it will be to vindicate his fair fame. He will ever be remembered as a young patriot of spotless life and purest purpose; honest, true, and gentle, dutiful to every obligation, unselfish and generous to a fault;

an undaunted soldier of the Union, who never struck a blow at an unarmed enemy, but carefully and kindly respected the claims of defenceless women and children; an accomplished gentleman, a sincere Christian, a faithful comrade, who, not recovered from the almost fatal illness consequent on losing a limb in battle, went forth to brave every hardship in the hope of aiding in the release of our captive soldiers from the dungeons of a merciless enemy, who, for this, treated his dead body with savage ferocity, and hesitated not to forge his name.

"Peace to his ashes, where they now finally rest, amid the scenes of his boyhood, and by the side of his sainted mother! The laurels on the young and fair brow of Ulric Dahlgren will never fade while there are true men and women in the land to keep them green. The poet has truly said, —

> 'Ulric Dahlgren, in the story
> Of thy country's grief and wrong,
> Thine shall stand a name of glory,
> Bright in history and song.'

"On Tuesday, Oct. 31, 1865, his recently recovered body was brought to Washington, where appropriate services were held, preparatory to its removal to Philadelphia for final interment. The occasion was one of unusual interest: but a severe storm prevented the anticipated military display; and the body, having lain in state at the City Hall, where it was viewed by thousands of sorrowful hearts, was escorted by the nearest route to the Presbyterian Church in Four and a Half Street. The military escort consisted of the Eighth Regiment of Hancock's Veteran Volunteers, detachments of the Seventh, Tenth, Fourteenth, and Eighteenth Regiments Veteran Reserve Corps, and the Hundred and Ninety-fifth and Two Hundred and Fourteenth Pennsylvania Volunteers, all under the command of Brig.-Gen. Gile, of the Veteran Reserve Corps. The pall-bearers occupied the head of the procession, and consisted of the following officers, — Brevet-Brig.-Gen. D. P. Dewitt, Tenth Veteran Reserve Corps; Brevet-Brig.-Gen. D. B. McKibben, Two Hundred and Fourteenth Pennsylvania; Brig.-Gen. S. D. Oliphant, Fourteenth Veteran Reserve Corps; Col. J. W. Fisher, One Hundred and Ninety-fifth Pennsylvania; Brevet-Col. R. E. Johnson, Ninth Veteran Reserve Corps; Col. Charles F. Johnson, Eighteenth Veteran Reserve Corps; Col. F. E. Pierce, Eighth United-States Veteran Volunteers; Brevet-Col. John B. Collis, Seventh Veteran Reserve Corps. The coffin was placed before the pulpit, which was draped, as were also the galleries, with large American flags. The church was darkened, and lighted with gas; and, as every available seat or standing-place was occupied, the effect was most solemn and impressive. The President, and members of the cabinet, distinguished army and navy officers, clerks, citizens, and ladies, notwithstanding the inclemency of the weather, came together on this mournful occasion to pay their tribute of respect to one of the noblest young heroes that ever drew a sword in a righteous cause.

"At the conclusion of the introductory services, which were of a deeply impressive character, the Rev. Henry

Ward Beecher delivered a funeral oration, full of eloquent and tender words of eulogy, and marked by his usual vigor and earnestness.

"The burial casket was draped with the national colors, and garlands of flowers were strewn on the top. A splendid photograph of Col. Dahlgren lay at the head of the bier, as well as the following autograph-letter of Secretary Stanton, which accompanied young Dahlgren's commission as colonel, in which the Secretary thus paid earnest tribute to the hero's gallant services:—

"'WASHINGTON, July 21, 1863.

"'DEAR SIR:— Enclosed you have a commission for colonel, without having passed through the intermediate grade of major. Your gallant and meritorious service has, I think, entitled you to the distinction, although it is a departure from general usage, which is only justified by distinguished merit such as yours. I hope you may speedily recover; and it will rejoice me to be the instrument of your further advancement in the service.

"'With great regard, I am yours truly,

"'EDWIN M. STANTON.'

"The remains were escorted, at the close of the services, to the depot, and were taken by the evening train to Philadelphia, where they laid in state, in Independence Hall, during the night.

"The final funeral services were held in the morning; the Rev. J. P. Wilson, of Newark, delivering an appropriate discourse. The body was then removed to Laurel Hill, that beautiful "city of the dead," — so like our own beloved Mount Auburn, — escorted by six companies of the Seventh Regiment of the first army corps, and two companies of marines and city troops, who acted as a guard of honor. Among the distinguished officers present were Rear-Admiral Dahlgren, the father of the deceased, and Gens. Meade and Humphreys. His Honor the Mayor was also of the party.

"No loyal heart can fail to thank God with feelings of devout gratitude, as well for himself as for a brave officer and bereaved family, that the mortal remains of the chivalrous young hero were at last recovered from a ruthless burial in rebel soil, and brought home, — back to the scenes of his earlier years, — there to be finally entombed with all the honors due the highest type of Christian knighthood.

"A brief career was his; and yet how noble, how sublime, its well-filled record! How many and how brilliant were his exploits by day and by night! How well do I remember him — the last time I ever saw his manly face — as he appeared at Gettysburg! — so brave and hopeful, so full of zeal and patriotic ardor. It is impossible not to be inspired by his very presence.

"Soon after this he was severely wounded, and, when all hope was lost, suffered the amputation of his foot and ankle. In this condition he paid a visit to his father, then in command of our naval force before Charleston. Writing to a friend from that place, he says, 'I stay to take part in the great fight: if I die, what more glorious than the death of men fighting for their country?' Such a death, soon after, but not then and there, was his fate, — a noble and heroic struggle against all hope of success, and a death and burial such as would disgrace the fiendish warriors of a savage tribe.

"Ulric Dahlgren deserved a better fate than this, even at the hands of his enemies; for they had never found him other than a brave, honorable, and humane foe."

Only one more record, and the list will be reluctantly closed. John B. Marsh, a Union soldier, was a prisoner among the rebels, forced into their ranks, and, on deserting, was recaptured, and then shot. He succeeded in giving the following note to a fellow-prisoner: —

"Kind friend, if ever you reach our happy lines, have this put into the Northern papers, that my father, Rev. Leonard Marsh, who resides in Maine, may know what has become of me, and what I was shot for. I am to be shot for defending my country. I love her, and am willing to die for her. Tell my parents I am also happy in the Lord. My future is bright. I hope to speak to you as I pass out to die. "JOHN B. MARSH."

"One of the guards told Mr. Shipman, that when young Marsh was placed by his coffin, and ready to receive the fire of his executioners, he was told he could speak a word if he desired to. He took off his hat, and, looking upon them, cried out, 'Three cheers for the old flag and the Union!' then, swinging his hat, shouted at the top of his voice, '*Hurrah, hurrah, hurrah!*' and fell a noble martyr to the dear old flag." *

* New-York Evangelist.

Thus have our loyal braves passed on to their reward. We are proud of the record,* — we who love the flag in whose defence they died.

Thank God for the hope of meeting those among them whom we knew and loved, where Affection's amaranthine flower blooms in its undying beauty, while the angels will gather the immortal blossoms, and crown the ransomed children of earth with fadeless garlands!

---

* Many loyal towns are wisely preserving the names of their own heroes by erecting monuments to their memory. An elegant marble shaft, surmounted by an eagle, thus commemorates the heroic dead of Reading, Mass. The following ode, written by the author of these pages, was sung at the inauguration of the monument: —

Air, — "Pleyel's Hymn."

To this sacred spot we come,
Half triumphant, half in gloom;
Thinking of the brave and blest
Gone to share a patriot's rest.

Now the marble shaft we rear:
Hero-names recorded there,
Telling to all coming time
Of their patriot deeds sublime.

And though far from us repose
Some that bravely met our foes,
Near or far they all shall be
Honored by the pure and free.

Lord! may we life's conflict meet,
As they went, with willing feet;
Crowned as victors may we rise,
Meet our brave ones in the skies!

CHAPTER X.

THE MARTYR OF MARTYRS.

"Great in his grasp of thought, and good as wise, —
  Not one pale shadow on his fame to rest :
Honor, love, trust, and all that good men prize,
  Were well-worn treasures of his guileless breast.
We dare not count our loss, but strive to see
Through the thick darkness where God's light may be.

Bring for his honored head the laurel-crown ;
  Low at his feet Spring's loveliest blossoms spread ;
On spotless marble grave his fair renown,
  And write his name among our noblest dead.
Deep in the nation's heart his rest shall be,
Till time is lost in far eternity."

"L.," in the "BOSTON TRANSCRIPT."

ONE of the greatest men of modern times was ABRAHAM LINCOLN, and one of the best for his time and place. His name is more deeply graven in the hearts of the loyal American people to-day than that of any that adorns the storied shaft of any age. Nor is monumental marble needed for a man whose fame belongs not only to his country, but to humanity ; not only to the nineteenth century, but to the ages. It outshines the sun ; it will outlast the nation ; for it will live as the name of a Messiah, even till all nations shall be merged into that great kingdom whose endless duration was the burden of ancient prophecy, and is still the theme of immortal song.

Born amid the obscurity of log-cabin life in Kentucky, on the 12th of February, 1809, Abraham Lincoln, by dint of untiring effort and undaunted perseverance, aided by a good conscience and pioneer health, rose to eminence as a lawyer and a statesman, and on the 4th of March, 1861, took his seat in the chair of Washington, as the acknowledged head of the nation.

Then followed four years of sanguinary conflict. The Quaker blood of the new President asked for peace; but the rebel horde would not accept an olive-branch from him, and saw only in his inaugural address a declaration of war.

God reserved for this man, whom he had ordained to be a " Saul among his brethren" in more than one sense, the high privilege of issuing a proclamation, which, in all coming time, should rank with the Magna Charta and the Declaration of Independence, — the Proclamation of Emancipation, whereby the chains of slavery were broken, and millions made forever free beneath the glorious banner of our country. This proclamation came in force on New-Year's Day, 1863. For its issue, the colored people of our land now look upon him as their deliverer, — the Messiah who came to proclaim liberty to the captives, the Moses who should lead them to the Promised Land.

And truly he was like Moses: for he only saw the land; he did not stay to possess it. By the ruthless hand of a barbarous assassin, while seeking a little rest from crushing labors, in Ford's Theatre, at Washington, April 14, 1865, the great and good man was cruelly murdered. The news of the assassination darted along the wires, and a nation's eyes flashed fire: the intelligence of the death of this preeminent martyr followed, and a nation wept. And this is no figure of speech. Strong men shed tears as they heard "The President is dead!" and their home-circles were as one band of weeping mourners for him who seemed a personal friend to all. The funeral services all over the loyal North told again the grief at first manifested.*

This brief sketch of the life of the martyr of martyrs in our country's struggle is all that can here be furnished. Able pens have written his biography again and again; and the reader is advised to seek such records of a stainless life and heroic death.

---

* The following hymn, by the writer of these pages, was sung in Reading, Mass., on the day of the funeral: —

Air, — "Mount Vernon."

Hushed to-day are sounds of gladness
  From the mountains to the sea,
While the plaintive voice of sadness
  Rises, mighty God! to thee.

Freedom claimed another martyr;
  Heaven received another saint.
Who are we, thy will to question?
  Lord, we weep without complaint.

May we, to thy wisdom bowing,
  Own thy love in this dark spell,
While with tears a mighty nation
  Buries one it loved so well!

And O Thou who took our leader,
  With the Promised Land in view,
While on Pisgah's height we leave him,
  Lead us, Lord, the Jordan through!

A few incidents, however, in his life, may here be mentioned. Here is a record of his visit to Antietam, by John W. Garrett, Esq.,* which reveals the true nobility of the future martyr: —

"By his request, I accompanied President Lincoln, immediately after the battle of Antietam, to the scene of that sanguinary conflict, after passing over the Baltimore and Ohio Road from Washington to Harper's Ferry. I continued with him, by his desire, during the memorable period he spent with the officers and soldiers of the Federal army, and among the hospitals, and the wounded upon that bloody field. As in accord with the spirit of your fraternity, I will mention a scene which occurred in one of those hospitals, which bedewed many eyes.

"The President examined kindly and tenderly into the condition and care of the Federal wounded. He also passed through the hospitals where were placed the Confederate wounded. Many of these hospitals, in view of the large number of the wounded, were improvised from the barns upon and in the vicinity of the field of battle. Passing through one of these, the middle space of an extensive Switzer barn, where a large number of Confederate wounded lay, the President stopped about the centre of the apartment, opposite to a youth of striking appearance, probably of eighteen or twenty years of age. He lay looking very feeble and pallid. He held three straws in his hand, and was feebly moving

---

* Mr. Garrett was presiding at a banquet given by Baltimore merchants to the United-States Convention of Odd Fellows.

them to keep the insects from his face. The President asked if he had received all necessary attention. He replied that he had; that his right leg had been amputated. The President responded, 'I trust you will get well.' The youth, great tears rolling from his eyes, said, 'No; I am sinking: I shall die.' The President leaned tenderly over him, and said, 'Will you shake hands with me?' I remarked, 'This is President Lincoln.' He attempted to raise his hand, and gave it to the President. The President asked him, 'Where are you from?'—'From Georgia.' Again the President expressed the hope, still holding his hand, that he would recover. 'No,' said the youth; 'I shall never see my mother again: I shall die.' The President still held his hand, and fervently ejaculated, whilst he wept, and his tears mingled with those of the sufferer, 'May God bless you, and restore you to your mother and your home!' Amid all the sad scenes of that field of carnage, coming forth from that sanctified spot, I said, 'Mr. President, such kindness will make missionaries of good will of the soldiers who return South to their homes.' The President then expressed his wishes generally to those accompanying him, that all the wounded and all the sufferers should be kindly treated, and, in the course of conversation thereafter, expressed sanguine hopes, that at an early day, instead of such scenes of suffering, scenes of concord and of good feeling, and a restored Union, would be speedily realized."

The following letter from the President is also a proof of his sympathy with the bereaved who mourn the loss of patriot friends. The lady who received this letter was a poor widow, residing in Boston. Her sixth son, when the letter was published, was lying in a hospital.

EXECUTIVE MANSION, WASHINGTON,
Nov. 25, 1864.

DEAR MADAM, — I have been shown, in the files of the War Department, a statement of the Adjutant-General of Massachusetts, that you are the mother of five sons who died gloriously on the field of battle. I feel how weak and fruitless must be any words of mine which should attempt to beguile you from the grief of a loss so overwhelming; but I cannot refrain from tendering to you consolation that may be found in the thanks of the Republic they died to save. I pray that our heavenly Father may assuage the anguish of your bereavement, and leave you only the cherished memory of the loved and lost, and the solemn pride that must be yours to have laid so costly a sacrifice upon the altar of Freedom.

Yours very sincerely and respectfully,

To Mrs. BIXBY, Boston, Mass. . A. LINCOLN.

The manner in which Secretary Seward came to know of the death of President Lincoln was singularly touching. A correspondent of the "Philadelphia Bulletin" says, —

"Mr. Seward had been kept in ignorance of the attack on the President, his physician fearing that the shock would be too great for him to bear; and all newspapers were rigidly excluded from his room. On the Sunday following the assassination, the Secretary had the bed wheeled around so that he could see the tops of the trees in the park opposite, just putting on the spring foliage ; when his eye caught the stars and stripes at half-mast on the War Department, on which he gazed a while, then, turning to his attendant said, ' The President is dead ! ' The attendant stammered, and changed color, as he tried to say nay ; but the sagacious old man said, ' If he had been alive, he would have been the first to call on me ; but he has not been here, nor has he sent to know how I am : and there's the flag at half-mast.' The old statesman's inductive reasoning had told the truth ; and he lay in silence, tears coursing down his gashed cheeks as the dreadful truth sank into his mind."

The following well illustrates the character of the martyr of martyrs. It is from the pen of a correspondent in the "New-York World."

" I am sitting in the President's office. He was here very lately ; but he will not return to dispossess me of this high-backed chair he filled so long, nor resume his daily work at the table where I am writing.

" There are here only Major Hay, and the friend who accompanies me. A bright-faced boy runs in and out, darkly attired, so that his fob-chain of gold is the only relief to his mourning garb. This is little Tad, the pet of the White House. That great death with which the world rings has made upon him only the light impression which all things make on childhood. He will live to be a man pointed out everywhere for his father's sake ; and, as folks look at him, the tableau of the murder will seem to encircle him.

" The room is long and high, and so thickly hung with

maps, that the color of the wall cannot be discerned. The President's table, at which I am seated, adjoins a window at the farthest corner; and to the left of my chair, as I recline in it, there is a longer table, before an empty grate, around which there are many chairs, where the Cabinet used to assemble. The carpet is trodden thin, and the brilliance of its dyes is lost. The furniture is of the formal cabinet class, stately and semi-comfortable. There are bookcases, sprinkled with the spare library of a country lawyer, but lately plethoric, like the thin body which has departed in its coffin. They are taking away Mr. Lincoln's private effects, to deposit them wheresoever his family may abide; and the emptiness of the place, on this sunny Sunday, revives that feeling of desolation from which the land has scarce recovered. I rise from my seat, and examine the maps: they are from the coast-survey and the engineer departments, and exhibit all the contested ground of the war. There are pencil lines upon them, where some one has traced the route of armies, and planned the strategic circumferences of campaigns. Was it the dead President who so followed the march of empire, and dotted the sites of shock and overthrow?

"Here is the Manassas country; here the long reach of the wasted Shenandoah; here the wavy line of the James, and the sinuous Peninsula. The wide campagna of the Gulf country sways in the Potomac breeze that filters in at the window; and the Mississippi climbs up the wall, with blotches of blue and red to show where blood gushed at the bursting of deadly bombs. So in the half-gloomy, half-grand apartment roamed the tall and wrinkled figure, whom the country had summoned from his plain home into mighty history, with the geography of the Republic drawn into a narrow compass, so that he might lay his great brown hand upon it everywhere. And walking to and fro, to and fro, to measure the destinies of arms, he often stopped, with his thoughtful eyes upon the carpet, to ask if his life were real, and he were the arbiter of so tremendous issues, or whether it was not all a fever-dream, snatched from his sofa in the routine office of the prairie State.

"There is but one picture on the marble mantle over the cold grate, — John Bright, — a photograph.

"I can well imagine how the mind of Mr. Lincoln often went afar to the face of Bright, who said such kindly things of him when Europe was mocking his homely guise and provincial phraseology. To Mr. Lincoln, John Bright was the standard-bearer of America and Democracy in the Old World. He thrilled over Bright's bold denunciations of peer and ' privilege,' and stretched his long arm across the Atlantic to take that daring Quaker innovator by the hand.

"I see some books on the table, — perhaps they have lain there undisturbed since the reader's dimming eyes grew nerveless, — a parliamentary manual, a thesaurus, and two books of humor, ' Orpheus C. Kerr ' and ' Artemus Ward.' These last were read by Mr. Lincoln in the pauses of his hard day's labor. Their tenure here bears out the popular verdict of his partiality for a good joke. And through the window, from this seat of Mr. Lincoln, I see, across the grassy grounds of the Capitol, the broken shaft of the Washington Monument, the Long Bridge, and the fort-tipped Heights of Arlington, reaching down to the shining riverside. These scenes he looked at often to catch some freshness of leaf and water, and often raised the sash to let the world rush in where only the nation abided; and hence on that awful night he departed early, to forget this room and its close applications in the *abandon* of the theatre.

"I wonder if that were the least of Booth's crimes to slay this public servant in the stolen hours of recreation he enjoyed but seldom. We worked his life out here, and killed him when he asked a holiday.

"Outside of this room there is an office, where his secretaries sat, — a room more narrow, but as long; and, opposite this adjunct office, a second door, directly behind Mr. Lincoln's chair, leads, by a private passage, to his family quarters. This passage is his only monument in the building: he added or subtracted nothing else. It tells a long story of duns and loiterers, contract-hunters and seekers for commissions, garrulous parents on paltry errands, toadies without measure, and talkers without conscience. They pressed upon him through a great door opposite his window, and, hat in hand, came courtesying to his chair, with an obsequious 'Mr. President!'

"If he dared, though the chief magistrate and commander of the army and navy, to go out by the great door, these vampires leaped upon him with their Babylonian pleas, and barred his walk to his hearthside. He could not insult them, since it was not in his nature; and perhaps many of them had really urgent errands. So he called up the carpenter, and ordered a strategic route cut from his office to his hearth, and perhaps told of it after with much merriment.

"Here should be written the biography of his official life, — in the room where have concentrated all the wires of action, and whence have proceeded the resolves which vitalized in historic deeds. But only great measures, however carried out, were conceived in this office.

. . . .

"As I hear from my acquaintances here these episodes of the President's life, I recall many reminiscenses of his ride from Springfield to Harrisburg, over much of which I passed. Then he left home, and became an inhabitant of history. His face was solid and healthy, his step young, his speech and manner bold and kindly. I saw him at Trenton stand in the Legislature, and say, in his conversational intonation, —

"'We may have to put the foot down firm.'

"How should we have hung upon his accents then, had we anticipated his virtues and his fate!

"Death is requisite to make opinion grave. We looked upon Mr. Lincoln then as an amusing sensation; and there was much guffaw as he was regarded by the populace: he had not passed out of partisan ownership. Little by little, afterward, he won esteem, and often admiration, until the measure of his life was full, and the victories he achieved made the world applaud him. Yet, at this date, the President was sadly changed. Four years of perplexity and devotion had wrinkled his face, and stooped his shoulders;

and the failing eyes that glared upon the play closed as his mission was completed, and the world had been educated enough to comprehend him.

"The White House has been more of a republican mansion under his control than for many administrations. Uncouth guests came to it often, typical of the simple Western civilization of which he was a graduate; and, while no coarse altercation has ever ensued, the portal has swung wide for four years.

"A friend, connected with a Washington newspaper, told me that he had occasion to see Mr. Lincoln one evening, and found that the latter had gone to bed. But he was told to sit down in the office, and directly the President entered. He wore only a night-shirt; and his long, lank, hirsute limbs, as he sat down, inclined the guest to laughter. Mr. Lincoln disposed of his request at once, and manifested a desire to talk. So he reached for the cane which my friend carried, and conversed in this manner: —

"'I always used a cane when I was a boy. It was a freak of mine. My favorite one was a knotted beech stick, and I carved the head myself. There's a mighty amount of character in sticks. Don't you think so? You have seen these fishing-poles that fit into a cane? Well, that was an old idea of mine. Dogwood-clubs were favorite ones with the boys. I s'pose they use 'em yet. Hickory is too heavy, unless you get it from a young sapling. Have you ever noticed how a stick in one's hand will change his appearance? Old women and witches wouldn't look so without sticks. Meg Merrilies understands that.'

"In this way, my friend, who is a clerk in a newspaper-office, heard the President talk for an hour. The undress of the man, and the triteness of his subject, would be staples for merriment if we did not reflect that his greatness was of no conventional cast; that the playfulness of his nature, and the simplicity of his illustration, lightened public business, but never arrested it.

. . . .

"It will not do to say definitely in this notice how several occasional writers visited the White House, heard the President's views, and assented to them, and afterward abused him. But these attained no remembrance, nor tart reproach, from that least retaliatory of men. He harbored no malice, and is said to have often placed himself on the stand-point of Davis and Lee, and accounted for their defection while he could not excuse it.

"He was a good reader, and took all the leading New-York dailies every day. His secretaries perused them, and selected all the items which would interest the President: these were read to him, and considered. He bought few new books, but seemed ever alive to works of comic value. The vein of humor in him was not boisterous in its manifestations, but touched the geniality of his nature; and he reproduced all that he absorbed, to elucidate some new issue, or turn away argument by a laugh.

"As a jester, Mr. Lincoln's tendency was caricatured by the prints, but not exaggerated. He probably told as many stories as are attributed to him, but not all that are attributed to him. Nor did he, as is averred, indulge in these jests on solemn occasions. No man felt with such personal intensity the extent of the casualties of his time; and he often gravely reasoned whether he could be in any way responsible for the bloodshed and devastation over which it was his duty to preside.

"An acquaintance of mine, a printer, once went to him to plead for a man's life. He had never seen the man for whom he pleaded, and had no acquaintance with the man's family. Mr. Lincoln was touched by his disinterestedness, and said to him, —

"'If I were any thing but the President, I would be constantly working as you have done.'

"Whenever a doubt of one's guilt lay on his mind, the man was spared by his direct interference.

"There was an entire absence, in the President's character, of the heroic element. He would do a great deed in *dishabille* as promptly as in full dress. He never aimed to be brilliant, unconsciously understanding that a great man's brilliancy is to be measured by the 'wholeness' and synthetic cast of his career, rather than by any fitful ebullitions. For this reason, we look in vain through his messages for 'points.' His point was not to turn a sentence or an epigram, but to win an effect, regardless of the route to it.

"He was commonplace in his talk, and Chesterfield would have had no patience with him. His dignity of character lay in his uprightness. rather than in his formal manner. Members of his government often reviewed him plainly in his presence; yet he divined the true course, while they only argued it out.

"His good feeling was not only personal, but national. He had no prejudice against any race or potentate; and his democracy was of a practical rather than of a demonstrative nature. He was not Marat, but Moreau; not Paine and Jefferson, but Franklin.

"His domestic life was like a parlor at night-time, lit by the equal grate of his genial and uniform kindness. Young Thaddy played with him upon the carpet: Robert came home from the war, and talked to his father as to a schoolmate. He was to Mrs. Lincoln as chivalrous on the last day of his life as when he courted her. I have somewhere seen a picture of Henry IV. of France riding his babies on his back: that was the President.

"So dwelt the citizen who is gone, — a model in character, if not in ceremony, for good men to come who will take his place in this same White House, and find their generation comparing them to the man thought worthy of assassination. I am glad to sit here in his chair, where he has bent so often, in the atmosphere of the household he purified, in the sight of the green grass and the blue river he hallowed by gazing upon, in the very centre of the nation he preserved for the people, and close the list of bloody deeds, of desperate flights, of swift expiations, of renowned obsequies, which I have written, by inditing at his table the goodness of his life and the eternity of his memory."

The following graphic picture, from the inimitable pen of "Carleton," shows how the freedmen regard their great deliverer: —

"I was standing upon the bank of the river, viewing the

scene of desolation, when a boat, pulled by twelve sailors, came up stream. It contained President Lincoln and his son, Admiral Porter, Capt. Penrose of the army, Capt. A. H. Adams of the navy, Lieut. W. W. Clemens of the signal corps. Somehow the negroes on the bank of the river ascertained that the tall man wearing a black hat was President Lincoln. There was a sudden shout. An officer, who had just picked up fifty negroes to do work on the dock, found himself alone. They left work, and crowded round the President. As he approached, I said to a colored woman, —

"'There is the man who made you free.'

"'What, massa?'

"'That is President Lincoln.'

"'Dat President Linkum?'

"'Yes.'

"She gazed at him a moment, clapped her hands, and jumped straight up and down, shouting 'Glory, glory, glory!' till her voice was lost in the universal cheer.

"There was no carriage near; so the President, leading his son, walked three-quarters of a mile up to Gen. Weitzel's headquarters, — Jeff. Davis's mansion. What a spectacle it was! Such a hurly-burly, such wild, indescribable, ecstatic joy, I never witnessed. A colored man acted as guide. Six sailors, wearing their round blue caps and short-jackets and bagging pants, with navy carabines, were the advance guard: then came the President and Admiral Porter, flanked by the officers accompanying him, and the correspondent of 'The Journal;' then six more sailors with carabines,

—twenty of us all told,—amid a surging mass of men, women, and children, black, white and yellow, running, shouting, dancing, swinging their caps, bonnets, and handkerchiefs. The soldiers saw him, and swelled the crowd, cheering in wild enthusiasm. All could see him, he was so tall, so conspicuous.

"No wonder that President Lincoln, who has a child's heart, felt his soul stirred; that the tears almost came to his eyes as he heard the thanksgivings to God and Jesus, and the blessings uttered for him from thankful hearts. They were true, earnest, and heartfelt expressions of gratitude to God. There are thousands of men in Richmond to-night who would lay down their lives for President Lincoln,—their great deliverer, their best friend on earth. He came among them unheralded, without pomp or parade. He walked through the streets as if he were only a private citizen, and not the head of a mighty nation. He came not as a conqueror, not with bitterness in his heart, but with kindness. He came as a friend, to alleviate sorrow and suffering, to rebuild what has been destroyed."

The correspondent of a Chicago paper, who accompanied Gen. Grant on his visit to the grave of Mr. Lincoln, thus describes the burial-place of the lamented President:—

"We went this morning (Sept. 13, 1865) to Oak Ridge; and some day we hope to give a detailed account of that wild burial-ground. It is about two miles from the city, and consists of a tract of land of about eighty-eight acres, which is in future to be considered as the Springfield burial-ground proper. The remains are still unburied, and lie in the reception-house, just as they came from Washington, watered by the tears of the nation. A guard-tent is pitched opposite to this house of the dead, on a rising knoll surrounded by trees. Three sentries guard the sacred remains night and day; and the stone doors are kept open, so that the air may circulate freely through the place. An iron gate protects the remains from a too close intrusion; although one can see the two coffins, — those of the father, and of the little son who was carried here from Washington with him to their final resting-place."

With the mention of the place where our country's martyr of martyrs rests, this volume closes. Its pages contain a glorious record of noble deeds; and no loyal heart can ponder the endurance, valor, patriotism, and Christian excellence, of the soldiers of the Cross and the Union, without feeling a commendable pride, and, at the same time, a grateful sense of obligation to the patriots of our army and navy; gratitude also to God for so inspiring their hearts, that, when the nation's life was threatened, they were willing even to die in its defence.

May the lessons of the past admonish our nation that righteousness alone exalteth! and may the peace now secured be perpetual, because based on the immutable principles of justice and humanity!

INDEX.

A.

A Boy-hero 156
A Brave Standard-bearer 65
Admiral Dupont 152
Admiral Farragut 124
Admiral Foote 150, 151
Alabama 108
A Naval Victory 121
Andersonville 312
Andersonville Cemetery 321
A Patriotic Family 75
Atrocities of the Rebellion . . . 323
Attack on Sumter 135

B.

Ball's Bluff 56
Battle before Richmond 177
Before Vicksburg 280
Brownell the Avenger 338

C.

Capt. Porter 114
Capt. Richard Derby 172
Capture of Beaufort 135
"Carleton's" Letter from Richmond 232
Charles Homans 36
Charles Warren 80

Chattanooga 283
Christian-Commission Incidents . 340
"Cincinnati" 115
Col. Canfield 328
Col. Munroe 50
Col. Hendricks 278
Commodore Foote praying 332
Count Schwabe's Benevolence . . 299

D.

Dahlgren's Ride into Fredericksburg 197
Dahlgren's Defence 345
Dahlgren's Funeral 354
Daylight and a Truce 128
Dead, — en Bivouac 189
Death of a Hero 74
Death of Col. Baker 340
Death of Gen. Mitchell 342
Death of Gen. Lyon 342
Death of Chaplain Fuller 343
Death of Major Camp 343
Death of Snelder 343
Death of Trask 343
Death of a Nephew of Goldsmith . 344
Death of John B. Marsh 345
Destruction of the "Nashville" . 118
Dorothea L. Dix 285

E.

Eighth Massachusetts Regiment . 29
Eleventh Illinois 250
Elizabeth Comstock 296
Ellsworth 337
Emotions during Battle 61

F.

Falmouth 340
Father and Son on the Battle-field . 74
Fifteenth Massachusetts Regiment 219
Fifty-fourth Virginia Regiment . . 253
Florence Nightingale 285
Fort Donelson 245
Fort Steadman 229
Fort Sumter 14
Fort Wagner 147
Fredericksburg 202, 206

G.

Gen. Frémont 266
Gen. James S. Rice 82
Gettysburg Battle 210
God's Flag 49
Gough's Testimony 80

H.

Hero of Gettysburg 220
Heroes of Ball's Bluff 164
Heroic Massachusetts Soldier . . . 107
Hervey Dix 58
Hospital Sketches 286
How Gen. Lee went into the War . 18

I.

Impromptu, by "Mabelle" 294
Incidents: Antietam 175
Indiana Hero-boy 76
Indiana Soldier 78

In the Wilderness 196
Iowa: Western Patriotism 68

J.

John B. Marsh 357
John Bright 367

K.

"Kearsarge" 108

L.

Last Interview of Two Heroes . . . 327
Last Words of Ladd 337
Letter from J. G. Smith, Jun. . . . 166
Letter from Lieut. C. P. Abbott . . 169
Letter from Sharpsburg, — "Carleton" 170
Letter from Col. Dahlgren 352
Letter from Admiral Dahlgren . . 346
Libby Prison 304
Library for Soldiers 295
Lieut. G. P. Stevens 70
Lieut. J. William Gront 72
Lieut. Hanaford's Escape 316
Little Tad 365

M.

Mabelle's Fair 295
Margaret Fuller Ossoli 285
Massachusetts Bravery 55
Massachusetts Troops 191
Massachusetts Thirty-fourth 200
Mrs. Frémont 265
Mrs. Hayden's Poem on Vicksburg 279

N.

Navy Letters 330
New-York Seventh 29
Nineteenth Mass. Regiment . . . 180

O.

One Leg more for his Country	66
Only a Private	84

P.

Picket Guard	188
Pittsburg Landing	270
Prairie Ridge	273
President Lincoln at Antietam	362
President Lincoln's Letter	364
President Lincoln at Trenton	369
President Lincoln's Playfulness	371
President Lincoln with his Children	373
President Lincoln in Richmond	374
President Lincoln's Grave	377

S.

Secretary Seward	364
Secretary Stanton's Letter	355
Sergeant Kernan	15
Sergeant Frye	69
"Shenandoah"	155
Sheridan at Five Forks	223
Sheridan's Ride	226
Shooting Prisoners	307
Sixth Massachusetts Regiment	46
Soldiers' Prayer-meeting	334
Somebody's Darling	254
South-Carolina Victories	132
Starved to Death	320

T.

Tale of 1861	26
The Call to Arms	17
Massachusetts Soldier's Wife	22
Gloucester Mother	46
The Marblehead Woman	45
Patriotic Girl	47
Brave at Home	51
First American Flag in England	49
Enlistment	52
"Monitor"	87
"Monitor" and "Merrimack"	91
"Cumberland"	93
"Congress"	95
"Whitehall"	100
"Cumberland" Heroes	104
Sailor	107
"Clifton" to the Rescue	127
Blowing-up of the "Westfield"	130
Hancock Farmer	202
Blind Soldier	326
Vermont Soldier	340
President's Office	365
Third Ohio	255
Thomas Starr King	47
Thomas F. Power	102
Through Baltimore	24
Tramp, tramp, tramp	301
Trumpet-song	209

U.

Ulric Dahlgren	345
Unalloyed Patriotism	66

W.

"Wabash"	135
"Weehawken"	140

Z.

Zagonyi	266

www.ingramcontent.com/pod-product-compliance
Lightning Source LLC
Chambersburg PA
CBHW022334230426
43664CB00040B/605